Nothing Ventured
Nothing Gained

Christopher Pantall

EDWARD GASKELL *publishers*
DEVON

Edward Gaskell *publishers*
6 Grenville Street
Bideford
Devon EX39 2EA

First Published 1998

© Christopher Pantall 1998

ISBN 1-898546-27-4

Nothing Ventured
Nothing Gained

Printed and Bound by
Lazarus Press
Unit 7 Caddsdown Business Park
Bideford
Devon EX39 3DX

DEDICATION

Linda Pantall
a wonderful wife who helped me so much
at the beginning of the Pioneer Years

and

Demelza (Melz) Jane Pantall
My beloved daughter
at present studying for her degree at St Andrew's University

ACKNOWLEDGEMENTS

The author's acknowledegements and thanks are due to the following people and institutions:

Mr John Vince, who is the author of many books including *Vintage Farm Machines* as well as being a contributor to the *Countryman Magazine*, was of great help. His assistance was invaluable, supplying rare photographs of a binder, thresher, international tractor and a side rake.

The Ford Motor Company for kindly supplying a photograph of a 1920s Ford Model T motorcar.

Daniel and Carol Price, owners of the Three Counties Hotel, Belmont Road, Hereford HR2 7BP who are kindly supplying the venue for the launch of this book.

My sincere thanks to my publisher, Edward Gaskell (Lazarus Press) who despite being overloaded with other manuscripts, was convinced that *Nothing Ventured, Nothing Gained* would 'make a marvellous read'.

INTRODUCTION

Leaving one's wife and child and bidding farewell to your beloved country to go and seek fame and fortune in a foreign land may sound like the stuff of fairytales but in the 1940s a young Englishman – dissatisfied with his rural Hereford existence – decided on such extreme measures in pursuit of a better future.

Turning his back on all that he knew and loved, 27 year old Christopher Pantall set sail for South Africa, convinced that great opportunities lay ahead. And they did. Although penniless and forced to work his passage caring for cattle on a ship that nearly foundered – even during this long and often turbulent voyage – Christopher believed his luck was changing.

Over the next twenty years, through a combination of hard work, bright ideas, good business decisions and luck, the author pioneered the poultry industry in South Africa, and succeeded in making the fortune which he could only dream of as a young man.

Contrary to the perceived belief within the poultry industry at that time, Christopher held it was *offal* in poultry feed which was one of the main causes of salmonella. Consequently he mixed his own feed, excluding the *offal* while including vitamins. This foresight 50 years ago eliminated diseases in his market niche – Sunnyside Oven-Ready Chickens.

Nothing Ventured, Nothing Gained, Christopher Pantall's autobiography, chronicles life in rural England in the 1920s, giving an insightful description of a way of life that has all but disappeared. His depiction of war torn London in the 1940s – and its effects on a country lad – is an evocative account.

Nothing Ventured, Nothing Gained is an informative and fascinating read about how one man's vision, grit and determination catapulted him into realising his dreams in South Africa, enabling him to retire at an early age and return to England where he could now freely dabble in the country pursuits that had called to him in his childhood.

CONTENTS

1st PHOTOGRAPHIC SECTION

between pages 192-193

2nd PHOTOGRAPHIC SECTION

between pages 224-225

PART 1

THE FUTURE'S NOT OURS TO SEE

1

It was six am on a wet December morning in 1918, Monday 12th to be exact, when Christopher took his first peep at this wicked world. A month and one day after the end of World War One. Christopher was the second child and a year and four months younger than his brother Richard.

Very few babies were born in maternity wards in those days so the usual trend was for the local midwife to be in attendance at home. Plenty of hot water was always available, heated by large tin or copper kettles swung over an open fire from a long iron bar. More water could be heated in a large copper basin with a fire below. These types of coppers were very popular and could hold up to twelve gallons.

Mrs Lewis, the midwife, who was ably assisted by her daughter Mary, was the first to speak, "There now Mam, you just lie quiet like. He's a bonny boy and must be at least an eight-pounder. Mary, go and tell the boss he's got a new groom and tell 'im to cum upstairs."

Mary duly hastened away whilst Mrs Lewis put young Christopher in the arms of his mother and began to tidy up the room.

Down below William Pantall, father of the baby, could be heard walking across the flag-stoned kitchen floor as he

made his way to the creaking oak stairway. He was carrying
an oil stove to help heat up the bedroom as it was a cold
miserable morning.

On entering he put the heater down and went straight to
his wife Janet's side. She was now sitting up holding the
baby. He bent down and kissed her gently.

"What a clever girl you are!"

Janet just smiled. She knew he was pleased. It was
another boy. He would be more help on the farm.

Kilkington Manor had been in the Pantall family since the
sixteenth Century. It was a large rambling Manor House with
over two hundred and fifty acres set in the beautiful
Herefordshire countryside, nine miles from Hereford, two
miles from the nearest village and over a quarter of a mile
from their nearest neighbour.

Looking very pleased Will said, "I'll come up later and see
you, you must rest now."

He went out to the wood shed and filled a bucket with
wood and coal. On entering the kitchen he set about the task
of re-building the fire that had, by this time, being neglected,
nearly gone out. The grate gave more heat to the chimney
than to the cold kitchen. The stable door, excellent for ventilation in the summer, allowed the wind to whistle across the
large kitchen, down the steps into the cellar and out again
through an uncovered barred window. Candles were flutter-
ing but the sturdy paraffin hurricane lamps showed no signs
of movement from the breeze.

By now it was seven and time to commence the daily
work on the farm. Will told Mary to make some tea as he
hurried off to the cart shed where the farm hands were waiting, holding up their lamps.

Will said, "Well, Boys, we have a new foxhunter!"

Tom Watkins, the wagoner, was the first to shout out,
"Well done, Boss!"

It was pitch black and all carried oil lamps as they went
on their way round the farm. Tom went off to feed the horses,
Bill Harwood to feed and milk the cows. Jack Hicks, the
youngest of the farm hands, went off to chop swedes in the

pulper for the young cattle and Alfred Holland (Pug was his nick name) to feed the ferrets for he was the general workman who, in the winter months, caught rabbits and laid hedges.

John Jones, the foreman went straight to the sheep from his house, so usually arrived at the farm buildings for his break at nine, but this morning he hurried through the task of moving hurdles and got up to the barn as it was getting light. Pug saw him and shouted, "Johnnie, the Gaffer's had a boy!"

John smiling said, "Pug, he could never do that, it must be the Missus."

By this time, back indoors, Mary had cooked the breakfast of porridge ham and eggs with large chunks of home made bread and butter.

Christopher's mother, Janet, was a champion butter maker and had exhibited at most of the big shows before she married. It was whilst at the Royal Show in Yorkshire that she had first met William, known to his friends as Will.

Janet and Will's first born, young Richard, was down and sat eating his porridge amidst the chatter of Mary and Ethel. Ethel was the daily help and Mary was now employed full-time to assist Janet. Will, who still kept his coat on, polished off two large rashers of home cured ham.

"Now, you two, anyone would think you'd had the baby. Pass down the tea!" he said.

Although the custom was fast dying out, cider was also placed on the table. Before tea became generally available, cider was the main drink on all farms, particularly in Herefordshire, nearly every farmer making his own.

Although a wet and miserable day, Will felt at peace with the world and at eleven am trudged up the stairs in his hob nailed boots so, although she had been dozing, Janet was now fully awake and greeted Will with a big smile.

"I can't stay here for long, there is so much to do with Christmas just around the corner," she said.

Will told her not to worry but to sleep. He was off to Weobley, five miles away, to get the baby registered.

11

Usually, on wet days, he would take Tommy and the trap but today he decided he would ride horse- back. Jack was instructed to saddle-up the hunter 'Little Woman'. The grey mare which stood at 16.2 hands was duly saddled and Will took a short cut across the fields to join the pot holed road to Weobley.

He stopped at the Red Lion there and handed over the horse to the ostler before making his way to the tap room where he was met by the inn keeper, Dan Evans and neighbour Ned Roberts, who enquired, "Well, come on then Will, is it a tup or a ewe?"

"Don't be so vulgar Ned!" chirped in Nellie Williams the barmaid. "But I'll bet a pint of cider it's a girl."

Will, wet through, but beaming, replied, "Nellie, it's too cold for cider so I'll have a whisky!"

"So it's another boy... and what'll you call him?"

"Well Nellie, Janet and I knew it would be a boy so Christopher Robert is his name!"

At two pm and closing time, Will walked with Ned up the cobbled street of Weobley village to the Registry office where Mr John Williams, the registrar, entered in big bold handwriting Christopher's pedigree in his book. He then made out a certificate and handed it to Will saying, "Five shillings if you please... and may the colt grow into a fine stallion."

"Thanks John I'm sure he will!"

Ned had come over to Weobley for some salt for killing a pig on the morrow so he geared his cob to the gig, threw in the block of salt and, with Will already mounted, together they made their way back home.

Ned lived the closest to Will's farm, about a quarter of a mile away at Hinton Farm. It was six pm when Will arrived at Kilkington Manor and the farm hands were getting ready to go home. It had long since been dark and after an eleven hour day which had begun and ended in darkness, Jack held the oil lamp whilst Will took off the saddle and bridle.

"Jack, give her a whisking down and some hot bran will you?"

"Yer rides' er too hard Guvnor."

Will made no reply but headed for the house to change out of his wet clothes.

That night the rain stopped, the stars came out and clear frosty air completed the first day of Christopher's life. The usual farm duties continued during that winter whilst Christopher continued to thrive leading a normal healthy baby's life.

The cuckoo comes in April, sings his song in May,
Tunes his song in the middle of June and then he flies away

Janet was soon back to the busy farm life but even busier with the increase in her family. Pug was a great help to her. In his thirties he was also a family man with two boys and a girl under five years of age. Pug and his family lived in a thatched cottage about two miles away in a village called Staunton-on-Wye.

No matter what the weather, Pug had not lost a day's work in the nine years he had been at Kilkington. His mode of transport was an old bicycle, which was prone to punctures. His father before him had been a skilled craftsman in hedge laying and rick making but, above all, he had passed on to Pug the art and skill of rabbit catching.

In the winter months Pug loved this work, for work it was, as the rabbit population had to be kept down. Pug was proud of his ferrets and called the five of them by their pet names. He was an expert at laying snares and enjoyed the thrill of poaching a pheasant occasionally.

He opened the back kitchen door and stepped inside. It was not yet seven and a beautiful April morning.

"Morning Mam. ' Erd a cuckoo jus' now. ' E be early this year."

"Good morning Alf," (Janet always called him by his proper name) "What a beautiful morning to hear the cuckoo and a lovely morning to let those baby chicks out for the first time."

"Yes Mam, I'll go now and make a wire pen roun' the chicks 'ouse."

Pug had the job finished by break time. Between nine and

nine-thirty he always stopped for bread, cheese and cider. After his break he lifted the lid off the coop and out came fifty Rhode Island Red chicks, glad to be alive on a warm cloudless morning. Young Richard, Christopher's brother, was at Pug's side, full of glee and wanting to catch a chick.

This morning was busy especially for Tom, the wagoner, who had been at the farm since six feeding the horses ready for the day's work. Tom had been a wagoner all his life and was now in his early sixties. He had been at Kilkington for fifteen years and lived in a small two-bedroomed cottage called 'Meres Place' on the north side of the farm. He kept a lovely garden of vegetables and his wife prided herself on her splendid flowerbeds. Their daughter, Molly, had grown up and married a painter on a neighbouring estate. This particular morning Tom was ridging land for potatoes with his two favourite horses, Boxer and Bonnie. With a jar of cider at the top of the field for refreshment, Tom could plough or ridge as straight as a gun barrel.

"Whoa there me beauties!" shouted Tom as he came out onto the end of the field.

Tom loved to natter with anyone who was near. The nearest was Jack, a lad of fourteen, who had just left school and was now serving his apprenticeship to become a wagoner. Jack was being trained by Tom and was busy harrowing the adjacent field.

"Nah, don't drive em so 'ard lad, or yerl kill em!"

Jack smiled, stopped his team from harrowing and joined Tom over a horn of cider.

"A strappin' day for spud planting, bain't it?" said Tom, drinking his horn mug of cider. "The Gaffer'll be 'ere in a minute."

Will came into sight, sitting on a cart full of seed potatoes with the team of potato planters and Barney the old sheep dog following in his wake. Sitting beside him was young Richard. Will had one arm around him whilst the other drove Tommy, the farm's general purpose horse.

Will drew up beside Tom saying, "Tom, we will start at the far end."

14

"Better get them mangold seed in, it's gonna rain, mind." Tom replied.

The potato planting gang set off for the far end of the field which, already ridged-out was ready for planting. Buckets began to rattle as women and children carried them to the nearest sacks of potatoes which Will was depositing down the rows. Amidst a good deal of chatter planting commenced.

By the end of the afternoon it was completed and the mangold seeds were also set using a two-row drill pulled by Tommy. That night it rained.

2

So the summer came and along with it the haymaking. It started one Monday morning at the end of June, Pug let out the chicks which were now quite big and well feathered. Richard came down the garden path on his own, chattering away and helped Pug to feed the chicks. By nine Christopher was in the pram on the front lawn. Although Janet kept an eye on him, his wants were now attended to by Mary.

Jack had started early, at six, and was cutting clover in Ashton Cross field with the new Bamford mowing machine. There were few such machines on farms, the hay still being cut by hand with a scythe. Two young horses, Jolly and Lion, were pulling the machine and, by lunchtime, the eight acres had been cut into very tidy swathes awaiting some sunshine which would make the clover like hay. At noon Mary bowled the pram, with Christopher gurgling away but not yet able to sit up and take notice, into the field to watch Jack. The clover had a lovely fresh smell and the bees' were busy taking pollen from the fallen flowers.

Although several storms of rain fell in the ensuing days, on Thursday Will came with his hunter 'Little Woman' hitched to a Swathe Turner which turned two swathes at a time. She was very quick and Will, sitting on the machine, was able to control her with a pair of long reins.

Saturday was a lovely day. The clover by then was ready for loading onto large four wheeled wagons. There were four in all, each one taking it in turn to be hitched up in front of the hay pitcher. This machine was operated by a chain attached to a wheel that revolved as the pitcher moved forward. It gathered up clover or hay with a spiralling attachment conveying it up onto the wagon where Pug and Jack were waiting to lay the clover in layers. Tom was driving the two horses that pulled the wagon and pitcher. After the first one was loaded Pug and Jack roped the clover down onto the wagon.

"Pug, where did you put they 'orns for the zider?" asked Jack.

Pug walked to the nearby hedge and brought back the horns. The three men sat down for a few minutes to have a drink.

Tom said, "Lovely now en it? The hosses will enjoy this in tha' winter. A bit of good stuff an' all."

"Aye, but mind you, it could rain yet!" said Jack.

They all looked up at the second wagon, Pug chirped in, "We best get this in today then, young 'un is Christened tomorra'."

Teatime came at five o'clock. Janet sent Mary out to the field with a basket of homemade scones, bread and cheese and a jug of tea. By seven the field had been cleared. Four loads were pulled into the barns to await unloading on the Monday.

On the last Sunday in June, Christopher Robert was to be christened. His nannie, Mary, dressed him up in a lovely shawl and bonnet and bowled the pram up to the church, only ten minutes away.

His godfathers, Uncles Fred and Bert, accompanied by their wives and Auntie Edie who was to be his godmother, walked down the lane and then up the road to the church. It had started to rain, fortunately only an odd shower, so no one got really wet. The parson was waiting on the steps of St.

Mary's church and all the family walked in to the font. After a few prayers, the Christening started.

Christopher, lifted from his pram, began to cry at being looked at but Janet took over and soon there was contentment. However, as soon as the parson holding Christopher splashed a spot of water on his forehead and began chanting the words, "Christopher Robert I baptise thee in the name of the Father and of the Son and of the Holy Ghost", the baby let out a big yell and Janet, once again, had to take over.

After a short service everyone, including the parson, returned to Kilkington to set about enjoying a good spread of food, which Janet and the girls had prepared, with an enormous Christening cake, made, beautifully iced and decorated by Janet.

All the farm hands, neighbours and friends were there. Tom and Pug brought their wives. John brought his wife and his two-year old son who was delighted to see such a wonderfully large cake. The evening, with the sun still shining, encouraged the guests, who had plenty of room, to sit down on the large lawn. Sweet smelling roses of the Daily Mail variety climbed the wall by the sitting room windows – the flower garden was a picture.

By this time, Jack, Pug, Tom, Bill and friends, who had been given an extra ration, were quite merry. Mary and Ethel began a singsong. Tom broke up the singing by raising his cider horn and exclaiming loudly,

"Gaffer and Madam, I drink to yee and young un, God bless ya!"

Pug, not to be outdone said, "Na look Gaffer, we do appreciate yourn goodnis. Bess' of luck to ya' and the Missus!"

The following week haymaking started in earnest and the cuckoo was heard for the last time. Although shearing had taken place a month previous, no new growth of wool had yet started. The sheep looked lovely and clean in their summer outfits and the lambs so funny chasing each other and then trying to find their mums. The whole countryside was now in full summer array, the grass so green, the oak trees in full leaf. That year the old saying, 'If the oak is out before the ash we shall have a splash but if the ash is out before the oak, we shall have a soak', favoured the oak because it was two weeks ahead of the ash. There was an abundance of strawberries and plenty of new potatoes and peas.

§

Haymaking came and went and harvest time arrived. Will was the only farmer in the area to have a modern binder. The machine cut the corn six feet wide, which then travelled up a canvas conveyor belt and into a narrow box like affair where spikes pushed the corn into a cradle. When the sheaf was large enough it was tied with boltin string and was then cut off to fall to the ground where it was picked up by the men following behind and stacked in stooks of six sheaves.

The binder was a wonderful invention, pulled by two horses for there were no tractors then. Will bought one of the first tractors in the county of Hereford. It was an International with a chain-wheel drive, a magnificent machine at that time.

In the middle of August Janet bought, at a farm sale, seventy young cockerels, fifteen geese and twenty ducks, to fatten ready for the Christmas market. These were all under Pug's special care. He made the pens ready for the cockerels and geese but the ducks were put on the pond having their own little duck cot. Pug's first remarks were, "Look Missus, by Christmas they'll be hevvy uns."

Michaelmas passed, the bays were full of corn and several ricks had been made.

October arrived with the harvest festival service at St. Mary's church, always held on a Friday. The church, as usual, was packed out with not a spare seat to be had. The Pantalls used their family pew, third from the front on the left-hand side. It had been the family pew for over two centuries.

Kilkington harvest dinner always followed. Both the children delighted in this occasion. Neither boy had attended the church because they were still too young.

Goose was always the chosen meat. Janet kept a small flock (mostly for Christmas) and Pug was an expert in feathering the birds. The down was kept for pillows.

At this harvest dinner, along with the parson and his wife, were all the local agricultural workers who joined in too. There was plenty of cider to wash down the goose, sausages and potatoes. Several large 'spotted dick' (suet puddings) followed full of currants and Lyles Golden Syrup. The whole Kilkington gang had a wonderful time singing songs until the early hours of the morning.

It was the custom in those days that no overtime was paid to the farm workers but, in return for them working so hard throughout haymaking and harvesting, they were allowed to drink all the cider they wanted. In fact, the local blacksmith, Chris Jones, would shoe a horse for no payment but several horns of cider. Often he had to walk home being too drunk to ride his bike. There were several horses working on the farm but not all payment was taken in this way. As the blacksmith's shop was two miles away the horses had to be walked there when shoeing was carried out.

November arrived and with it cider apple picking time. The apples were shaken down from the trees and put into hessian sacks before being emptied into carts. The apples were then put into a circular stone basin about twenty yards in circumference. In turn a heavy circular stone was placed in this trough and by placing a strong piece of timber in the centre, it became a wheel. Pulled by a horse travelling round and round the outskirts of the basin, it crushed the apples into pulp. This was then shovelled into the cider press.

The press consisted of pieces of matting, each holding about twenty shovels of pulp: about fifteen of these sections were layered then with a board laid on top screwed down and this pressed the cider out of the fruit. It gushed out of the press into large bucket-like containers that were emptied into wooden casks. A certain amount of water was added to each cask of cider as otherwise it was too strong.

The common Herefordshire name for cider is 'scrumpy.'

Each barrel of cider had its bung removed from the top to

enable the cider to ferment and spill over. About six weeks later, when the fermentation had steadied the bung was secured and the barrel was ready to be tapped. Will bottled about one hundred bottles, corking them with a specially made corking machine. The bottles were then wired to secure the corks.

Christopher was now growing rapidly, keeping the house-hold awake at night, believing he had never been fed. The bottle was always at hand, the milk straight from the cow. There was no such thing as pasteurisation – or disposable nappies in those days.

3

November 1919 was a busy month, what with threshing corn, pulling mangolds and swedes for the cattle, harvesting sugar beet, ploughing, then planting the corn. At seven am on the second Monday in November the Gaffer (as Will was called) went to the stable and met his men.

"We are going to thresh the wheat today, the weather is holding. You all know what to do!"

Tom said, "Gaffer, do you want Tommy and the cart?"

"Yes! Jack, you take the sacks round ready with Tommy."

Pug chirped in, "I'll help John and set up the tack."

John filled up the tractor with paraffin and petrol. When the engine was hot enough to ignite the paraffin the tank was switched over from petrol. However, on this morning, John turned the tap too soon. A splutter and it stopped.

Pug chimed in, "I told ya you was too quick!"

"Know all!" John retorted.

The carburettor had to be drained to start the procedure all over again. No easy task, it took a great deal of patience, it couldn't be rushed.

Eventually it started and the Kilkington gang was ready. Jack went to the bay of wheat and with a pitch fork lifted the sheaves of corn onto the thresher. Molly Watkins, Tom's daughter, lifted each sheaf, cut the string and put the sheaf at the entrance of the drum (a large heavy cylinder).

Pug, using a pitchfork, little by little pushed the sheaves of corn into the cylinder which was driven by a long belt attached to the threshing box from a drive wheel on the tractor. The machine made a lot of noise.

The corn was separated from the chaff by riddles and the chaff fell to the floor. The corn travelled along an escalator and dropped into a heavy sack.

Looking after the corn was Will's department. John raked the chaff out from under the machine and then helped Will to load the sacks of corn onto a wagon.

Tom looked after the boltins. The straw went from the threshing machine into yet another machine called the 'Boltintyer'. This packed the straw tightly turning it into what was known as 'a boltin of straw'. It was tied automatically with string and released from the machine when heavy enough to trip out. Tom used a pitchfork to pass it to Bill Harwood, the cowman, who loaded the boltins onto a wagon.

Harwood was the son of a wealthy industrialist, well educated and well spoken. The story went that he had ran off from home with the parlour maid, married her, then his family disowned him. He had enough money to buy a little cottage on the boundary of Kilkington where he lived for a good many years. He knew nothing about farming but was a quick learner.

During his lunch hour it took him twenty minutes to walk home, twenty minutes to eat his lunch, and twenty minutes to be back by the hour.

Harwood said, "Look here my man, I can only handle one at a time."

"Jump around a bit more then!" Tom replied.

At nine they stopped for half an hour for bait and cider. It was dusty work.

Will made straight for the house where a bowl of porridge, followed by the usual ham and egg awaited him. Richard was running around with a toy horse and Christopher was still sleeping. Janet and the girls were butter making.

Pug only had a few minutes break because he had to feed his ferrets and the poultry. The hens were now laying, roosting in a little shed by the pigsties, but all day they were free ranging except the twenty five special cockerels that were in a fowl pen being fattened for the Christmas market. The hens were let out every morning but closed up at night to prevent Reynard the Fox from having a meal.

December came in with a flurry of snow that soon disappeared, giving way to a lot of rain. The Black Mountains, about ten miles away, capped with snow, heralded the first signs of winter. An old Herefordshire saying goes, ' When ye' can zee' the mountains, it's gonna rain and when ya' can't see 'um, it's raining.'

The 12th of December brought Christopher's second birthday.

"I can't believe the year has gone so quickly!" Janet said to Will.

So much for Christopher's birthday – he was strong and healthy.

At the beginning of December one of the two fat pigs had to be killed. The pig killer, as he was known, was Frank Hicks. He lived in the village of Staunton-on-Wye. During the winter he was kept busy killing pigs for both the farmers and farm workers most of whom bought a piglet in the Spring and during the following months fed it on scraps and meal. The pigs were not killed humanely, like today, but were led to a bench, pushed onto their sides, and held down by the men whilst the pig killer despatched them. After the pig was gutted it was carried into the dairy and hung up by its throat, there to stay for twenty four hours whilst the meat cooled off and set. The following day Frank would come back and cut it up.

The hams and sides were cured with salt for a couple of weeks. Then the two hams were placed in muslin bags and hung up in the kitchen on hooks in the beams that had been in situ for possibly three hundred years. Pieces of ham were then cut out for cooking when required. The sides were hung up, lengthways, on further hooks to be sliced for bacon. The two pieces of the carcass known as the spare rib and ball rib were only lightly cured. They were delicious roasted. Also the chine, part of the backbone which was very tender and tasty with the pickled cabbage and onions that Janet made during the autumn. Finally came the trotters and scratchings, which were very fatty and made up into balls of nutritious meat. The head Janet made into brawn set in basins for slicing when cold and the jelly had set. Although today bacon, ham and pork are bought from the butcher or super-market, they do not have the taste of the home cured meat as in days gone by.

Country folk, particularly farm workers, not only kept the pig but a goat for its milk, chickens for their eggs and cockerels for their Sunday lunch! Rabbits were plentiful and cheap for those not able to catch them.

The 18th December soon came, the seven days before Christmas Day when the poultry had to be killed and dressed. Plucking was done by hand. A goose would take the longest. Pug would organise the pluckers, about six of them. There was no transport and they had to walk over a mile from the village to Kilkington to be there by seven thirty. Mrs.Handley looked after the dressing and, in between household chores, Janet also assisted. When the birds were ready for packing they were first laid out on thick slats already in position on the stone in the dairy and left to cool for twenty-four hours. A great deal of chattering went on during the plucking and every now and again Pug would chirp in, "Ya' old gas bags, been over a yer' since ya' had a tung' wag." Or some other wisecrack. They all worked hard and for a few pence, but a few pence went a long way then.

Three days before Christmas the poultry were all loaded onto the dray. This was a flat-bottomed wagon that could easily be pulled by one horse.

Jack set off very early for Hereford market using his favourite horse Jolly. The distance was nine miles and he had to be there in time for H.P.Barnsley's Christmas poultry auction.

Tom had been in the stable since five am to give Jolly a good feed and prepare her nosebag for the return journey.

"Now look 'ere lad, don't take 'er too fass." was Tom's instruction on Jack's departure.

"Erl be good for a point to point tamorra." Jack hastily replied.

Tom had also given 'Little Woman' a good feed and Will and Janet left about an hour later. Tom had hitched the mare up to the trap, a favoured vehicle as the two wheels had rubbers attached to the outside making it more comfortable for travelling. By trotting they could cover the journey in about two hours.

When they arrived at Barnsley's auction, part of the Hereford Cattle Market, Jack was already there, waiting. The birds were labelled and recorded. A good many dealers were there to inspect the poultry prior to auction.

There was a huge amount of poultry and plenty of buyers. The geese sold for ten pence and the cockerels for one shilling per pound, so they averaged seven shilling each. The ducks sold for eleven pence a pound, about six shillings each. Janet was quite pleased with the result. There were also a great number of turkeys to be had making about one shilling and five pence per pound. Afterwards Will and Janet made their way to Broad Street to Mrs Harris's café where they had a good lunch followed by some Christmas shopping.

Jack had fed Jolly and had gone on his way home long before dark but Will and Janet had to light the paraffin lamps on each side of the trap. The light was not very good so a slow trot was necessary. It was not unusual for a fox to cross the road a few yards ahead and frighten the horse.

The Great War had been over in 1918. Christmas 1920 was here. Food was scarce and expensive. Though there were few luxuries such as sugar, flour was plentiful, yet the quality of the bread was poor.

At Kilkington few commodities had to be bought as the farm was self-sufficient with milk, cheese, poultry and eggs, meat and all their own vegetables. The garden was separated into four sections. At the very top the first one was about eight yards in length, twenty yards wide with a path at one end and the house at the other, it had branches of Doyenne du Comice pears overhanging. This patch, being very sheltered, was always reserved for early potatoes, Sharps Express or Arran Pilot. The second, over the path, had firstly two rows of raspberry canes and then general vegetables. It was about twenty yards x thirty yards with another two large patches of ground beyond. The third was lower still with about thirty gooseberry bushes and ten blackcurrants. It was divided by a hedge, from the remaining part, which was a small orchard with Conference Pears, Worcester Permain apples and one tree we called *seek no further*. At the bottom of this orchard was a big rubbish pit for old buckets, etc. and adjoining was a lovely patch of rhubarb! In this area were four beehives that were looked after by Mr Barber, the manager of Garnons Home Farm. Up the northerly side ran a hedge of hazelnuts and filberts. It came up to the lavatory. The ferret hutches stood by the lavatory path. This is all part of 'The Glory of the Garden'.

4

The next ten years went quickly by. It had been a hard decade for the working classes: children had to work in factories and coal mines and they were always hungry. Farming was at a low-ebb, many farmers having to sell up their few head of stock and try to get jobs. There was no 'dole'. The unemployed had to apply to the parish for some relief. It was only a few shillings per week.

Paddy, an Irishman, came to this country after the war to work on trench digging, but his real love was forestry. The nearest he could get to a forest was to buy branches from tree fellers. On Garnons Hill, woodmen were cutting out 'suckers', saplings that had sprung up at the base of large trees and branches which needed pruning back. Paddy got the contract to remove these suckers and had a ready market for them.

They had to be moved down 'rides': these were woodland roadways and very muddy. It would be difficult to use any other method than Paddy's. This was four donkeys hitched up two by two pulling a large bundle of branches to the roadside. Paddy loved yelling at the donkeys who of course were as stubborn as he was. Paddy could be heard shouting through the wood.

"Yer lyzy beggers, dig 'em irons in!" One donkey only had half a shoe, another none at all.

"Shore and begorra' I'll make yer go if yer wanna go!"

1930 found the Kilkington gang still the same, though Tom, the wagoner, was to retire and Jack Hicks to take his place. Pug had been busy all winter laying hedges. This involved cutting and layering young branches to enable the hedges to fill up at the bottom and prevented the stock from getting out through the gaps. He still found time to catch rabbits and in 1929 had caught two hundred and eighty. When sold on Hereford Market they made about one shilling and three pence each.

During the decade, on December 5th 1921, Alan Wallace had been born, followed the year after on December 26th 1922 by Jean Isobel.

When Christopher was four years old in January 1923, he started the elementary school in Staunton-on-Wye, two miles from Kilkington.

Richard was now five and a half and together the boys would walk the four-mile round trip, wet or fine. As there was no such things as school lunches Janet made up sandwiches, which with cake or buns, were all wrapped up in the Hereford Times.

School began at a quarter to nine and ended at four pm The two boys left home at eight to arrive in time and got home around five.

The infant school mistress was called Miss Metcalf, she was the sister of the Headmistress, Mrs Markham.

The summer came and went. Will could not wait for his sons to become useful. By the time Christopher was six years old he was expected to work on the farm and the boys were regularly kept home from school to help with threshing the corn. They began at eight am and finished at four with Christopher cutting the string holding the sheaves. Richard, being stronger, had the job of raking the chaff out from under the thresher.

Will and his brothers had been fortunate enough to have wonderful parents who had had a total of seven children. Of the four boys and three girls, two died from Tuberculosis: many people died from T.B. at that time.

They were successful farmers and farmed Old Letton Court. It was good agricultural land through which flowed the River Wye. All the children received private schooling. The boys were sent to Clive House in Hereford where they had a good education until they reached eighteen years of age when they were set up in their own farms. Their parents' main priority was to educate the family.

Even today under New Labour with their demand for education for all, there will be many who just have not got it 'upstairs'. Christopher's Father was one of these. Lazy, he never did any of the heavy work, and bad tempered, he had a habit of placing his tongue between his teeth when in a temper. Following his education, his Father had set him up with ten thousand pounds in the bank and Kilkington Manor, well stocked with all the implements needed for farming. Christopher's Grandfather was not only a successful farmer but also a champion ploughman, and later in life, became a well-known judge.

At the age of seventy-eight he retired to Eardisley, a lovely village north of Hereford. The house had a big garden and an adjoining paddock. He was accompanied by his dog 'Rags'. Grandma had died in her early seventies.

It was customary in those days for farmer's wives to make cheese and butter and to sell this together with their surplus produce, eggs etc. in the 'Butter Market' on Market Day held on a Wednesday in Hereford.

Janet found that the quantity of milk she was getting from the farm was not enough so she purchased two and a half gallons from Mr Price at Scutmill Farm every Monday as this was the day she made soft cheese, known as 'Welsh Cheese' for market. She was pleased to have this milk as a couple of Mr Price's herd were Guernsey's, noted for the richness of their milk, whereas the cows at Kilkington were Shorthorns and Crossbreds nothing like the quality of Guernsey milk.

Delivery was quite a problem as there were no vans. It

had to be carried in buckets from Scutmill Farm down the long drive over a stile and up Pool Meadow walking quite a distance to join the lane to Kilkington. Janet bought the extra half a gallon to allow for spillage!

Christopher's Mother was a clever woman, well educated and astute. She had been brought up on a modern farm at her home Fyfield Hall, Ongar, in Essex, owned by the Watt White family: there she had learned the art of making cheese and butter, cakes and pastries. Her stall in Hereford's Butter Market was very well known, the quality much appreciated.

Will was very jealous of her ability for she far outshone him. He had his Father's money – but no ability. He farmed badly never appreciating that 'what you put into the land you will get back'. He put in nothing.

One morning, around eight am in 1925, Christopher happened to be in his parents' bedroom, a large oak panelled two windowed room leading on the one side to a passage to all other bedrooms. On the other side were the back stairs, oak, creaking and possibly as old as the house. The front stairs were at the other side of the house. Janet was attending to Jean. Christopher was seven years of age. They heard Will coming up the stairs. He burst into the bedroom in a fit of temper, putting his tongue between his teeth and uttering abusive language. He began kicking Janet, knocking her to the floor and with his hob nailed boots continued to kick her all over. She was screaming with pain, Christopher was screaming too, in anguish having received a clout from Will's fist, knocking him to the floor. Swearing, Will departed downstairs. This incident was to live with Christopher for 73 years, like a ghost to appear every day, more so during the last forty years.

Janet had two cats, pedigreed and valuable. Will ordered Pug to kill them. Pug would normally have refused such an order but, having a family to support and with jobs scarce, he could not. His wages were thirty shillings per week!

Will continued to ill treat Janet. Instead of helping her with her profitable sideline with the sale of produce he was incensed with jealousy and hatred. If he'd had the brains he would have realised this income of hers was helping the finances in very difficult times.

Broad-leafed clover was much in demand and Kilkington land was very suitable. He could have grown fifty acres by under sowing in a cereal crop. He always sold a good sample of this clover at the top price but grew only a small amount.

1925 was a lovely summer following a wet spring. Due to moisture, crops of all sorts were heavy resulting in much growth. Due to the sunshine haymaking was off the mark in June as was the first cutting of clover used in the winter as horse fodder. Clover is sown in the spring and usually undersown with another crop such as barley planted previously then left to grow until the following summer. Another crop is produced in late September but this time the flowers are left to seed, cut and harvested in early October hopefully with the help an 'Indian Summer'. When matured the clover is put in a rick. Inclement weather in the autumn makes the clover very difficult to harvest.

That year was a real 'Indian Summer' – and time for fruit picking. Cox's Orange Pippins were ready as were the numerous wasps that ate the windfalls.

Harvesting finished, there were seven bays of corn in the French barn, three bays in the lower barn, known as 'the barn'.

Of course there were still the potatoes to be lifted to say nothing of the ploughing and planting. Christopher was too young to take part in any of these projects but was always present helping where he could.

In 1926 Janet was forced to seek a Separation Agreement and this was to be heard at Weobley Police Court. Janet had applied for custody of the children. Will objected and in Court he forced some of his employees to tell the Magistrate a pack of lies about her. She was accused of ill treatment and neglect of the children. These employees realised that their jobs were at stake so lies they told. Will wanted to keep the children for cheap labour. He was given custody. Janet was awarded maintenance but Will never paid her a penny!

Janet opened her shop, The Lilac Dairy – Home Made

Prize Products, at 8 Widemarsh Street, Hereford and rented a house at Lugwardine, two miles from Hereford. She was allowed once a month the custody for one day of her children. This was of little inconvenience to Will but imagine Jean the youngest at only four years old, having no mother. The eldest, Richard, was only nine. The children at Kilkington were in great distress – WHAT A MISERABLE BUSINESS. Sue Roberts from Hinton would come over and get them, including Jean, ready for school and organise their breakfast.

The local gossip was all about Janet, "Fancy leaving little children to fend for themselves."

She had no option. The Court at Weobley kicked her out, aided and abetted by Will. He did not help or suffer. He employed a housekeeper who was no substitute for Janet. Sandwiches for school consisted of 'bread and scrape' and were like brickbats for there was no such thing as sliced bread then.

From the age of six until he left Kilkington, Christopher went to St. Mary the Virgin's Church on most Sundays, attending the eleven am Service together with Evensong at six thirty. From four years of age he also went to Sunday school at two thirty.

The Reverend G. O. Lewis was the parson for a good many years, having succeeded the Rev. G.R. Ellwood. Reverend Lewis did not serve in any other Parish. This was one 'living' which came from about one thousand acres of common land in Staunton-on-Wye. This land was let to farmers and Will rented a large acreage.

Graves were dug manually. The Churchyard was kept tidy by the Rector's gardener, John Roberts, his son Dan was about Christopher's age. In later years the Rev. Lewis transferred to Tupsley, Hereford. The Rectory was sold and the 'living' was joined to two other Parishes.

During 1925 Will bought a car, a new model Ford T. CJ.7517. It had oil lamps for night driving and the canvas hood was fastened to the front mudguard by a leather strap. The petrol tank was under the front seat that had to be removed in order to pour in petrol through a funnel from a two-gallon tin. The car was started by cranking a handle at the front with one hand and then holding out the choke with a piece of wire with the other. The tyres had tubes and punctures were frequent. A 'jack', with a long handle, was provided for changing a wheel. It was a lengthy affair. The repair of any puncture had to be done at the Ford motor dealership, R P Ravenhill. Reg Ravenhill and Will were great friends. The Ford T was sold for scrap in 1934.

Petrol, which was kept in a separate compartment was delivered in two-gallon cans every fortnight on a Friday, along with Tractor Vapourising Oil. The 'T.V.O' was stored in a specially constructed round tank holding several hundred gallons and five gallon cans were filled from its tap before being carried to another tank which could hold about a hundred gallons. It was a hard task that could have been made easier with a little thought.

Petrol in 1930 was one shilling and a penny three farthings (six new pence) per gallon

A custom in those days was the Annual Pleasure Fair. It was not only held in Hereford but in villages such as Eardisley, Kington etc. Always held in May, it was known as the May Fair, and lasted three days and three nights.

At a May Fair held at Eardisley, Christopher climbed onto a roundabout and held on to one of the moveable upright supports that joined the moving platform. When it gathered speed he became giddy and was thrown off into the crowd, unconscious. After being carried to the Red Cross tent he came round and then went to his Grandad's house, close by, to make a complete recovery.

5

Wednesday 7th May 1930, being Market Day, Will and the housekeeper were away for the day. Christopher was sick all that day and had been the previous night, although nobody had taken any notice. When Will returned from Hereford at five o'clock, he took the boy to see Dr Steed at Staunton surgery. By now Christopher was very ill. After examining him the doctor confirmed it was an acute appendicitis.

"Will, get Christopher to hospital quickly," Dr Steed ordered, "I'll telephone through." The telephone was a difficult instrument to use – trial and error – and one had to keep winding a handle saying, "Hello, Hello!" There was no emergency line. Eventually the doctor made contact with Mr Wood Power at the General Hospital and asked him to stand by to operate.

Will took Christopher by car to the hospital ten miles away where he was wheeled straight into the operating theatre.

Mr Wood Power sharpened his knife and made a five inch incision from the naval almost to the testicles and removed the cause of the appendicitis, an orange pip. Christopher was put on Oxford Ward where he eventually came back to life.

Nurse Vaughan, a probationer, who kept him comfortable went on to become the Matron of Hereford General Hospital. The stitches came out after eleven days.

It was a long operation, not like today and they used chloroform that made you very sick. Christopher had lots of visitors, many of whom came by pony and trap as cars were very scarce. Janet visited him everyday with all sorts of goodies.

After three weeks Christopher was allowed out but had to have the dressings attended to which was done by a nurse at Ferndale House, White Cross Road, Hereford. This house was owned by T A Matthews – Christopher's Uncle Tom, being married to Will's sister Lula. He was Hereford's main solicitor having made a name for himself defending Dr Crippen. There was little evidence for the defence and Crippen was found guilty of murdering his wife and hanged. The press had their papers full of the case. Dr Crippen tried to escape to America after the murder but was brought back by the Police. T A Matthews built up a well-known and efficient practice. When he attended Court at Dorstone, he often defended poor clients and never charged them. Today, T A Matthews & Partners are one of Hereford's best established firms of solicitors.

Christopher was collected from hospital by his Uncle Tom and stayed at Ferndale with 'Uncle and Aunty' for six weeks. It was the first 'holiday' he had ever had.

In 1930 APF Chapman was Captain of England cricket team.

On June 6th, 7th and 8th 1930, it was the Three Counties Agricultural Show: Hereford, Worcester and Gloucester: each county holding it in turn. Nowadays it is held permanently at Malvern.

Letters. Postage stamps one and a half old pennies.
Driving licence for a car: five shillings.
Age for driving: 17 years.
Motor licence: six pounds.

June brought haymaking time, so Will said to the Kilkington gang, "The weather is good, Jack take your favourite horses and cut Woodles Green meadow!"

Jack responded, "I will 'av to grind them knives then!"

Pug chirped in, "Gaffer, the clavver be gittin' a bit 'ot, better open 'un up a bit!"

"You'd better go and do it then!" retorted Will.

The clover had been cut and harvested two weeks before and was heating up. Along with Woodles Green there were Ten Acres, Three Ricks, Middle Meadow, Little Meadow, Scutmill and Portway meadows all to be cut for hay.

That evening Christopher, then twelve years old, was turning the hay in the Woodles Green meadow. Whilst he was cleaning the hay from the main shaft, the horse moved. Christopher caught his right hand in the cogs and received a nasty gash. He managed to unhook the horse and led it home. Will put the horse in the stable before taking Christopher to the surgery where the doctor expertly stitched the gash, though the scar is still visible to this day.

Amid storms the haymaking proceeded.

One of the highlights of the day was teatime when, at about four o'clock, one of the girls came with a basket of sandwiches and scones and tea.

Mary called out to the men, "Come on yer vultures!"

They needed no calling and nestling down in the hay they soon devoured everything.

Tom said, "Now for a 'orn of zider and then we'll be alrite, tanks!"

The hay had to be unloaded into lofts above the cowsheds ready for the winter feed. This was always a seven am job, whilst the dew was still on the meadows.

On a fine Tuesday morning all was set to make a start on Portway Meadow where the hay was always made into a rick.

Tom said to John, "Nice day, 'en it."

Pug shouted to Jack, "Yew bring me more beddin' fer ta bottum!"

Jack did as he was bid,

"Ther' ya be," he said, as he off loaded bushes and sticks for Pug.

Will and the grey mare had already side raked several swathes, so Jack and Pug mounted the wagon whilst Tom drove his team of horses. The wagon was loaded and in getting down, Pug said, "Go ste'dy with zider. Jack forgot to brin' two casks."

Tom butted in, "You wer' to blame, twas uer fult!"

The weather held and nine loads of hay went into the rick.

"Gaffer, she be a good un'," said Pug, referring to the quality of the hay, "and I will enjoy thatching 'er but mind she don't get ot!"

"What happened to the rick knife?" asked Will.

"It be a gonner – got unda the wheel of the wagun!" Alf replied.

Haymaking over, the two boys were very tired. Milking at five am; breakfast at eight; school by nine; returning by five to work with the haymaking; then milking with the aid of hurricane parrafin lamps at ten pm

The children broke up for six weeks holiday towards the end of July. This was a long 'holiday' but during this period they hoed sugar beet, mangolds and potatoes and harvested the peas that would be used to feed the cattle.

On August 1st 1930 the men prepared to cut a field of oats in Ashton Cross field. This was to be done with a new McCormick 'binder'. In those days this was a wonderful invention. It could cut and tie sheaves, all driven from a large wheel which operated the whole machine. The binder was then pulled by two horses, later a tractor would be used. Today one can laugh at such a machine when a combine harvester can turn on a sixpence!

Tom brought the binder into the field, unhooking the horses whilst preparing the machine for operation. Tom loved his horses and let them graze by the hedgerow as he stood by.

John shouted to him, "Aren't you ready yet?"

"We are all ready!" Tom replied, "The Gaffer is cummin' so cum on me beauties and don't be scurred."

Will helped with the hooking up. Pug arrived ready for stooking, carrying a little cask of cider and said to Tom, "A noggin' afore ye go?"

Tom did not hesitate, wiping his mouth with his shirt-sleeve,

"Come on, me' hearties," he coaxed.

Will sat on the seat to control the cutting height and with a clatter of different noises, the binder burst into life and the oats went into sheaves very quickly. After six times around, Tom and his horses stopped for a blow. "Brin the zider," he shouted.

Pug replied, "Yew' wont' waak' strit!"

They were all happy and by dinnertime half the field had been cut. Tom fed the horses under a large oak tree with the freshly cut clover that he had brought on a barrow from the stable at seven that morning.

First time around, after dinner, 'Lion' the young horse put his foot in a wasp's nest that greatly upset him. He pulled himself away from the binder and set off across the field with Tom in pursuit.

"Wait yee 'ere," he shouted to the horse, "Why be thee running away?"

Eventually Tom managed to catch him and Lion was re-hooked to the binder and away they went, finishing before nightfall. Tom blamed the wasps for stinging one of his beloved horses, "I will bring a kettle of boiling water and fix 'em tonight!" he promised. And he did.

On the 22nd August, having cut, threshed and bagged up a field of wheat, approximately thirty bags were hauled to Moorhampton Station, about four miles away, by two horses and a wagon.

There were a good many rabbits in the field. Children from the village would come and chase them as they came out of the corn, hitting them with sticks if they could catch them, the sheaves of corn hindering the rabbits as they tried to run away.

Chores permitting, Richard, Christopher, Alan and their school friend Tom Gwilt cycled in the evening, one riding on the cross bar, up to the Scar on the River Wye, two and a half miles away where they all learned to swim with the aid of a car inner tube. It was swim or drown. They always took soap and a towel. This was the equivalent of the weekly bath.

Saturday night was bath night. The copper, which held about twelve gallons of water was built in for permanent use, it had a fireplace below to burn wood and to heat water. A bucket would be used to carry what was called 'soft water' from the rain buts. These buts were filled by the rain running off the roof of the house and down a spout. They were close to the back door, nevertheless it was heavy work having to lift the buckets of water about five feet high to empty them into the copper. The fire was lit and two hours later 'hey presto' the water was hot enough. The top of the copper was covered with a wooden lid to keep the heat and steam in. A tin bath about five feet long and two feet wide was placed on the cold slabstone kitchen floor in the middle of the kitchen in front of the open fire that had been well stoked up. Each child in turn stripped off and bathed, Jean first and then the boys. After drying, fresh clean underclothing and socks were provided and would last the week!

August 23rd being Richard's thirteenth birthday, the children had a party. They played cricket with all their school friends, drank lots of lemonade and cider and had a thoroughly enjoyable time.

In September the harvesting was nearly over. They were into cutting barley the last cereal to be cut. On the 15th they started back to school having finished the harvesting first. The 28th September was Janet's birthday and all the children spent the day with her at their Auntie Grace's place called Lanveangle in Wales, where Christopher loved to pick the whinberries on the mountain.

The summer was nearly over and was followed in late

September and October by early frosts.

On the 5th October 1930 the R101 Zeppelin crashed in France and was completely destroyed.

At Kilkington Manor a 'wireless' was installed. There was only one station, Radio Daventry, it was not very clear and only broadcast the news.

Although the Harvest Festival still took place, Kilkington's harvest dinner did not. Times were hard with cider making discontinued on most farms. The cider apples were being sold direct to H P Bulmer and Company of Hereford, who were just becoming well established as cider makers, supplying throughout the country.

'Bulmers Woodpecker', as the brand name was called, could be obtained in most hotels and public houses. The old tradition of 'a horn of cider' had died out.

In December there was a terrific thunderstorm, something very unusual for that month. Christopher was in the woodshed around eleven in the morning when a loud bang was heard with a huge flash of lightening followed by a clap of thunder. A thunderbolt had passed through the wooden side of the calves' shed, travelling through it for about ten yards, knocking the seven calves in the shed to the ground.

Bill Harwood yelled out, "Someone, Come quick!"

Will and John were there immediately to find Bill in a state of shock. The thunderbolt had just missed him; one of the calves was killed and two severely burned. The thunderbolt, a ball of fire the size of a football, went out through the other side and into another shed where two women were honing hedge bills with a grindstone, one turning the wheel and the other holding the blade on the wheel, thus sharpening it. Amazingly the thunderbolt passed between the women, not touching them, but giving them one hell of a fright. They should not have been handling steel in a thunderstorm for both could have been struck by the lightening. The Good Lord saved them.

Kilkington, being situated on a hill, was prone to lightening. A big oak tree had been struck several times in the past.

Pug came running from where the thunderbolt had gone into a hedge,

"Are you alright, Alf?" asked Will.

"Aye, I be an' all," was his retort. It rained for the rest of the day.

On the 12th December it was Christopher's twelfth birthday. He weighed six stones, was five feet tall, enjoyed good health and worked very hard. Christopher received many presents. A ten shilling note, dominoes, half a crown from Aunty Edie, a brush and comb from his Father and a bible from Mother.

A fox broke into the fowl pen on the 20th December, devouring four of the best cockerels. He carried two away and would have come back for the other two but it got light and he had to go back to his lair.

Two days later on the 22nd December Will had a birthday. The previous weekend they had been around the apple trees in a horse and cart gathering mistletoe and holly to decorate the house.

The highlight of Christmas came on Boxing Day when, it being Jean's birthday, Janet took all the children to the Pantomine; Dick Whittington and, of course, his cat. It was a wonderful treat. The following day they went to visit some friends and nearly got stuck coming home in the mud. They had to make use of the oil lamps seeing as best they could.

§

New Years Day, 1931 found Christopher, like all the other members of the family, up by six o'clock and straight out to do the milking. Both Richard and Christopher would milk about six cows, taking the milk and putting it through a cooler before having breakfast. Meanwhile Bill Harwood would have fed the cows with a mixture of corn and hay. They were now ready to be turned out for the day into one of the meadows.

Christopher was ready for his porridge, bacon and egg.

Returning back to work he met Pug and exclaimed, "Very Happy New Year to you, Alf!" Like his Mother, Christopher always called Pug by his proper name, "I'm afraid I can't come rabbiting with you today I'm a bit under the weather. In any case it looks like snow but I'm sure you'll manage on your own."

"Just yew' go back to bed, boyo," Pug replied, "Drink plenty of orange juice and I'll tell yee when I cum back ow' many rabbits I caught. It's not a good day, mind!"

For the rest of the day, and to the next morning it snowed. Christopher, still feeling ill, stayed in bed. He could see from his window the heavy snow fall and his Father said it was up to the top of the doorway. It was all hands making a path out from the house to the cowshed and stable.

It was still snowing heavily as Bill Harwood trudged in from his cottage over a mile away. Somehow the milk lorry managed to get through to collect the milk. Later the same day it changed to rain.

Christopher had the 'flu and stayed in bed for the next two days. The school organised an annual tea party but he was too ill to go. Dr Steed came to see him and gave him some medicine that helped a lot.

On the 7th January 1931 Doctor Steed was taken ill and went into hospital. He improved the next day but, on Tuesday 10th he died. A much loved and well-respected practitioner, it was Doctor Steed who had diagnosed my appendicitis two years previous. His funeral took place at St. Mary's Church, Staunton-on-Wye on Friday 13th. The church was packed. He would be sadly missed.

On the 23rd January Janet took the children to the Kemble Theatre in Hereford to see 'All Quiet on the Western Front'. It was a well-known film at the time. They also went to see 'Dawn Patrol' at the same theatre.

Parties at this time of year were very popular as well as holding their own at Kilkington they were always invited to the other farmer's parties. Their favourite was held at the Dales in Preston-on-Wye. They always had a lovely time there as the Dale children were similar ages. A good time was had by all.

Will sent twenty pounds of butter to market. It made one shilling and eleven pence per pound. Eggs were sold at eleven pence per dozen.

Pug caught fifty-four rabbits. Will took them to market and made two shillings and three pence each, a very good price.

School examinations took place in the March. Although difficult, Christopher received a total of 52 marks – the second highest of the boys.

The school at Staunton-on-Wye was a Higher Elementary. It was so popular that over one hundred local children together with some from the local parishes attended there. The Headmaster was Mr George Markham. Across the road the school owned a five-acre piece of land which was used as a playing field. It had a pavilion and was mainly used by the boys. On Friday afternoons instruction on various sports was given by the Headmaster.

Reg Bigglestone did not turn up for school one Friday. In the afternoon he appeared in Weavers Orchard, which was opposite the school playground, where the Headmaster, Mr. Markham was giving a lesson to the children. Reg was mimicking him pulling faces and making gestures. However, Monday morning came, Reg was in his class and Mr. Markham called, "Bigglestone come here!" Taking his cane from the desk, he ordered, "Bend over!" He gave him six of the best across his backside. Reg knew he deserved it as, holding his bottom, he limped back to his place in the class.

Christopher was elected Captain of Blue House, the other one being Red House. Cricket was played against the other schools, both home and away. On the twelfth of June they played Marcle at home. Staunton made seventy-two runs, Christopher being responsible for twenty-seven of them. His heroes were Walter Hammond for batting and Harold Larwood for bowling (Marcle managed just thirty-five).

In the winter they played soccer. Whilst the Blues were the better side at Cricket, Reds excelled at football. There were no tennis courts, but the Trumpers at Red Barn Farm, close by, had a grass court and there Christopher learned to play. He still plays and enjoys the game.

Jack Hobbs made his one hundred and fiftieth century in May 1928. He was later Knighted. The origin of the 'Ashes' dates from 1882 when a mock epitaph on English cricket was published in Australia, concluding with the statement, 'The body will be cremated and the ashes taken to Australia'.

At Harvest time Jack, Pug, Christopher and Tom, the wagoner, went into the field and pitched all day. Christopher had to lift a sheaf of wheat, which was very heavy, onto the wagon where Pug loaded it. Jack was pitching the other side. Although Christopher was young and strong, it was very hard work.

On the 18th September Hay sheep sales started and Will bought thirty ewes for breeding. Christoper and Tom, a buddy of Christopher's from school, drove the sheep five miles from Kington to Eardisley. The ewes were put into a field owned by Grandad where they stayed under his watchful eye for two days before Tom and Christopher drove them to Kilkington.

Christopher was helping Jack to take the sheaves of corn that had got wet from one of the bays at the lower barn. The horse and cart into which they were to load the sheaves was beside the bay. The horse decided that standing still was not for him and started to move off. There were a few children playing in the area and Arthur Thomas was looking on.

Jack shouted, "Whoa', you bloody hoss!"

Arthur pointed to the children and yelled at Jack, "Language! kids about."

Panic over, about ten minutes later the children were making a nuisance of themselves climbing a ladder.

Arthur shouted, "Come down, you'll break your bloody necks!"

One Sunday morning, Len the postman as he was known, called in at the Warren, a cottage occupied by Murray

McGee, an Irishman, "Come on in, Len, 'av a 'orn of zider, zrink it all, the barol be empty." Len did as he was bid and left. Shortly afterwards someone else called and before they could utter a word Murray said, "Sorry, I can't offer ya' a 'orn of zider, old Len tha' postman thrunk ta' bloody lot!"

January 1st 1932 began with snow and a hard frost. Everyone helped with the threshing. Father owned his own threshing box and the International tractor so we could thresh corn when it suited us. It was dusty work, very laborious and needed a team of seven men to complete the operation. The drum, which was the main part of the machinery was circular and heavy, revolving at great speed, thrashing out the corn which dropped through a riddle onto an elevator and thence into a sack at the front. The straw went to the rear and into the 'boltin' tyer which produced a large compact easy to handle boltin of straw. One of the men took these boltins, passing them on to the next whose job it was to pack them into a bay. One worker raked the chaff, whilst another looked after the corn which flowed into the sacks. The thrashing box made a good deal of noise.

Easter came and with it two weeks holiday. Unlike most children, for Richard and Christopher it meant a lot of work. Christopher did manage a few hours fishing on a Sunday evening where he would meet up with Bill Watkins.

Bill was a coarse fisherman (all fish except salmon and trout) who helped Christopher to cast bait of maggot or worm. On one particular Sunday in May Christopher met him at the 'Scar', a well-known picnic spot on the River Wye. Christopher had no proper fishing gear: he used a Greenheart spinning rod belonging to his Father who had never used it. It was a solid rod more suitable for catching a forty pound salmon, with a heavy spinning reel. He had no money to buy a light springy rod and decent reel. However, he arrived for an enjoyable couple of hour's relaxation.

"Good evening, Mr Watkins."

"Good evening, Chris, they're not biting very well. Put up your rod, tack up and fish below me!"

Christopher had to learn the hard way and copy

Mr Watkins, who was a coal merchant from Moorhampton railway station.

He put a worm on a rusty old hook and cast the line towards the river but on the way the line got caught on a thistle. He wound it back in, put on a fresh worm and cast again. This time he was successful but had too much weight on the end of the line and it sank into the weed.

Mr Watkins caught a lovely big chub that he placed with his net on the bank. It weighed four pounds seven ounces.

"Well done, Mr Watkins!" Christopher praised as he withdrew his line to the bank.

Mr Watkins was using maggots for bait and gave some to Christopher but with no success.

Later in the year Christopher would put sheep dip into a wasp's nest at night, the following morning digging up the nest covered in dead wasps and wasp grubs. They were excellent for catching chub.

He had a good many enjoyable Sunday evenings fishing during the Summer. One Sunday he had watched General Pitman, a friend of the landlord, 'play' a twenty-two pound salmon and became 'hooked' on fishing from that day. The General was so excited as he landed his catch that the memory remained with Christopher all his life. In future years he was to enjoy the sport, catching hundreds of salmon in Scotland, Ireland, Norway and Greenland. He would even one day own one of the best salmon stretches on the River Wye at Ballingham; would catch a forty-pounder on the River Tay and two more of these at Ballingham but first he would have to make his fortune.

The beginning of June being sheep shearing time John brought the sheep in to the top orchard putting about twenty into an enclosure in the barn. A large sheet was placed on the floor where the shearing machine was located. The machine was made up of a large wheel with a circumference of about six feet attached to a chain, joined to an attachment that was driven by a spindle. A length of cable attached to a shearing head enabled John to manoeuvre around the body of the sheep. The wheel had a handle that was used to crank the mechanism into life. Christopher had the misfortune to be allocated this job, standing in one place all day, cranking the machine. It was hard work and very boring.

It took John ten minutes to shear a sheep, about six per hour. The fleeces were carefully rolled up and stacked in a pile and placed on a platform to one side of the barn. After an hour, his back aching, it took John a few seconds to stand up.

"Oh, this really is a backbreaking job!" John was a clever man, always cheerful who worked very hard and was not a cider drinker.

Christopher begged, "I wish I could have a turn!"

"Youngster, ye 'av a go!" Pug had arrived on the scene.

Christopher eagerly said to Pug, "Alf, catch me a sheep!" Pug did as he was bid and John gave Christopher a lesson.

This shearing machine was replaced a short time later with a petrol engine, driving the pulley with six shearing heads, then later still with an electric version.

In Australia they shear a sheep in three minutes but our breed, called Clun Forest, are much larger and have ten times more wool on their coats. John had about two hundred ewes and three hundred lambs to shear. Before the sheep were shorn they were washed in Maddle Brook which was dammed for the purpose. Each sheep was washed thoroughly, a paddle being used to move the wool around in the water.

In November it was time to knock the apples and pears off the trees then gather them up from the ground. The apples were made into cider; the pears into perry. Most of the apples belonged to the Strawberry Norman and Kingston Black variety, special cider apples that tasted foul. The pears, which were not great in quantity, belonged to the Perry variety. All the fruit was picked-up by the women from the village and placed in hessian sacks, emptied when ready into a horse and cart and then taken to the cider mill. There the apples were emptied into a crusher and the pulp put into the cider press. When the buckets were full they were in turn emptied into different sized barrels holding from twenty to a hundred gallons. Christopher usually got this job. Cider making would take several days. Five large barrels were made ready in the cellar at Kilkington just waiting to be filled. This was done manually carrying the cider by barrel on a cart. With a tap over the edge a bucket could be fitted underneath, filled and then carried through the back kitchen and down the steps into the cellar.

Cider in this form before it had fermented was strong and lovely to drink but could sometimes cause diarrhoea!

Christopher said to Pug, "Alf, we need more buckets!"

Pug retorted, "I'll go and find zum then!"

"I will have to leave this now and go to the sheep." John said to Will.

Will replied, "John, on your way see if the horses need any hay. Jack, bring another load of apples!"

"Which ones?"

"The Kingstons."

When finished there were the five barrels, each holding fifty gallons of cider. Two would be used for bottling in the spring. The barrels were left with the top bung-hole open to ferment for two months. They were then 'bunged' down ready to be tapped. This fresh rough cider was now known as scrumpy. The barrels were all nearly new, only having being used previously for brandy which greatly improved the taste of the cider. They were known as brandy 'casks.' Ned Roberts of Hinton Farm made about five hundred gallons of cider. His work force, like many others in the county, as had been the custom for generations, received no overtime for harvesting, haymaking or shearing. Instead they were allowed to drink as much cider as they wanted. Most families drank it with all their meals.

Today relics of cider making can still be found at the entrances to most farms. The most common being the large round stone attached to a long heavy pole which sits in a circular basin. A horse was used to haul the stone round and round. Apples were fed into the basin to be crushed continuously throughout the day. The pulp was then removed into the cider press. The horse would be changed several times during the day.

Cider making made one's hands look dirty and rough. Christopher found it very embarrassing for he liked to play whist at which he was very skilled, winning many prizes at local whist drives.

On Monday December 12th 1932 it was his fourteenth birthday when the law allowed youngsters to leave school. Will was delighted, for Christopher was destined to work on the farm with no payment as was the custom.

His special day came with 'Many Happy Returns' and lots of presents from everyone and an especially big present from his Mother. He was fourteen and felt very grown up. The following Friday was his last day at school. At three pm Mr Markham, the Headmaster, bid him stand in front of the class next to him as he addressed the youngsters.

"Today is a special day for one of our class. Christopher Pantall, Captain of the Blues, is leaving us today. I must say he has done exceptionally well as a pupil of this school rising from the infants to the top of standard eight and passing all exams with top marks. He has been popular and shown great skill as a cricketer, both bowling and with a bat. Although always scoring highly a century has always eluded him, but last year when playing Dymock, he made sixty-two not out. We are sorry to lose him and wish him well. So let's give him a good clap and say Goodbye and Good-luck!"

Christmas came and, as usual we spent most of our time feeding stock. At the end of the year the Clover Thresher arrived. It was a special machine and had to be hired. It was similar to the Corn Thresher. On the Thursday afternoon the hissing of steam and thumping of an engine heralded the arrival of this four-wheeled monster as it trudged up the drive pulling the threshing box. With a couple of celebratory 'toots' it ground to a halt, pulling up beside the clover rick. Coal had already been placed there ready for heating the water.

Christopher had the job of carrying the water to make the steam. Using two buckets at a time he emptied the water into the boiler. A dusty, dirty job and endless work but it was a very good machine and thrashed the clover clean.

On one trip he met the operator of the box, "Am I keeping up with the water?"

"Yes laddie, you are doing well. Where are you bringing it from?"

"I'm having to pump it from a well in the yard because all the taps are frozen!"

The pump had a long heavy iron handle and before starting to fill the buckets, he had to pour some water down the outlet pipe to prime the pump before water would rise. This procedure for every two bucketsful!

"What is the yield like and the sample?" Will asked John. The machine was able to separate out any light clover seeds.

"Very good." John replied. "Not many seconds!"

It was a very good sample of red clover and the yield excellent. It was sold for what was a high price at that time, sixty-seven shillings and sixpence per pound.

PART II

TO BE A FARMER'S BOY

6

On New Years day, 1933, having now left school and being fourteen years of age, I looked forward to what I was destined to do, work on the farm at Kilkington.

My first day's work began at seven in the morning, milking four cows, pouring the milk into a cooler through a strainer and into a five-gallon milk churn stamped with the name 'Cadbury's'. It was then time for a breakfast of porridge, bacon and egg with bread and butter. Father always sat at the top of the table, Richard on his left with Alan beside him and Jean beside me on Father's right. It was a hurried affair.

During the time it took us to have breakfast, Bill Harwood would have fed the cows, calves, yearlings and other stock with hay and a mixture of pulped swede and oatmeal. Although New Year's Day, it was no holiday for farmers. However Pug and I went rabbit catching taking his ferrets, a spade (a very important tool specially designed for digging out rabbits) and about twenty rabbit nets. Pug owned four ferrets, a hob (male) and three jills (females).

He suggested we went to Ashton Cross hedgerow. We arrived at the first rabbit warren and carefully laid our nets. Pug put a jill ferret in the top hole and she made her way down the warren seeking a rabbit. Occasionally a rabbit would bolt, running out of the warren and into the net. Other times there were no rabbits in the warren so we would pick up the ferret and nets and go on to the next hole.

On this occasion we bolted three rabbits into the nets but at the next the ferret got attached to the rabbit. This was where the 'liner' was useful. This was a ferret with a collar around its neck that pulled a long line. When put down the hole it would lead us to the ferret which was gripping the rabbit. Either kneeling or lying down we would then reach in for the rabbit, sometimes being nipped on the fingers by the ferret in the process! I pulled the liner back and Pug called the ferret. We had to dig to reach a rabbit trapped at the end of a five-yard hole. We caught twenty-eight that day!

After work we had a singsong in the kitchen. I went down to the cellar and drew some cider. We still had half a cask left and the 'scrumpy' was in 'good fettle'. We had a few horns left over from the previous year and made up the number with mugs. There were mince pies, dollops of cheese, bread and biscuits.

I started it off by asking Jack, Arthur Thomas from the cottage in Barn Lane, Tom, Bill Harwood and Pug to sing 'To be a Farmer's Boy'. They were so hopelessly out of tune (not enough cider had been consumed) it had to wait until 'Shook' – Arthur's twenty year old daughter – arrived and got us going by singing a few ditties then broke into 'To be a Farmers Boy'.

Learn to sow, to reap and to mow and be a fermer's boy ya. And to be a fermer's boy.

Before she could continue we were interrupted. One of the horses, Jolly, had got her foot stuck in the stall. Heaving and groaning we got her loose. I didn't feel too well so I left the party – which went on for hours! So ended New Year's Day. After the next morning's chores, Richard, Pug and I went rabbit catching around Sedgepit and caught thirteen rabbits. It was a showery day: frosty weather is always best for rabbiting. They were worth more money when caught in nets but provided a lot of sport when shot. The rabbits would run like blazes across the meadow, a good marksman could shoot every one. The rabbit population had to be kept under control and the only method was to catch them. We usually caught over three hundred every season. Rabbits cause a lot of damage eating young plants and grass. Ten rabbits eat as much as one cow.

Saturday was cold and unpleasant. The school held its Annual Fancy Dress Ball. Many pupils went to a lot of effort which helped to make it a huge success. On this occasion I went as Primo Carnera, the well-known boxer, all I wore were shorts and a pair of plimsoles – as they were called at the time – trainers today. It was my last fancy dress ball at the school but I didn't get a prize, just very cold!

The following week we were all invited to a party at the Dales of Huntley Court, Preston-on-Wye. Their children, Marjory, Betty, Dorothy and Arthur, were our age. We looked forward to it every year, always having a good time, and we reciprocated in turn.

By February the weather was becoming milder. The frosts were less and we were getting ready for spring-cleaning. On February 8th I went with the pony and cart taking two pigs to Hereford for sale and where Father sold the clover seed.

Some years earlier, on Richard's twelfth birthday he'd had many presents including a Raleigh bike from Mum. At this time there were no bicycles in the family so I had to walk. In the following years I was very fond of whist and what were known as whist drives but getting there was not so easy. If Richard was not using his bike, he would hire it out to me for one penny per session, bang went my rat money!

Although bicycles were not very plentiful, most of the working class owned one. They were free wheel and fixed wheel and, for those who could afford it, a Sturmy Archer three speed, not to be compared with the mountain bikes of today.

If I went to Hereford I would hire Richard's bike or walk, often many miles. I would take my boots for soling and heeling to the cobbler at Mansel Gamage three miles away. This too was a walking job.

On Friday 17th I went to a whist drive which was held at Moccas situated just over the other side of the River Wye. At this time, the bridge over the road into Preston-on-Wye and the surrounding area, was accessible but two or three years later a big flood partially washed the bridge away leaving it unsuitable for vehicles ever again. Whist drives were often held in various parishes to raise funds for the church amongst other things. At this particular event I took first prize – a very good penknife – which I kept for many years eventually giving it to Horace, the gardener at Lugwardine House when it became too heavy to carry around for the small amount of work it had to do.

On the Saturday it was very cold and snowed all day to a depth of over four feet, staying on the ground for a good many days. The following Friday a big blizzard blew up and we had one of the biggest snowstorms for years.

Imagine using the lavatory at a time like this. It was down the garden path, about twenty yards from the back door, and comprised of a small hut with a tiled roof. Using a bowler hat for size a hole was cut in a piece of board and secured by nails in the sitting position and a pit was made below. It had a plentiful supply of lime and was cleaned out every winter. The *Hereford Times* sufficed as toilet paper. The call of nature on a freezing night was horrendous especially if a fox or rat cross your path on the way!

7

In March all the farm staff appeared to have influenza including Pug, Jack and Tom, the wagoner. Only Bill Harwood seemed to be free of it. There were no inoculations or any cure for 'flu in those days. It was a matter of it taking its time.

At the end of March I found a blackbird's nest in the garden containing three eggs and a thrush's nest holding two. There were also several sparrow nests. Crows were nesting in Lower Stands Banks wood, below. The remarkable thing was that all the birds were nesting at the same time with the exception of the pheasants that usually nested in May and the pigeons in August.

An item of great interest to me took place on April 3rd 1933 in New Zealand. Walter Hammond made three hundred and thirty six runs in the Test Match England against the New Zealanders, a record. Don Bradman did not make as many runs and he was a very famous batsman.

We were now in *'Oh! to be in England now that April's there and some morning would meet one unaware.'* This particular morning, April 10th, there was a hard frost. Everything was white and caused a lot of damage to the blossom.

May Fair day was held on the first Wednesday, Thursday and Friday in May and was followed by the Three Counties Agricultural Show at Worcester on the first weekend in June. I went along with the rest of the family on the Friday. It was very hot. It is worthy of note that, in those days, there was no need to lock doors, day or night. Our doors had neither a lock nor a bolt. There were just no robberies.

Many of the farm implements had improved during the previous ten years. There was now a diesel Ford tractor pulling a four-furrow plough. (The one-way six-furrow plough, hydraulically controlled was yet to be invented).

The Combine Harvester was replacing the binder and the bailer, cutting and threshing the corn then taking the loose straw and hay and bailing it into neat bales, thus doing away with endless days of threshing. The Combine Harvester was the 'death knell' to the threshing box.

Possibly the best invention (since the bow and arrow became a secret weapon) was the mechanical hedge trimmer. Linked to the hydraulic system on a tractor it would drive a flat shear-like blade that could be raised or lowered according to the height of the hedge. The hedgebill, used by hand, became extinct. What a blessing!

On October 1st Alan, Jean and I spent the day with Mother. We went to the 'pictures' and saw 'The Kid from Spain'.

Next day I helped Tom to take eighty-five sacks of black oats to Moorhampton station. I drove one of the wagons pulled by two horses, Tom the other. The oats were sold to Griffiths and Hartland, Corn Merchants, Hereford, for four shillings and eight pence per hundredweight.

All cider fruit was now sent off by horse and wagon to Bulmers, Cider Makers. Our cider-making days were over.

Running at the side of Woodles Green Lane was a wood called 'The Brinks.' Full of wood pigeon it was also home to the woodpecker. With their glorious green and black plumage flashing they flew around in pairs. You could hear their rat-a-tat-tat echoing through the sunlit wood in their search for grubs in the trunks of trees.

At the beginning of October I went by train to stay with Uncle Dudley and Auntie Edie at Whittle-le-Woods, Preston, Lancashire for the my first holiday since having my appendix operation five years earlier. One evening we went into Blackpool to see the illuminations. I was very impressed. Blackpool Tower was a wonderful sight, known world wide for its beautiful organ and ballroom. After a week I returned to the 'grind.'

On the Sunday I went to church in the morning then picked twenty-six pounds of chestnuts from Stands Bank Woods in the afternoon.

November 5th saw Bonfire night. Although showery the evening was bright and crispy. We had a Guy Fawkes and twelve and six pence worth of fireworks. Sparklers, Catherine wheels, jackey jumpers and a few rockets. Guy Fawkes was burnt on a huge fire consisting of hedge trimmings and with sweets, cakes and pop we had a thoroughly enjoyable evening. We also made our own 'bangers' or, as we called them, 'carbines'.

Another simple form of portable lighting employed on the farm and on bicycles was acetylene. Calcium carbide in lump form was placed in a holder at the base of a lamp. There was a small water reservoir that dripped at a slow pace. A small jet with two holes for the gas could then be lit and when covered by a glass produced a strong glow accompanied by the hissing sound of the water and carbide reacting.

We would collect empty Ovaltine tins to make our carbines. They had close fitting lids that you prised open with the end of a teaspoon when making up the explosive. A small hole was pierced at the base of the tin, two or three lumps of carbide and a good spit and we were off. With the lid well rammed on the tin would be placed on its side with a foot pressing it to the ground. A long 'England's Glory' match was applied to the hole and with an enormous BANG! the lid would be blown about ten yards. We never thought of the damage to our feet if this went wrong!

§

That December I was fifteen and confirmed at Letton Church by the Bishop of Hereford. Letton is a Parish two miles from Staunton-on-Wye. It was the first confirmation to be held there.

Boxing Day, December 26th was Jean's birthday which we celebrated on the last day of 1933 and which Jean, Alan and I spent with Mother. She had made lots of lovely goodies for us and we played games for most of the day. We all had a jolly good time.

My Mother still had her little shop (the Lilac Dairy) in Widemarsh Street. Here, with the aid of an assistant, she sold all kinds of homemade food. She made a variety of sandwiches, cornish pasties, beef steak and kidney pies, veal and ham cutlets, ham and egg cutlets, fish cakes, salmon cream cakes, sausage rolls and cooked meats. She was a silver medalist and a BDFA and was an excellent cook. The demand for her products became so great that she really needed a larger shop.

Another 'speciality' of 'The Lilac Dairy' was the homemade stone-ground bread. This was made with locally grown wheat and ground by the wheel. When in season various fruits such as strawberries would be placed on the pastries followed by a blob of clotted cream. What a treat!

Mother's shop became very popular due to the demand for whole-meal bread. Housewives placed daily orders for loaves and office workers for sandwiches. Poor Mum was working day and night. After closing the shop at half past five she would slave over the kitchen stove often until midnight.

8

Father sold our Model T Ford for scrap – he could not find a rear axle for the car as spare parts were impossible to obtain. It was only eight years old. Poor 'old Liz' as we called her fetched seven shillings and sixpence and was replaced with a second-hand Citroen, KA7957, bought for Father by Grandad and costing him twenty pounds.

I could not count the times I harnessed a horse to pull that car up the drive after Father had tried to bump-start it by putting it into gear and running it down the drive which was five hundred yards long.

He would shout, "The car won't start!"

"Oh! no, wot' again!" I would reply.

It would always be me, not Father, who would have the task of harnessing the horse. After several attempts with this strenuous business the car would start. We called this heap of junk 'The Flying Bedstead'.

Every year, we always 'walked' a puppy foxhound for the Radnor and West Hunt. It was common practice for most farmers who enjoyed the hunt to take a puppy into their household from when it was weaned until it was first ready to be trained. This way they were 'socialised' and thoroughly 'domestic,' though working dogs.

After having walked 'Passtime' for eight months we took her back to the kennels at Tetley, near Eardisley. At the 1936 Annual Puppy Show, one year, we won a trophy for 'Truman'. I still have this trophy today! One year we walked two hounds. When they were about nine months old and about to go back to the kennels they started hunting together on their own and could be heard going 'full cry' across the countryside. They were too young, of course, to catch a fox and soon came back home.

On January 9th 1934 all the family went to Cousin Jean Yates' birthday party held at the Falcon Hotel, Bromyard. We had a wonderful time. Jean's mother, Auntie Ciss, was a widow. Her husband, Uncle Tom, was returning from the Falcon, on horseback, one wet and stormy night to his farm which had a long drive with a series of gates (cattle grids were unknown on that farm). He was drunk and as he tried to open one of the gates he fell off the horse and broke his neck. After the death of her husband, Auntie Ciss farmed the place herself and did very well too. It was one of the best hop farms in Herefordshire.

That January my Great Uncle Tom died. He was eighty-five, a well-known and much respected farmer in his day.

On Sunday evenings we used to ride off on our bikes to see Grandad. He was always cheerful and accompanied by 'Rags', did all the gardening. When we arrived he was always pleased to see us. He would usually start off with, "Come on in," before placing his bible safely on the sideboard.

"How is Jean?"

"Very well, thank you."

"What have you been doing on the farm?"

Our reply would depend on the time of the year. In the summer it would be "Very busy Grandad. We have finished haymaking in Portway!"

"The winter oats are to be cut next week."

"Your Father?"

"He's well, been to Lancashire this week."

"Doing what?"

"Seeing a housekeeper."

Grandad had a very good housekeeper, Mrs Pound, who would bring us some cake and biscuits.

"How is the cider Grandad?" one of us would ask.

"Have lots left," he would reply.

We always made a barrel of cider for him every November. We would bid him farewell and cycle back home.

I helped to finish cleaning the clover seed in the middle of January. When completed it yielded thirty five hundred weights of top grade seed that sold for ninety-five shillings a hundred weight, an excellent price.

The following day John and Peter Ravenhill came for a day's rabbit shooting. These were the sons of Reg Ravenhill, the Ford Agent and Fathers friend. They were about our age. I had a 4.10 shot gun, given to me by Uncle Fred. Twenty-five Eley Furlong cartridges cost two shillings and nine pence. We shot twenty- eight rabbits and had a party to finish the day off.

On January 30th I shot three rabbits with the 4.10 with only three shots!

In February, I took two fat pigs to Hereford Market in the pony and cart. They sold for nine pounds each. The round trip took me four hours. Father, who had come in by car in about half an hour, bought me a pair of hob nailed boots, size ten, costing twenty three and sixpence. In addition, he gave me six pence to spend on a haircut. The barber always gave us back a penny which we spent on fish and chips.

My sister Jean Isabel, nicknamed Bell, went to catch the bus from Kilkington to Hereford. The bus stopped at Portway, the main road and a mile away from the farm. She missed it. There was only one bus each day so she had to walk the nine miles. She was only twelve years old. She had been working in the house and with so much to do forgot the time. Father was too mean to take her by car!

Children were safe walking country lanes and roads. Jean often took her dog Barney for a walk down Woodles Green Lane which was 'far from the madding crowd', and so peaceful with the birds singing. Skylarks could be seen in abundance. You would see one rise from the ground and soar up towards the sky singing its little heart out. When it rose up to over fifty feet it would stop, hover and continue to sing before making its way slowly back to earth, still in full song. The mistle thrush was another singing bird that would sit at the top of a branch of an old oak tree and warble its lovely song. The blackbird too was a popular bird but the mistle thrush had by far the superior voice. The robin, sparrow, chaffinch etc. were then quite plentiful.

Magpies were not common, they were shot by keepers and farmers. These are destructive birds that either kill the newly hatched birds or eat the eggs in the nest. When they find young birds starting to fly, magpies will congregate and set about killing them. The parent birds will cry warnings but can do nothing. After making a nest in a hide and sitting for twenty-one days waiting for their chicks to hatch and then having continually fed them until they are strong enough to fly, to see their young attacked and killed by the magpies is very distressing. This is why, today in 1998, there are so very few wild birds because the magpie, the most destructive bird of all, is protected and numerous. Only a few Estates can afford to employ keeper's who try to keep the jay and magpie at bay by shooting them, as do a few farmers, trying to protect the few birds in their gardens and paddocks. Town people think magpies are beautiful birds having no idea that they are responsible for the absence of wild birds singing in their neighbourhood. Between the wars there were also plenty of red squirrels to be seen, soon to be almost taken over by the grey squirrels introduced from America by accident. These bred so quickly that they over-ran our red squirrel, now only seen in Scotland. Grey squirrels will eat small bird eggs and, unlike red squirrels, do much damage to young trees by stripping the bark, mostly for fun. Mink is also a destructive escapee having fled from fur farms and multiplied during the past twenty years. Mink can climb so no nest is safe.

On Monday, March 5th, I took 'Doll' the pony with the

cart to Hereford and collected two barrels of spray, weighing three hundred weight each, for the apple trees. I started out at half past two and arrived back at eight in the evening, in the dark, with no lights and drenched to the skin.

Tuesday March sixth was the first day of the Cheltenham Festival that was as famous then as it is today for steeple chasing. Father went on the Wednesday and lost money as usual.

On the Saturday, we threshed corn all morning finishing at one-thirty. I rode the bike to Edgar Street soccer ground in Hereford where I watched Hereford United beat Kidderminster Harriers three to two. When I arrived home later I helped with the bottling and wiring of two hundred bottles of cider finishing well after midnight. Special note: Father locked up the bottles in a cupboard under the front stairs! Occasionally if we were lucky he would open a bottle on a Sunday. Later that day he took Auntie Lula at Ferndale one hundred bottles of the cider.

On Tuesday, Father went to Shrewsbury Market and bought three calves. I took Doll and the cart, and collected them off the nine pm train at Moorhampton.

On March 23rd the Grand National Steeplechase was held at Liverpool and won by Golden Miller. This horse was owned by Miss Dorothy Pagett, a very famous race horse owner.

Flat racing was always held on a specially constructed course with no jumps or ditches just gradual inclines to make the 'going' harder.

Fox hunting was very popular at this time throughout the country. In Herefordshire we had two famous packs, the Golden Valley and the Radnor and West Hereford. Father used to hunt occasionally but we, as boys, were not allowed to hunt because of the time it could take up.

Father was keen on fox hunting. When younger he had hunted regularly two or three times a week with the Radnor & West Herefordshire Hunt and always kept a good hunter,

'Little Woman'. She was from Ireland and I think, at the time, she would have been about three years old. I only heard of the incident but apparently the mare put her foot in a rabbit hole tripped and threw Father to the ground breaking his leg. I do remember him being in hospital, I must have been about five at the time and recall quite clearly his leg in the air strung up with a chain. It got better but he never really hunted again.

On Sunday, Jean, Alan and I went with Mother to Builth Wells (up in the Welsh Mountains) We had a picnic by the River Wye, enjoying the wonderful food Mother had prepared.

I went to Monnington Farm to see Uncle Walter towards the end of March. He was very ill with T.B., and because fresh air was recommended, he was in an outside tent. Tuberculosis at that time killed thousands of people. There was no cure. Uncle Walter died, so did Auntie Maggie and, over the next few years, six of my friends died from it. Herbert Wadley, my best friend, died in just six weeks.

Tom Jones who, with his Father, rented 'The New Inn', Staunton-on-Wye, was confined to an outside cubicle. He always had plenty of visitors but gradually became worse and very soon was a 'gonner'.

At the end of March, the hounds met at the Portway Hotel. After the 'stirrup cup' the hounds drew a nearby cover. I followed the hunt and the hounds found a fox in a spinney and followed it to Garnons Hill about two miles away.

Garnons Hill was steep and densely covered by bushes and ferns but first the fox ran through two other spinneys. I was standing in a ride, close to a large growth of ferns when the fox with about ten hounds on its trail made for the fern.

Foxes give off a strong odour that the hounds can smell and this is the attraction that causes the hounds to chase the fox. It's this scent that they follow, possibly never seeing the fox.

The fox stayed in the fern and the hounds, after a delay, went in and caught it. (It is worthy of note that foxhounds, like Labrador dogs, have a soft mouth and do not tear foxes apart). The whipper-in arrived, jumped off his horse and took possession of the fox, ordering the hounds to stand back. Then the master arrived and kept the hounds back. The huntsman held the fox down on the floor with his boot and took from his pocket what appeared to be a 'Priest'. When used by fishermen to despatch a salmon, it can be either be piece of wood, around five or six inches in length and about the same size as a fountain pen, but with a head broader and about an inch in length, or a metal rod larger and heavier more suitable for painlessly killing the fox!

I was now with the huntsman and could not see a mark on the fox where the hounds had caught it. The dead fox was handed to the whipper-in who passed it over to the hunt staff to dispose of. Foxes breed very rapidly, vixens usually having two litters of four cubs per year. They kill lambs and poultry, devouring them. They have a 'lair' in which they live and breed. Like rabbits, the population has to be controlled. *Hunting foxes is not a cruel sport!*

On Saturday 7th April 1934 the Radnor and West Herefordshire Hunt held their annual point to point at Weobley. The expression 'point to point' comes from steeple chasing, which is from a point, i.e. a church steeple, to start the race and another point, i.e. another church steeple to finish the race, possibly one near a pub!

The course would be jumping all farm fences and hedgerows, gates, ditches and brooks, (barbed wire at this time was not invented) crossing fields and meadows but with the church steeple in sight. Hence, point to point. Of course, a jolly good time with plenty of liquor followed. The hunters used in those days were cobs. They were very sturdy with shortish legs and bred for hunting, usually their tails were docked to prevent injury.

In Herefordshire there were many packs of hounds with the hunts. They were with the Radnor & West Herefordshire, the North Herefordshire, the Golden Valley, the Ledbury and South Herefordshire. There are hundreds of packs throughout the country, some being famous such as the Quorn and the Beaufort. Hounds are always counted as 'couples'. Packs would have about thirty dogs, that is fifteen couples.

At this time farming was going through a 'bad patch'. Father could not afford to keep a hunter for our use, at least that is what he said, but, thinking about this now, hunting would have been enjoyment. We did ride his hunter 'Little Woman' to visit the cattle on the commons (land we rented from the church) I remember jumping a five-barred gate for the first time, it was thrilling.

During 1934 Father went to eleven point to points whilst Richard and I were working on the farm.

On Wednesday April 11th, Market Day, Father sent to market fifteen fat sheep. These would be yearling lambs and during the past three months they would have eaten swedes off the field. Hurdles, moved each morning, gave them about one yard of fresh grazing each day (electric fences are simpler!) A sheep cratch was filled with hay and troughs with a mixture of home grown milled barley and oats. With only the light from a hurricane lamp I would spend many evenings milling the barley and oats. The lambs topped the market at seventy-two shillings each. Two fat bullocks also went and they made eighteen pounds each.

On Saturday April 14th I went to Burley Gate, near Hereford, to the North Herefordshire Point to Point and won six shillings (6/-) on O'Dell. She won the Farmers' Open.

The following Wednesday we sent in the last of the fat sheep, fifteen in all, again they topped the market at seventy-five shillings. The next day Father sold two ricks of hay at three pounds, three shillings a ton.

May 2nd and Father, Richard and I, went to Worcester to see Australia play Worcester. Don Bradman made one hundred and ten runs, not out.

By 1934 cars were becoming more plentiful. The Ford Popular two-door saloon was now being manufactured at Dagenham, Essex, by Henry Ford and cost one hundred pounds. Henry Ford said, "You can have any colour car you like as long as it's black." A Deluxe Ford cost one hundred and thirty five pounds.

The Morris Cowley and Morris Oxford were being manufactured at Oxford. A Morris 10 cost one hundred and seventy two pounds. The Austin-Seven tourer and Austin
Cambridge were in great demand. The Bentley, an open
tourer, could obtain a speed of one hundred miles per hour
and took part in racing at Brooklands. The most reliable car
for sheer luxury was the Rolls Royce manufactured at Derby.
"THE MOTOR CAR WAS HERE TO STAY".

Very soon petrol pumps were to be seen on major roads.
The petrol was pumped in to car tanks by pumping up the
fuel by hand filling first one gallon bottle, then filling the second whilst the first emptied by gravity into the tank of the
car. One gallon of petrol cost one shilling and seven pence
half penny.

Lorries and vans began to appear, roads being constructed and repairs done to old roads. Some were being tarred for
the first time.

Horses were still used on farms but tractors were becoming more plentiful. A Ford tractor cost one hundred and forty
pounds and ran on TVO, Tractor Vapourising Oil – paraffin.

Players Navy Cut cigarettes cost sixpence for ten and
eleven pence half penny for twenty. Woodbine cigarettes were
sold in packets of five and cost three pence. In each packet of
Players was a photograph of a well-known footballer in the
winter months and a cricketer in the summer.

On May 14th my Mother moved from a house in
Lugwardine to the Upper House, Staunton-on-Wye. This
meant we could see her more often but it was more difficult
for her as she now had to travel ten miles to her shop in
Widemarsh Street, instead of the two miles from Lugwardine.

The start of three days sawing wood for the winter began
on May 17th. The saw was a circular blade attached to a
heavy steel bench with a pulley to drive it with a belt from
the tractor. I would help to lift the timber onto the saw
bench, this was heavy work and then in the evening we'd
load a barrow and wheel the logs into the log shed, stacking
them with the aid of a paraffin lamp.

Shearing started on the 21st. I sheared twenty-nine ewes

myself. The following Saturday Father went for a week's holiday to Chorley, Lancashire to stay with Uncle Fred who ran
Ridgewood Dairy Farm. He drove his Citroen, 'The Flying
Bedstead', which did not break down. He left me a list as
long as my arm of 'things to do' during the week.

On June 6th, 'Windsor Lad' won the Derby at fourteen to
two. I put four shillings on him!

On Friday September 21st, Father's Citroen broke down
again. A mechanic fixed it.

The best fixing for the car would have been an 'England's
Glory' match.

We picked apples all day for the market on the 25th, Cox's
Orange Pippins, Blenheims and Newton Wonders.

On the last Friday in September Harvest Thanksgiving
took place at St Mary's church. It was packed full of worship-
pers.

On October 20th twenty aeroplanes, British, American,
Dutch and Australian set out from Mildenhall aerodrome for
Australia in a race for a first prize of ten thousand pounds
and a Gold Cup. Amy Johnson, now Mrs.Mollison, led the
field but broke the undercarriage of her plane whilst landing
en-route. C.W.A. Scott, an Englishman won the race in three
days. Captain Cook, who was the first person to discover
Australia, had taken three years.

On leaving school Percy Morgan, a friend from school,
was given a job as a gardener for the wife of the treasurer to
the Jarvis charity. After three weeks he decided gardening
was too much like hard work so he said to Mrs. Blenkin,
touching his cap, "Mam, I want to leave!"

Mrs. Blenkin who was busy cutting flowers to decorate the
house was somewhat taken aback. Percy was a good lad who
worked hard and did as he was told. Turning around to face
him she said, "You know Percy, a rolling stone gathers no
moss!"

Percy replied, "I know Mam, but a still one don't gather
much.

At the end of the week Percy left.

On September 22d, two hundred and sixty men were

killed in the Wrexham Coal Pit disaster. They were buried alive. An explosion was the cause of the disaster.

Wednesday December 12th, I became sixteen.

Market Day. Rabbits selling for nine pence each
Coxes Orange Pippin apples for 3 shillings per
hundredweight.
One fat bullock, weighing seventeen hundredweight,
sold for twenty- eight pounds.

On December 18th, Father paid the rent for Kilkington, one hundred and twenty pounds for the half year to the owners, the Cotterells. They owned Garnons, an estate of around ten thousand acres.

Pantalls had been their tenants for four centuries until 1967, when my brother Richard bought Kilkington upon the death of Sir Richard Cotterell when death duties forced the sale of land. At last Kilkington was in the ownership of the Pantall family.

I finished the year of 1934 with a new pair of boots, size ten, costing twenty three shillings and sixpence. Father bought, to share between three of us, a new bike from Cons. of Hereford at three pounds, nineteen shillings and sixpence, the cheapest in the shop.

'Good luck to all the rats and the same to all the cats,
it does not matter how I try,
my traps the rats will defy,
but all things in rat scandal
they do hate the words C R Pantall.'

9

January 1st 1935 found me continuing with my rat catching contract. In those days rats thrived and multiplied because of the corn bays and ricks. With the introduction of the combine harvester there were no more corn ricks. New type of poison and gas ensured rats were nearly exterminated. However in 1935 they were numerous. Father paid me a penny half penny per rat. In 1934 I had caught fifty-two! A colony of rats will eat a lot of corn but you could only catch them in the winter months when ricks of corn were still available to lay the traps in.

I packed the remainder of the apples stored in one of the old bedrooms. We kept tons of desert apples there over the winter because from January onwards they would sell at a higher price. It was always very cool in the bedrooms. I took a load of Cox's Orange Pippin and Blenheims to market on the dray where they made three shillings per hamper of fifty-six pounds.

An interesting family event took place on Tuesday January 22nd 1935. Cecil Pantall, father's cousin, was married at Stoke Lacy Church to Miss Orgey and father went to the wedding. Cecil is alive today, aged 94, and living at Sutton St. Nicholas Parish, near Hereford.

Father sold the clover seed to Passey and Nott, Corn Merchants, of Hereford. Forty-five hundred weight, fetching seventy shillings per cwt.

In February Mother decided to live with Auntie Elizabeth at Riverside House, Fyfield, Essex. Poor Mum had a raw deal in life.

Our threshing machine broke down so we hired one from Williams of Preston-on-Wye. It threshed and bailed, the bails being tied with wire. The charge, seven shillings and sixpence per hour!

Moles were on the increase so I started setting traps killing the moles instantly. They had to be skinned as soon as possible and I tacked the skins on boards to dry out then sold them for ten pennies each to Robinsons of Hereford, 'Furriers of the West'.

Whilst rabbit catching on Monday February 11th, 'Trueman' the foxhound we were 'walking' for the Radnor & West Hereford Hunt, came from a field of kale about four hundred yards away with a live rabbit in his mouth and carried it over to me. It was a fully-grown rabbit and before despatching it I could see it did not have a mark on it. Proof enough that foxhounds have a 'soft mouth'.

Rabbit catching for this season 468.

At the end of February father, Richard and I had a wonderful day in London. We went down by early train and visited St. Pauls; the Houses of Parliament; Buckingham Palace; and saw the King and Queen leaving for Eastbourne. It was the first time Richard and I had been to London. The journey took three hours, the same time it takes today. We were lucky not to hear 'British Rail regrets the delay'.

March 14th Golden Miller won the Gold Cup at Cheltenham for the fourth time in succession.

At the North Herefordshire Point to Point in April, I bet on two races and lost on both.

That Sunday Jean cooked a lovely dinner of pork, cauliflower, potatoes and gravy, followed by a rhubarb tart. She was just twelve years old!

I had been having pain in my right big toe for which I went to Hereford General Hospital for X-rays and to see a specialist. It was not getting any better so I went to see Mrs. Drew at a village called Ameley. She was a fourth generation bonesetter. She found that my toe was out of joint and put it back together again, charging three shillings and sixpence. It stopped the pain but to this day I have a right foot with a stiff big toe!

Monday May 6th was King George V and Queen Mary's Silver Jubilee. We celebrated the occasion by having a sports day followed by a tea party in the village hall.

On June 15th Garnon's new cricket pavilion was 'opened 'by Lady Lettice Cotterell. I often went to the cricket ground but I did not have time to play in any of the matches, there was always too much to do on the farm.

Now we are busy making hay,
the rats are making the best of play.
But wait until the winter comes again,
I will catch those stagers without a wee bit of pain,
but although I cannot trust the cats,
I put a bob on my dear old traps.

We burned chiefly wood on all fires but to cook we used coal that had to be collected from Moorhampton Station by horse and wagon. We collected two and a half tons for our workers and three tons for ourselves.

On October 8th I went to stay with Uncle Fred and Auntie Doris at Ridgewood Dairy Farm, Preston, Lancashire. Whilst there I went on his round with the milkman at six in the morning. I found it very interesting. If a customer wanted half a pint it was ladled out of the milk churn and poured straight into their jug. Most dairy deliveries were done with horse and cart but we delivered in an Austin van. We sold fifteen gallons of milk between us that morning.

I also went to the Blackpool illuminations, inside the Tower, and Auntie Doris took me shopping in Manchester. It rained but the shops were wonderful. We went to Southport, a lovely quiet town, and visited the Winter Gardens there which were very neat and tidy. I had a good holiday.

When it was time to leave I packed my bags and caught the eleven fifteen train from Preston arriving home at four. I started work straight away, milking, and hauling sacks of corn from the thresher to the granary, finishing at eleven that night.

The whole gang at Kilkington helped pull the sugar beet. It began with two horses pulling a plough-like contraption down the drill, which lifted the sugar beet out of the ground. We then pulled up the beat by hand, chopping off the leaves and throwing the beet into a tump to be loaded onto a horse and cart and then on to a large wagon. Two horses pulled the wagon to Moorhampton Station where it went by rail to Kidderminster Sugar Beet factory to be processed into sugar. Today the sugar beet is lifted out by a machine with a hydraulic system, topped and put into a trailer before, with the aid of a mechanical chain, being put into a lorry and sent to Kidderminster – involving no manual handling.

On November 14th, 1935, The Conservative Party won the general election.

On November 21st we made one hundred and fifty gallons of cider, fifty gallons of which was for Grandad.

At the end of November I ploughed all day in the bottom field with a double furrow plough and three horses. These ploughs were very heavy and awkward to handle. It was hard work to drive three horses taking three days to plough ten acres.

Today a tractor ploughing six furrows and travelling four times the speed of horses would be finished in four hours with the driver sitting comfortably in a waterproof cab on a specially designed seat and with a radio on full blast.

On Monday January 20th, 1936 King George V died. He was a great shooting man, loved the sport and was a good shot.

Life on the farm went on as usual. On March 21st the Radnor and West Herefordshire Point to Point was held at Weobley, followed on the 28th by the North Herefordshire's held at Burley Gate. I backed O'Dell and again won two pounds.

From November 12th milk producers, like us, sold milk direct to Cadbury for one shilling per gallon. We supplied Cadbury with two hundred and seventy seven gallons of milk during the following March.

Mother came down from Essex to see us. We all spent a lovely day with her on Easter Monday. At the end of April Father bought a second hand Morris Oxford Six. It could exceed fifty five miles per hour. He got ten pounds for the old Citroen!

In May, Richard who was now in the Shropshire Yeomanry, Territorial Cavalry regiment, went with the Garnons Troop for training to Salisbury Plain, returning from camp two weeks later, twenty pounds better off.

Saturday September 5th was wet again. It had been a very wet summer, the corn knocked down by the rain, was difficult to cut. That night we all went to the Kemble Theatre to see 'Things to Come' but in my diary I have written 'I don't think they will!

Sunday the following day found us loading wheat from the field in front of the house, fourteen loads in all.

'Six days shalt thou labour, but on the seventh day do all odd jobs'.

We hope to get harvesting finished for a Harvest Thanksgiving Service on Boxing Day this year.

On October 10th, the Weobley and District farmers ploughing match took place at Weobley. A few days later Tom Gwilt, a big friend of mine, left to live and work in Newport

Monmouthshire. 'The best boy as ever a crow flew over.'

At the end of October Father sold ten tons of wheat and all the malting barley at ten shillings a hundred weight. This was the price for top quality milling and brewing cereals.

On December 10th King Edward V111 abdicated to marry the twice-divorced Mrs. Simpson. The following day the Duke and Duchess of York ascended the English throne as King George V1 & Queen Elizabeth.

Alan was confirmed at St. Mary's Church, Staunton-on-Wye on December 17th.

On December 18th 1936 being eighteen years of age, I joined the Shropshire Yeomanry. A good many farmers' sons joined which entailed some evening and weekend training. Richard and I were obliged to join up because our landlord, Sir Richard Cotterell was a major and Garnons troop was his. It met at Moorhampton Hotel every Thursday evening. The hotel supplied a large room, and in the middle was a table spread with all types of instructions and maps. The Officers were mostly landlords like Sir Richard. Privates, corporals and sergeants were the less educated 'buggers' like me. Several weekend courses were held at the Shrewsbury headquarters. It had all the facilities, kitchen, sleeping quarters and a large parade ground. On the outskirts of Shrewsbury was a shooting range with point 303 rifles being used. I excelled in this type of warfare, winning prizes and was picked to represent 'C' Squadron at Bisley the following Summer where I met a lot of competition and didn't win anything!

In May 1937 the Garnons troop made their way with their horses to Moorhampton Station to embark for two weeks training at Porthcawl in Wales. The army paid twenty pounds for the use of each horse. I hired a hunter from a farmer at Madley. The two weeks were no holiday. Between five am and six pm lots of exercises and manoeuvres. I was Bren Gun carrier for our troop. On one occasion a General paid us a visit. We were on parade. Next to me was a lad from Oswestry. The General remarked what a fine chap he was. Bill, the lad in question replied, "I'm a good doer Sir."

(a 'good doer' was a remark used to describe cattle)

We had all had a ration of rum and the General said to Bill, "Did you like the rum?"

Bill replied, "Yes sir. If my Mother had brought me up on that stuff, I would be sucking her now."!

The exercises consisted of cavalry warfare riding in line and changing pace to order. The horse I had hired was a mad uncontrollable sod. At Porthcawl station, when saddled up the Officer in charge said, "Independently mount!"

I mounted, the horse reared straight up and landed on its back with its four legs in the air. I managed to slip out of the big uncomfortable saddle. It took guts to remount him. On another occasion he bolted, charging straight past the officers in front. I could not stop him. We arrived back in camp in record time and Sgt. Major Milward gave me a right ticking off. The camp over, we returned to civilian life.

On December 20th, Jack took a load of dressed poultry on the dray to H P Barnsley's Christmas sale of poultry. The birds had all been killed and dressed by our gang of women from the village, with Pug in charge as usual, the only difference being that my mother was not there to put the finishing touches to these birds. Presentation was, as today, very important to attract buyers. Her absence was felt amongst the women – there wasn't that happy atmosphere we had experienced in mother's presence.

We had chickens, chiefly cockerels and some geese. The geese made seven-pence-half-penny per pound, the chickens eleven-pence-halfpenny. They would have made more if mother had been there. These prices were very low indeed.

In 1936, 'dole' for farm labourers was introduced by Stanley Baldwin's government. He became Prime Minister in 1935 and remained so until 1937.

On the January 9th 1937, we had a party to celebrate both Jean and Alan's birthdays. Jean invited Elizabeth Richards and Kathleen Morris, two school friends and Alan invited Robert Richards and another friend. Many of our farming friends including the Dales of Preston-on-Wye and the Roberts of Hinton were also invited. We played games and the grown-ups played cards and chatted.

The first three months of the year passed in the same routine as other years. My diary records Good Friday, March 26th 1937. 'Rolling and harrowing the lower field all day'. At night, after milking, the grinding and pulping would commence which was laborious work. To begin, the Blackstone engine had to have its tank filled with paraffin before a heating stove, permanently attached to the front of the engine, was lit and became hot enough for the paraffin to ignite. The saying 'Patience is a virtue' applied to this task. About two tablespoons of methylated spirit was poured into a cup-like holder, fixed to the lamp, after lighting it took about two minutes to heat the paraffin. The lamp had to be pumped and gave off a hissing sound when the heating stove was hot enough to receive more pumping, heating the ignition on the engine. It was a 'guessing game' as to when it was hot enough to start but it usually took about ten minutes. The engine had two large wheels on each side and a smaller offside wheel driving the belt operating the mill. The operator stood beside the large wheel, placing his right foot at the bottom and using his right arm to turn it faster and faster until, with a 'choo choo', the engine started running at a very fast speed.

Whilst the engine was heating, I filled the mill hopper with oats. By pulling a lever I transferred the belt from one pulley to another which drove the mill, setting it to grind whatever was required, from flour to kibbled oats. Another lever set the chaff cutter in motion. Whilst the hopper was being filled, I went up a ladder to the loft, carrying a hurricane lamp, and fed boltins of straw and hay into this two bladed machine, having sharpened the knives with a file before I began. I would have to go down to the mill several times, filling the hopper with more corn. If the bin was full of flour I would have to fill a sack, carrying it on my back to the granary, about two hundred yards away, also carrying a lamp to guide me up some steep wooden steps where I would drop the sack on top of the heap.

When the chaff cutting was finished, I would change the

pulley over to the pulper, putting in the swedes or turnips to be crushed.

At midnight I would turn off the engine, go into the house and fill a bucket with soft water from the buts to wash the dust and flour away. I needed nothing to help me sleep and was up again at six o'clock.

Nature brings out the daffodils and primroses in March and April then, in May and June, the trees are in full leaf. Bluebells 'herald' the arrival of summer.

Haymaking and harvesting took place as usual but we'd had a new Fordson tractor in April, costing one hundred and thirty pounds, which used T.V.O, with petrol to start. This was done with a cranking handle at the front. If paraffin had leaked into the carburetor it meant emptying and beginning again – cranking the engine placed a huge strain on the shoulder. I found the most successful way to start the Fordson was to let it run on petrol for about two minutes before changing over. All over the country tractors were replacing the horse for pulling the haymaking wagons and binders. The most popular tractor was the little Ferguson, adaptable for most jobs, including ploughing. Cabs were to become compulsory in later years. Diesel tractors soon became available. John Deer and International with Fordson were popular for ploughing four furrows.

§

Early in 1937 I decided to leave Kilkington and with it the farming world. The future was not bright for me. Father, unlike Grandad, was not a successful farmer and any hopes I may have had of being financed and set up on a farm were a pipe dream. Here I was at twenty years of age working my guts out for no payment at all. I decided to try to join the Metropolitan Police Force. I would be a little cog in a great big wheel and would see how others lived: the rich, the middle class, and the poor, like me.

On January 14th I wrote to the recruitment centre at New Scotland Yard requesting an application form. I received an early reply with forms to fill in (since leaving school at four-teen I'd had no further education or even the opportunity to write my name). On February 15th I heard back from them informing me that my weight of eleven stone three pounds was under the average for my height and advising me to re-apply in six months time. I needed feeding up!

First thing every morning I took the cover off a milk churn and helped myself to a cup of rich creamy milk. I also decided other 'goodies' would help including Cadbury's milk chocolate. For this I needed cash. When Father went to market on Wednesdays I used to take a ferret to an open rabbit warren (no hedges) lay nets and, with a bit of luck, would catch one or two. Also on the quiet I would shoot a cock pheasant. In years gone by such poaching would have had you shipped off to Australia! That night I would take the bird and rabbits to the local shop. The following day Mrs. Kinsey, the shopkeeper, would hand them over to a game dealer – rabbits fetched a shilling each and a cock pheasant, half a crown. Occasionally, time permitting, I would lay rabbit wires. I became quite an expert with these, laying them in quiet spots where they would not be seen, and – creeping out in the early morning – with a bit of luck, find a rabbit or two to put in my hiding place.

In that six months I raided the cake larder numerous times, never missing out on a meal and came up for seconds whenever the opportunity arose. My chocolate store, I ate half a block each day, was hidden in the hay in the cow shed. This was supplemented from Mrs Kinsey's shop, often on tick!

On September 1st, having gained a stone, I was invited to visit the Police Station at Weobley for a preliminary written examination. I was feeling very nervous, not having prepared for this exam. I cycled to Weobley, parked my bike outside the police station, then the sergeant took me into a quiet room for the test, English, Mathematics, and General Knowledge.

On September 8th, I heard from the Metropolitan Police Force. I had passed.

On the 7th January 1938 we held a party at Kilkington for all our friends. We had been to them lots of times during 1937. There were twenty-three of us altogether including the Dales of Huntley Court, whose parties were out of this world. My two particularly favourite people were Dorothy Dale and Eileen Manning.

On Wednesday January 12th it was market day. Rabbits made four shillings a brace.

It was the time of year when the social side of village life took place. Most Friday evenings dances were organised in the village hall (commonly called the hut) which attracted many young girls from neighbouring villages.

On Saturday January 15th, it was the annual school treat. This involved a good old eating session of buns, cakes etc. followed by games such as musical chairs, blind man's buff and so on. I could not attend because I was too old, but Alan and Jean did.

On January 18th I went to drill at Moorhampton Hotel for the first time. It consisted of map reading, mock battles and beer drinking. I did not like beer so I drank lemonade.

Below Kilkington Manor and gardens, adjoining the drive stood a hand pump. It was situated on a very steep incline (about forty-five degrees). When pumped with some considerable effort it forced water up a long one-inch pipe into a two hundred-gallon tank stored in the roof of the wool room above the kitchen. It was cold water only, for use in the kitchen. From an early age, whatever the weather and with the aid of a hurricane lamp father would take Richard and I down to the pump once a week. He would put one hand on the topmost part of the handle (the easiest place) the other in his pocket, whilst Richard and I operated at the lowest point, pushing the handle up and down. It took all of forty-five minutes, was very hard work and we never did completely fill the tank. At very little cost Father could have fitted a 'Blakes Ram Pump' making it a much simpler task but nothing was cheaper than using 'the boys'. (See photograph of Kilkington)

On Sunday January 30th it snowed. Father and I pumped. This had become a regular Sunday chore. I could have told him not to be so lazy, pull his hand out of his pocket and do his share but he ruled us with a rod of iron. If I had confronted he would have been the worse off. He was short in height, five feet eight inches but as by then I had decided to leave I decided against it.

On February 19th I went to Ludlow on the annual week-end course with the Garnons troop 'C' Squadron. We celebrated their annual dinner and on the Sunday had rifle drill and lectures finishing at noon. I was paid twelve shilling and three pence.

On Sunday April 10th I went to the first mounted drill at Garnons the stately home of Major Sir Richard Cotterell – Commanding Officer of 'C' Squaron, Shropshire Yeomanry. I rode Little Woman and at the end of the exercise we had some fun jumping. She performed like a Point-to-Pointer.

April 24th saw the second mounted drill at Garnons. About twenty of us, including Trooper Reg Trumper from Staunton came with me. We had a map reading exercise and pretended that we were being attacked by enemy aircraft – in reality we would have been blown to smithereens.

On Friday April 29th 1938, Sir Samuel Hoar presented his Budget in the House of Commons.

Petrol.   Up ld. from 1/5 to 1/6 per gallon

Tea.   2d on tea. From 2/2 to 2/4 per lb.

Income Tax. Up 6d.

Cigarettes. Ten for sixpence,
*   20 for Elevenpence halfpenny.*
*   Cigarette cards in each packet.*

On Saturday April 30th, it was the Cup Final.
The result: Preston North End 1 Huddersfield Town 0

On May 2nd, Ernie Williams who had been at Kilkington for three years as general workman helped me to roll and harrow the beet ground in the lower field. Not only was Ernie a very nice chap he was excellent at his job. Ernie was later to leave Kilkington, taking a job as a tractor-driver at Newent, Gloucester. Unfortunately he contracted T.B. returning home to New House Cottage where he died.

On Saturday May 21st, we members of 'C' Squadron, Shopshire Yeomanry loaded our horses at Hereford Station after riding them over from our homes. We left at half-past eight in the evening for the Gower, near Swansea, for two weeks annual camp, arriving at half past five on Sunday morning. We fed and watered the horses then went into a large tent for breakfast where I soon learned 'S.O.S' (*Stretch Or Starve*) and '*What Does Not Fatten Will Fill*'. We had to queue holding a tin dish and cup. When my turn came, a rasher of bacon was slapped on my plate from a pig which had outlived any other in the country, along with what turned out to be scrambled egg and doorsteps – bread that put your teeth to the test.

We found the latrines, a pole over a pit. Toilet paper here was the *South Wales Echo*. After a bellyful of army grub the only laxative to move it was TNT.

The horses now had to be groomed. I had Little Woman and she disliked army life with hundreds of strange horses around her. She had been 'shod' by our blacksmith on the Thursday prior to camp.

We had been up since five, fed the horses with Welsh hay (no clover or ryegrass in it) and a small ration of oatmeal. If the horses arrived at camp fat, they would not return home in the same state! If they arrived thin, they would only just last the fortnight. We had to muck out using an old wheelbarrow, which was on its last legs, to convey the droppings to a pit close by. Our next job was to clean and polish our tack that included our army boots. I always used chromium-plated stirrups, as did everyone else but the Army made us use their stirrups which were made of steel and the buggers took a lot of cleaning.

Colonel W W Hayes commanded the Shropshire Yeomanry. Major Lonsdale was second in command. Major Sir Richard Cotterel commanded 'C' Squadron and his second-in-command was Lieutenant Davenport, leader of Garnons troop. They each had a groom and wore chromium plate stirrups!

The Officers were all landlords and lorded it over us but without us farmer's sons there would not have been a Yeomanry.

Colonel Hayes was always one of the first to arrive at the stables (this was not an enclosure but where the horses were tied up in a line). He was happy to be seen pushing a wheelbarrow full of horse muck, and *mucked* in with us all, helping where he could.

We spent Monday, our first day, on Troop Drill that was tiring and difficult work. We spent the afternoon foot slogging and map reading and again in the evening after feeding and mucking out our horses.

On the Thursday, after three days of drill, I was again appointed Bren Gunner for the Garnons troop and in the evening spent four hours on line guard.

Payday : To Date – One pound and fourteen shillings

The following Sunday was church parade. I was ordered to go on main guard for two nights, two hours on and four hours off on a twenty-four hour shift.

On Thursday, 'C' Squadron declared 'war' on 'A' Squadron in mock battle. This was all very exciting but I never did find out who won.

Friday was Sports day. Garnons troop won the cup for the best troop in the Shropshire Yeomanry during camp.

On Saturday June 4th at half past five in the morning we left camp and went by train home to Hereford arriving at six in the evening. Camp was finished for 1938 and a damn good job too!

Alan and I went to the Three Counties Show which took place on the following Wednesday and were amazed to see what improvements had been made to farm implements even in twelve months.

Father took Jean to Portsmouth for a holiday with Uncle Bert and Auntie Katie and at the end of the month I went to Ludlow to shoot for 'C' Squadron Shropshire Yeomanry in the Trained Men's Cup. I was fourth using .303 rifles.

On July 2nd I went to Bisley, a famous shooting range, to represent them in the T.A.R.A. Competition. There were very many competitors from all over England.

I practiced target shooting all the next day, distances from one hundred yards, seven hundred yards up to two thousand yards. I was shooting for the Queen Mary & Kings medal. Although I shot well it was not good enough, it was won by a Sergeant Major in the Monmouthshire regiment.

On the Tuesday we shot for the Secretary of State and the Wantage Cup. I enjoyed these competitions but due to the numerous entries it was a hurried affair. I was rankless and had to rush in when I had the chance. I was the last competitor and was sure my entry was not recorded!

On Wednesday July 6th I left Bisley and went to Sandhurst College for a tour of inspection. In the afternoon I travelled to London then on to Fyfield Hall where I stayed the night with Uncle George and Auntie Lizzie, spending some time with Mother.

The following day I travelled back to London then by train to Hereford.

Father was at the Royal Agricultural Show at Cardiff

On Saturday August 6th I went with Mother to see George Robey in 'The Ship of Wrath' followed by a good supper.

On August 18th I reapplied to the Metropolitan Police Force.

On the 23rd Richard was twenty-one and had lots of presents including a gold watch from Mother.

On September 8th I heard that I had passed all my exams for the Police Force and was now invited to take another exam in London.

On September 15th 1938, our Prime Minister, Mr Neville

Chamberlain, flew to Germany to discuss the present crisis in Czechoslovakia with Herr Hitler but Hitler was not interested. The following Sunday the outbreak of war seemed imminent. Parks throughout the country were being dug up and air raid shelters installed below ground. All Reserves were called up and mobilisation was expected at any time. On Friday 23rd gas masks were issued to people all over the country.

On the 26th I went to London. Sandbags were being laid at all strategic points. War was expected at any time. The following morning, at half past eight, I went to New Scotland Yard and passed my medical examination, followed by a written and oral examination. I went before a Selection Committee and after taking the Oath of Allegiance was given thirty years service. I finished at five o'clock and returned to Hereford.

On Thursday September 29th Mr. Neville Chamberlain flew to Munich to attend a Four-Power Conference. Herr Hitler, Germany; Signor Mussoline, Italy; Monsieur M Doladier of France; and Mr Neville Chamberlain; Great Britain. On Friday September 30th, The Four-Power Conference came to an agreement. Wearing a black coat and top hat, Mr. Chamberlain stepped from a twin engined Dakota airoplane at London airport waving a piece of paper declaring *Peace in Our Time*. Hitler had made this agreement.

On October 3rd it appeared *Peace Had Returned Again*.

On the 8th Weobley & District Agricultural Improvement Society held the annual ploughing match at Bearwood, near Hereford. This was possibly the last ploughing match to be held with horses pulling the plough. Ten years later it would be all tractors with not a horse to be seen!

On Sunday October 16th 1938, I packed my few belongings ready to leave Kilkington after twenty years. Since the age of six I had worked for my Father with no wages except for the odd sixpence now and again. I now received, after fourteen years of hard work, the magnificent sum of thirty shillings less my train-fare to London. My total cash to start out on my own was less than Father would put on a horse at the races!

Monday October 17th 1938 I left Kilkington for London to join the Metropolitan Police Training School at Peel House, Buckingham Palace Road, Westminster.

PART III

INTO BATTLE

10

From Tuesday 18th October 1938, instead of working with my hands, I had to 'work my loaf.' I decided that now I had left Kilkington I would work hard and make a success of my new career in the police. I was offered the prospect of a thirty-year contract and sent to Peel House.

The word Police means generally the arrangements made in all civilised countries to ensure that the inhabitants keep the peace and obey the law and particularly the FORCE OF POLICE OFFICERS employed for this purpose.

There were twenty recruits in our class, all a pleasant bunch of lads. We each had a little cubicle with a bed and washbasin with a tap. This was better than Kilkington to say nothing about the flush lavatory along the corridor!

At six am we were 'on parade' with a pair of plimsoles and a light shirt (I had no PT kit). Off we went around a block of houses at full trot then back for a session in the gymnasium. This was the procedure each morning. Afterwards a quick breakfast from a kind of help yourself cafeteria offering coffee or tea, bacon, eggs and toast etc.and not a tin plate or mug in sight! We were in the classroom by 9 o'clock sharp.

I was now a policeman and started in the eleventh class,

moving down one class each week of training. Each week we covered a different aspect of police work and were tested every Friday on the subject. If we made under sixty percent on the test it was 'Goodbye'.

Our instructors were older and very experienced sergeants, each with his own speciality. We visited police stations, courts even the mortuary where we reckoned the bodies had been for months.

October 31st was my first payday. I received twenty-five shillings and could now buy some more clothes.

§

On November 4th a dance was held at Peel House. Hundreds of girls seemed to flock there but this country bumkin kept well out of the way. Instead I took my cousin, Stephanie Matthews, to see Will Hay in 'Hay Hay America'.

Although Hitler had stated 'Peace in our Time', no-one trusted him, so sandbags were continuing to be placed by newly dug shelters, anti-aircraft guns were appearing in parks and more people in uniform appeared daily.

On Friday November 11th there was a mini exam. Five questions had to be answered in half an hour with fifty marks to be attained out of a possible seventy. I passed the exam with a score of fifty-six. Of the twenty in our class four failed.

I went to St. Peters Church on Sunday and the following day seventh class began under Sergeant Mack. During one of the lectures he asked had anyone a photograph of home. I produced from my inner pocket a snap of me stood by the tractor at Kilkington. He took one look and roared with laughter. I never understood why!

One Thursday Sergeant Wheatley set us a First Aid examination. A maximum of one hundred and twenty marks could be achieved with a minimum of eighty. I attained one hundred and sixteen, losing only four marks.

The following Sunday I went out to Fyfield thumbing a lift

to Chigwell and spent the day with Mother, Uncle George and Auntie Lizzie. This was a lovely break for really we spent most of our time studying.

The next day it was sixth class and payday – twenty-seven and sixpence. That week we learned how to make an arrest and I bought a pair of boots for nineteen shillings and six pence.

On Sunday 27th I went sight seeing, taking in St Martin's in the Field and Nelson's Column with its hundreds of pigeons and thousands of visitors. I also visited Hyde Park and the Serpentine. The following weekend I went out to Fyfield. Mother had a suit made for me. My 'one and only'.

On December 29th I took my final examination and passed with flying colours. Next day I went again to see Mother and her family, the Whites. They always made me welcome. Mother told me that her Grandfather's name was Watt, famous for inventing the steam engine and the free wheel on a bicycle. Both she and the rest of her family kept the name Watt-White. Mother herself was a very clever woman and any brains I may have were inherited from her. We saw the Old Year out and the New one in on Saturday night and spent a thoroughly enjoyable weekend in all.

On Monday January 2nd I said my final good-bye to Peel House and was sworn in as a Constable of the Metropolitan Police Force by Sir Phillip Game, Commissioner, at New Scotland Yard. Fitted out with my uniform and helmet I was given the number of P.C.519N. The N denoted the division and I was to be stationed at Kentish Town and so began two years probation.

I was given lodgings at 98 Huddlestone Road, Kentish Town. I have written in my diary 'A blinking hole'.

I spent the next few days at Clerkenwell Police Court watching the procedure. The next weekend I changed my 'digs' to 163 Tufnell Park Road agreeing to pay Mrs. Carrot twenty-six shillings a week for full board and lodgings including my laundry. On payday I received two pounds, nineteen shillings and threepence.

During the next few days we new recruits received

instructions on 'how to fill in the various forms' and the pro-
cedures in dealing with the duties of a police officer on the
beat.

On the Monday I went on duty at six a.m., number two-
beat with an 'old hand', changing over at ten to number
three-beat with another officer. Two days later I had the day
off and opened a savings account with a deposit of three
pounds fourteen shillings and purchased my first provisional
Driving Licence costing five shillings.

A few days later, driving Mother's car, I took her and Jean
to visit Uncle Bert and Auntie Katie in Portsmouth.

We used to do regular Saturday duty at football grounds,
usually Highbury, and consequently saw some interesting
matches. We were there to stop the enthusiasts flocking onto
the pitch at the end of the match. We would also be sent in
the van over to Wembley for 'Cup Final' duty. A semi-final for
the F.A.between Portsmouth and Huddersfield on 25th
February saw Portsmouth into the final and then at the end
of April I saw them beat Wolves 4-1 for the cup at Wembley.

At the end of February I enrolled as a member of the
'North Western Polytechnic' (membership 6/8d) to take
Maths, English and Geography and, on March 2nd, I attend-
ed my first class.

A few days later saw me at Clerkenwell Police Court for my
first case to be heard. George (Ginger) Townsend, a coster-
monger charged with 'Obstruction & Obscene Language'. He
was found guilty and fined forty shillings, obviously not his
first time in Court. I also had my first suicide. A man had
hanged himself in a private house in Dalmeny Road. At the
Coroner's inquest which I attended a verdict of 'suicide whilst
of unsound mind' was recorded.

The next day Mum came over from Fyfield and we spent
the day together.

On March 30th I brought my first charge of 'drunk and
disorderly' in Kentish Town.

On Good Friday I went on night duty to Hampstead
Heath. A number of air-raid shelters had been located there
and a police presence was needed to make sure all was well.

The various police stations had sports teams and were very keen to co-opt new members, I joined the cricket team for Kentish Town and when we played Albany Street scored two runs! The final score was Albany Street 32, Kentish Town 11. The following week we played Caledonian Road, I took a wicket and scored 23, but we still lost!

One of the recruits, Terry, was very friendly. I went to his house on several occasions for late tea, he lived at Peaslake in Surrey. His Mother and Father made me welcome. He came with me down to Kilkington once and we had a good weekend. At Peel House we had played table tennis and I discovered I was better than the average player. It was good exercise and I enjoyed it. We were really too busy studying, though, to really enjoy ourselves or even to form friendships. We all ended up in different divisions at the end of the course anyway.

May 17th. Grandad was eighty-eight years old, still drove his car and did all his own gardening. The garden was big with two large greenhouses.

At the beginning of June, I registered at Kentish Town Labour Exchange with three other P.Cs for conscription. I then applied to the Royal Air Force to be trained as a pilot as planes had always held a fascination for me. I would have to wait twenty years before this fascination was satisfied when I owned and flew my own plane. On June 10th orders came through that Police Officers were an exempt category

The following Saturday I went to Hendon to take my driving test and passed. I hired an Austin 10 for the purpose from Junction Garage for ten shillings. I went to Fyfield on July 25th where we were harvesting all day.

The following month I took my six-monthly exam and passed with a ninety percent mark. The next day along with twenty-one others I had to go before the Superintendent for an interview regarding our efficiency. Mine was described by him as 'Excellent'.

My annual leave began on August 10th and I went home to Kilkington. I played cricket for Eardisley on the 12th and made thirty-two runs, taking four wickets. I was called back from leave on August 22nd. On the 24th Germany demanded Danzig and the Polish border. Three days later Sir Neville Henderson, the British Ambassador, arrived in Germany and was snubbed by Hitler.

I had developed a great taste for tennis and had joined the tennis club up in Highgate village. There I had met a very pleasant married couple who after some time offered me 'digs' in their home. They were ardent tennis players and I think they regarded housing me as part of their war effort. I stayed with them until the time when all single officers were required to lodge in police section houses and I found myself at Camden House.

§

It was a normal Sunday morning. The weather was fine, church bells were ringing, and traffic was light. A few people were gathering around Tufnell Park Tube Station. I was on duty standing near a police box at the top of Tufnell Park Road. It was eleven-twenty on September 3rd 1939. Standing beside me was an elderly civilian and an ARP Warden. The civilian looked at his wristwatch and said, "We'll know in a few minutes, eleven-thirty was the deadline!" This was the time given to Adolf Hitler to withdraw his troops from Poland or face war. Eleven-thirty came and with it the noise of sirens. God help us, after twenty-one years we were now at war again with Germany. They had been preparing for war for a number of years. Hitler planned to rule the world. The Germans were well equipped and well trained. We on the other hand only had a handful of trained men but 'RULE BRITTANIA'. At half-past-five that afternoon, France also declared war on Germany.

I did not ring in to Kentish Town Police Station, there was nothing to report. We all expected bombs to be dropped from German aircraft at any minute yet everyone appeared to be cool, calm and collected. When it became apparent that we were not in any danger from an air raid, our sirens sounded a long clear blast lasting about half a minute signalling the ALL CLEAR. Later in the day, King George VI broadcast to the nation giving courage and confirming that we were at war with Germany. What he did not say and would have been so appropriate was Nelson's famous address before the Battle of Trafalgar: 'England expects every man to do his duty'.

Police officers were issued with steel helmets and gas masks. Two days before, thousands of school children had been evacuated from London and other large cities to live with willing country folk. The evacuation was well timed and well organised. Bombing was yet to come as Germany was busy invading Poland. September 1939 saw very fierce fighting on the frontiers.

The Air Raid Precaution Service (ARP) had been set up before the outbreak of war and was made up of civilians who were not fit for conscription through age, some slight infirmity or a reserved occupation. Recruited from both sexes, they often had specialist knowledge or training. Equipped with a steel helmet, the statutory gas mask and a large torch, the wardens patrolled the streets and ensured that the 'Black Out' was maintained. Apparently a small pinprick of light could be seen clearly from the sky and enabled the German bombers to pinpoint their target with deadly accuracy. It was common to hear the order 'Put 'em out!' in the dark. Cars were driven without lights and created a whole generation of nervous drivers.

On Monday September 4th, London had its second air raid warning. Enemy planes were spotted in the distance but they did not come near London. (I think it was an exercise in preparation for the real thing). The *Athenia* was torpedoed from a German 'U' boat and there were no survivors. On the Wednesday a 'U' boat sank a British Ship with four hundred Americans on board and on Sunday September 10th Canada (part of the British Empire) declared war on Germany.

On September 15th, French troops were advancing on the Western Front between Luxemburg and Zaarbruken on the crack Ziegfried lines. Warsaw was being heavily bombed by German planes and Russia's army invaded Poland from the

Eastern front. On Monday September 18th a 'U' boat sunk *HMS Courageous*, all the crew were saved.

Poland capitulated to the Germans on September 28th. *HMS Royal Oak*, a famous battleship, was sunk by a 'U' boat in Scapa Flow, Orkney Islands on October 15th but England was free of air raids for the remainder of 1939.

In December on the glorious 12th, where most young men would be celebrating their twenty-first birthday with a party I was on duty from two in the afternoon until ten in the evening. I had a busy duty in Camden Town that included several reports and lots of warnings to motorists for leaving their cars unlocked whilst away shopping. Quite a contrast from 1998 when no one would dare leave their cars unlocked for not only would the contents be stolen but the car too.

There was good news on December 17th. The German battleship *Graf Spey*, which had sunk so many British ships including several with only children on board had entered the River Plate in the South Atlantic at Buenos Aires. Argentina was a neutral country so the *Graf Spey* had to leave the safety of the port. Outside the harbour were three British warships, ready and waiting to engage in battle with her. She steamed down the River Plate towards the open sea but suddenly before battle could commence her Captain scuttled her and she sank!

For the remainder of the year it was quiet on all fronts. Christmas was not a happy occasion. Polish people were being murdered in Poland, Jewish people sent to Concentration Camps and many people died from starvation and the bitter cold at 10 degrees below.

I was on duty all over Christmas, from two o'clock until ten pm My weekly pay was three pounds, three shillings and nine pence on which I paid two and four pence income tax. The latest reports from the Western Front were that the only fighting taking place was the British Soldiers snow ball fighting. Throughout 1940 it was to be 'Optimism to crush Hitlerism'.

11

O
n New Years day, 1940 there were no air raids and very little war activity. I began night duty. It was very cold and dark with no lighting permitted.

On February 12th, whilst on duty, I injured my left foot. The following day it turned septic and I was conveyed by ambulance to the Metropolitan Police Nursing Home, Chigwell Hall in Essex. This was a beautiful Georgian house, converted into a nursing home. I developed a temperature of one hundred and two but was well looked after.

On Sunday February 25th, British Summertime began. Three days later I left Chigwell Hall and went home to Kilkington, returning to London and resuming duty on March 5th. There were no air raids for the first part of the year although an occasional air-raid warning.

On April 23rd, Sir John Simon, Chancellor of the Exchequer, presented his budget. Cigarettes went up from ten for seven pence to ten for eight pence halfpenny. Beer up a penny to ten pence. Postage stamps rose from one-penny halfpenny to two pence halfpenny. There was a three pence increase on rolling tobacco.

On May 10th 1940, Germany invaded Belgium and Holland. Neville Chamberlain resigned as Prime Minister that day to be succeeded by the Rt.Hon. Winston Churchchill, First Lord of the Admiralty.

The following day British and French troops enter Belgium.

On May 19th there was very heavy fighting on the Western front. The Germans were advancing rapidly onto French soil with numerous tanks and fighter planes, the M.E.109s, M.E.110s and Junker bombers. We lost twenty-six Hurricane fighters, the Germans thirty seven M.Es that day.

By May 22nd the Germans had advanced to within fourteen miles of Paris. Two days later, they captured and occupied Boulogne only twenty-six miles from England. Fierce fighting was happening outside Calais too.

On Monday May 27th, King Leopold of Belgium deserted his country. Belgium surrendered to the Nazi invaders.

On 10th June Italy declared war on Great Britain and France. On June 15th the Germans occupied Paris the capital of France.

On August 28th the German airforce, having now consolidated their establishment in France and Belgium decide to bomb London on a big scale and there were two air raids on London docks lasting all night.

All young single policemen, 'volunteers', were detailed for night duty in the East End and Docklands. Six of us went from Kentish Town police station. It was my first real experience of bombing. We arrived at East India Docks at seven. I was assigned to a police party of eight to assist A.R.P. Wardens in the Whitechapel area. We didn't have to wait long for the warning sirens, followed by the drone of enemy aircraft, the anti-aircraft guns in full cry and the continuous whistling sound of bombs. Usually a stick of six bombs were released together, when the sixth arrived dozens more followed from other planes. There could be a hundred bombs on the downward flight at any one time and numerous incendiary bombs containing a highly inflammable substance designed to explode on impact. The explosions were terrible, fires everywhere with not enough fire engines to cope. Screams of Help! Help could be heard from many houses. I ran with two wardens to one of the bombed homes and tried to pull and dig out those trapped in the debris. We found one dead body and a man and two women who were trapped under piles of wreckage. We managed to release them and handed them over to the squad of first aid workers. I saw more dead bodies in that one night than in my worst imaginings, only having seen three people dead before in my entire life.

The anti-aircraft guns were flat out. Although bombs were still whistling down, we kept going into the wrecked houses. At three in the morning the guns were suddenly silent, the 'all clear' was sounded and we could assess where to go next. Several police and wardens were casualties. We worked through the debris until seven, helping many to get free. Fortunately most people had gone into the shelters. Two of the six policemen who went did not come back with us! We were back at the station by half past seven.

On Friday 30th we went again to the docks, this time to Canary Wharf arriving around three in the afternoon. I assisted with the traffic, mostly fire engines and ambulances, the bombs were falling even then. So many detours had to be made. On this particular day there were five different air raids. In the month of August, eight hundred homes in London were destroyed by air attack.

I had a rise in pay of eight shillings. My wages were now three pounds and eight shillings a week net.

Eighty-eight German planes were shot down in August.

Germany began using a different type of bomb. It was called a Delayed action bomb. About an hour after it landed it would explode.

On Saturday September 7th 1940 the biggest air raid yet took place. I went with six other constables to Whitechapel High Street. We were there at three in the afternoon when over a thousand enemy planes arrived to bomb Dockland and the East End. P.C. Russell and I were both buried by falling debris. I fell into a bomb crater. Our anti-aircraft guns were relentless and had many hits to say nothing of our fighter planes, the Spitfires and Hurricanes. We heard aircraft in spiralling dives, bombs were raining down every-where. Hundreds of cries for help could be heard from homes and warehouses in the area. An ARP Warden had joined us in our search for the crying voices when a building suddenly collapsed on us. Fortunately we were near the surface, the warden only suffered an injured leg, P.C Russell and I sur-vived without injury. We were lucky enough to have an ambulance nearby for the injured. There were many dead too and they were removed, certified later and then identified.

ABBREVIATIONS FOR REFERRAL

NK	*Kentish Town Police Station*
AFS	*Auxillary Fire Service*
ARP	*Air Raid Precaution*
ATS	*Auxilliary Territorial Service*
ACK ACK	*Anti-aircraft gun*
BEF	*British Expeditionary Force*
DA	*Delayed Action Bomb*
LDV	*Local Defence Volunteers*
UXB	*Unexploded Bomb*
WAAF	*Women's Auxilliary Air Force*
WRNS	*Women's Royal Naval Service*
WVS	*Women's Voluntary Service*
HE	*High Explosive Bomb*

Over 8 million people in London

London docks are Wapping
Whitechapel and Stepney
One farthing $1/4d$
Sixpence $2 1/2$ *new pence*
One shilling 5 new pence
Half a crown $12 1/2$ *new pence*

At eleven o'clock we made our way back in the dark to the police station to report in and have a cup of Bovril and a sandwich. The station sergeant sent me with another consta-ble to the Commercial Road to cordon off an area where a bomb had left a large hole in the road. We found the UXB about twenty-five yards down from the junction on the left hand side. Nearby was a depot for council hoardings and we managed to find enough of them to block the area with NO ENTRY signs. We then searched the nearby houses to make sure everybody had evacuated the area. There were fires everywhere and in spite of the bombs people were still walking about. I left our bomb and reported its position to a police patrol car. They would inform the bomb disposal squad. I expect there were many more unexploded bombs in that area still to be discovered.

The bombing of the docks continued until nine. Sunday morning we left the scene at about seven and returned to Kentish Town. I went straight to bed on a mattress under a table in the basement of Camden House. No sooner had I laid down when there was a thud and a terrific BANG. A H.E. bomb had exploded in the road outside. I put my uniform back on and went outside to assist any injured, eventually returning to my bed and falling asleep in my uniform. At three in the afternoon I got up, had some breakfast, then made my way up to the tennis club and enjoyed a few sets of tennis!

The RAF bombed Berlin and Hamburg. The industrial valley of the Ruhr where the armaments were being produced was continually under attack.

Back in the East End there were further air raids over London. Numerous barrage balloons floated in the sky preventing enemy planes from venturing too low. Nelson was still there, surveying the scene from the top of his column, a symbol to eight million Londoners who showed great courage, patience and determination.

On September 11th a bomb weighing one ton was dropped outside the door of St. Paul's Cathedral. It was a time bomb, but before it could explode, it was de-fused by the army. Arriving at Aldgate at seven that evening I was delegated to help with the congestion of people flocking into the tube stations to shelter from the continual air raid which was in progress. It was a sight never to be forgotten.

The tube station and railway lines were packed to capacity, stretched to the limit. People in general were very good-natured and understanding, tired, about ninety percent of them falling fast asleep on the hard concrete platform, despite the bombs dropping above. Along with two other PC's I made my way back up the street to help fire engines find their way to fires too numerous to cope with. Only the skeletons of houses remained. I witnessed bombs exploding in streets and on houses and shops. So many people were killed by the blast from the bombs. We had been talking to a man and his wife and they had only walked twenty yards away when we heard a stick of bombs coming and fell flat on our faces on the pavement. A bomb exploded nearby. When we got up to survey the damage the man and his wife were lying on the ground, dead. They had caught the full blast from the bomb.

We inspected several air raid shelters where all was well and then made our way to a police box to report our presence. On the way another stick of bombs was dropping towards us. Again we fell flat on our faces. My companion was O.K but I was buried under a pile of debris from a fallen house. With his help I surfaced and, except for scratches, bruises and a coat that was torn and filthy, was whole. It was soon daylight and the 'all clear' sounded. It was reported in the newspaper that one hundred and eighty-five German planes had been shot down by our fighters over London that night. We had lost seventy-four of our planes. I obtained twenty-four hour's leave and made my way to Fyfield where I slept soundly.

On September 13th three bombs dropped on Buckingham Palace, destroying the Chapel. There were now hundreds of A.A guns in London defending the City. Our fighters kept to the outskirts attacking German bombers and fighters on their way to and from London.

NOTHING VENTURED, NOTHING GAINED

Rationing had now been introduced and although bread, potatoes and vegetables were not included, baking became impossible when 'fats' were so limited. The adult ration for one week was:

Milk	*3 pts*	*Cheese*	*3 ozs*
Sugar	*8 ozs*	*Bacon*	*4 ozs*
Butter	*2 ozs*	*Eggs*	*1 if available or one ounce of dried egg per month*
Margarine	*4 ozs*	*Sweets*	*2.1ozs*
Lard	*3 ozs*	*Tea*	*2 ozs*
Jam	*2 ozs*		

Meat to the value of one and tuppence so long as the tuppence was spent on corned beef; children were allowed an extra half but of this 1shilling and ninepence, fivepence-half-penny had to go on corned beef. Sausages weren't rationed but very hard to come by.

I was on duty in the Kentish Town Road area on September 9th and part of Castle Road was cordoned off because of an UXB. I saw the engineers working there and went to see if any help was needed. The engineer in charge invited me to have a closer look! The bomb was in the centre of a small lawn, at the back of the house. They had dug around the hole made by the bomb, about fifteen feet deep and wide enough to put down a ladder. They were awaiting the arrival of another engineer before it could be defused so invited me, at my own risk, to go down the ladder and make an inspection. I thought that if it did explode I wouldn't know anything about it so anyway down I went. It was as tall as I was, six feet. On the top was a small casement from which I presumed the engineers were going to render it harmless, unless it exploded in the meantime! It was quite an experience meeting a bomb face to face.

I surfaced and whilst discussing the situation I noticed people at one of the windows of the house next door. I went immediately to the house and advised them to leave, which they did. Shortly afterwards the bomb was defused, hauled up and taken off to Hackney Marshes where it was safely exploded.

On September 16th there was a full moon, this meant the German bombers would be out in force as would our boys. I remember the names Cunningham, Cunningham and Conningham as being famous night fighters, particularly by moonlight. I was on night duty and as expected there was a heavy air raid on the West End.

The following day the Germans introduced us to a new secret high explosive weapon. A Magnetic Landmine, dropped from a plane by parachute, seven feet long and two feet wide, it exploded when in contact with steel. Its arrival was totally silent. They dropped one in the Euston Road that demolished several hundred yards on one side but it missed the stations. I was not then being called to extra duty in the East End because North London was itself receiving heavy raids. Three very large bombs exploded near Kentish Town Police Station and did much damage. A thousand-pounder fell thirty yards from Camden House but did not explode.

The RAF retaliated. On this and every other moonlit night extra planes were sent to bomb Berlin and the Ruhr. Reports from Berlin confirmed that fires were raging. Railway yards, oil depots, power stations were being blown to where 'ALL NAZIS SHOULD GO'.

Three days later on the Thursday at one thirty in the morning a H.E. bomb was dropped in the street fifteen yards from Camden House demolishing three dwellings. Camden House only suffered from broken windows on the lower floors where we were sleeping, but the upper floors, including my bedroom, were destroyed. One civilian was killed and several injured, together with two PC's. This incident was reported by the 'Raid-Reporter' the following day.

I awoke with the blast knocking my head against the table but I could have been killed.

In November Anthony Eden in the Commons stated that about forty-four thousand British troops were being held as prisoners of war by Germany and Italy.

On September 24th Germany sank a British ship loaded with children being evacuated to America. Only a few were saved, the rest drowned as the ship sank in the darkness.

September 27th was London's twenty-first night of being continually blitzed.

On the Saturday I was on night duty, riding my bicycle close to the North Western Polytechnic. It was about two in the morning and I heard a stick of bombs dropping in my direction. Was one meant for me? I jumped off my bike and bolted up the steps of the Polytechnic four at a time reaching the door just as the sixth bomb fell in the courtyard. The blast blew me through the doorway, which fortunately stood open. Luckily I was not injured. The Polytechnic was being used by a Police Group and as an ARP Centre. I was being welcomed by several colleagues when part of the building caved in, resulting in us all having to be dug out. Some received slight injuries but no one was badly hurt. This incident was also mentioned in the *Daily Express* Raid-Reporters the following day.

On the 5th October Kentish Town was fifth on the list for the number of bombs dropped on sub-divisions, approximately 275.

I had two days leave and went out to Fyfield where I was met by an anxious Mum and Auntie Liz.

"Are you alright?"

"Yes, Mum, why?"

"Because we know you had very heavy raids last night."

"I know, I was buried in the North Western Polytechnic but except for a bruise and a cut on my right hand I'm fine."

Uncle George appeared and I asked, "Is there any ploughing you want doing?"

"Yes, but first of all get some sleep," he replied.

In the early afternoon I filled the new Fordson tractor with TVO and started ploughing in the front field. I was ploughing in stubble from a crop of linseed already harvested. I thoroughly enjoyed myself, finding it very relaxing after London.

§

The following night I was on duty and the bombing was fairly heavy. One bomb fell on Camden Tube Station, killing several, injuring many.

October 15th was another hectic night. There was a full moon and bombs were falling everywhere. I was walking up the Holloway Road when I saw one fall on a factory where a few minutes earlier I had been talking to the caretaker. I ran back to what remained of some steps. The bomb had completely demolished the factory and lying on the ground in front of the crater was the man. A gruesome sight, his face had caught the full blast and was covered in blood and bits of skin with the teeth protruding. There was nothing I could do to help him so I headed for the police box to report the incident.

The night was still with a light mist showing up in the moonlight. Just before reaching the police box I heard a soft rustling noise. There was a piece of waste-land to one side of the road and there, about five yards away, in all its majesty, was a land mine, its parachute lying beside it, spread all over the road. When I touched the material I was surprised at how beautiful it felt, it was pure silk. I made my way quickly to the police box expecting to be told to clear the area of any inhabitants. I phoned through and told the police officer on the switchboard what I had discovered only a few yards away. A voice shouted, "FIVE ONE NINE, GET THE HELL OUT OF IT!" I did just that. He must have told the demolition squad because about half an hour later when walking down Junction Road I saw the UXB vehicle in the distance turn into St John's Road on its way to the Holloway Road. The UXB crews were very brave, they went from bomb to bomb defusing them. Sometimes they were too late and the bomb had exploded, at other times the bomb would explode in their presence and then they would all be killed. Although I helped to release many people who were buried under their homes and many times I fell through a roof, I don't think anyone was as brave during the bombing as those UXB crews.

I spent the rest of October carrying out relief duty, filling in where needed. The bombing continued and when on day duty and on my beat I helped in the search for live or injured people. There were so many casualties!

Meanwhile Hamburg, Germany's second largest city, was receiving continuous heavy bombing.

On November 14th Coventry, one of Britain's most industrial towns, received a merciless all night raid by the bombers. There were over a thousand casualties. The Cathedral, built in the fourteenth century, was destroyed.

Three days later a land mine fell by Chalk Farm tube station, it did not explode and was rendered harmless by naval experts. It weighed two thousand, two hundred and eighty pounds, was eight feet six inches long and three feet wide.

Because London is one of the largest cities in the world, one can appreciate how difficult it was to feed eight million in wartime and particularly during enemy bombing raids. London even then had a large immigrant population especially in the East End where there were many Chinese.

Housewives wondered where the next meal would come from. Rationing was not the answer to an empty stomach when you had been bombed out of your home but in all fairness without rationing it would have been chaos. Neighbours and the voluntary women's organisations worked wonders when confronted by dozens of displaced people. The remarkable thing was the cheerfulness of everyone, there was no television, and radio reception was poor, although 'ITMA' was a popular programme and the voice of Vera Lynn (the Forces Sweetheart) always welcome.

Every morning at approximately ten am William Joyce a British Citizen, a traitor to his country, known here as 'Lord Haw Haw,' would broadcast over the British radio propaganda for the Nazis. He would commence by saying, "JARMANY CALLING, JARMANY CALLING." He would then proceed with a lot of lies as to how near Germany was to winning the war telling British people to unite and capitulate minimising Nazi air losses with staements such as :

"THE TWO HUNDRED AND FIFTY GERMAN PLANES THAT BOMBED LONDON LAST NIGHT, THREE HUNDRED RETURNED SAFELY".

After the war ended this traitor was hanged.

I was very thankful to be able to stay at Fyfield where Mother, Uncle and Auntie made sure I had rest and food. I visited as often as time allowed, enjoying tractor work when I could and shooting in the winter months.

On Tuesday November 19th, Birmingham received a heavy all night air raid from German bombers. Bristol was heavily bombed on the 30th. In return we gave all German towns a good pasting.

On December 12th I had my twenty-second birthday.

Twenty six thousand Italian soldiers were captured by British troops in Egypt on December 14th and two days later we gave them a good caning in Libya. The Italians are no fighters and must regret ever entering the war against Great Britain. Mussolini was a great friend and admirer of Hitler and it was his fascism that drew Italy into the war.

On Christmas Day there were no air raids but two days later on the 27th there was a heavy one over London with hundreds of casualties. One of the heaviest took place on December 29th. Our fighters, who went up to intercept them, were able to see the enemy planes by the light of the fires below. The next day hundreds of police and fire brigades were brought in from outer districts to help cope with the fires. It was London's second great fire! St. Paul's still remained intact!

I was on duty at Kentish Town when a bomb demolished a house in Fortess Road where two sisters lived, members of our tennis club. The bomb had dropped around midnight and I spent from early morning until midday searching the debris for signs of life but with no success. I never saw the girls again.

German plane losses since May 10th 1940 had reached over five thousand.
German planes shot down over London since August 1940 – One thousand, three hundred and forty five.
Our losses: four hundred and sixteen planes, two hundred and eight pilots saved.

When war was first declared most places of entertainment closed but as people became almost accustomed to the bombings, dance halls and cinemas started to open again and people began to enjoy themselves again despite the risk.

I saw in the New Year at the Hammersmith Palais de Dance. The following day I went out to Fyfield to haul potatoes to Ongar station returning to late turn and the air raids.

On January 6th 1941 Miss Amy Johnson, first woman to fly solo to Australia, drowned when she bailed out of her plane into the sea. She was an aircraft transporter.

By January ninety four thousand Italian troops were out of the war and the British troops were advancing towards Tobruk.

On January 12th at half past eleven I was on duty. It was very cold with a little snow. I was searching for victims in a bombed factory and found an injured man trapped beneath a steel girder. I managed to lift it whilst he pulled himself out but I slipped into the bomb crater and injured my left foot. I hobbled out and found a phone to ring Kentish Town Police station in order to obtain assistance for the man, and also to report my own injury. An ambulance took him to the nearest first aid station. It was difficult to go via a set route because of the bombed roads and obstructions and many diversions had to be made. However it was marvellous how well the drivers of Government vehicles managed to avoid these obstructions. Their morale was high and they 'felt' for the injured, hungry and homeless.

By this time I couldn't walk as my ankle had swollen up and was very painful. I was dropped off at the Section house in Camden Town where I soaked my foot in hot water.

Tuesday morning I was taken to Denmark Hill Police Nursing Home and was confined to bed for three days. There were no heavy air raids, just heavy falls of snow.

I left the nursing home after a week and the following day went on sick leave to Kilkington for five days. The snow was so deep that I stayed the night at Ferndale. In the morning I managed to get to Kilkington through snow four feet deep. I did a spot of rabbiting whilst there and caught seventeen. I returned to a spell of night duty. It was very cold but quiet.

On January 28th Lord Woolton, Minister for Food, placed a control on poultry prices. Chicken producers were to be paid one shilling and eleven-pence per pound by poultry buyers; wholesalers two shillings; retailers two shillings and four-pence. Duck producers: one shilling and nine-pence per pound; retailers two shillings and one penny per pound,
Last weeks shipping losses from enemy action were:
British Ships: Eleven. Forty-thousand four hundred and twenty nine tons
Allied Ships: Three: Thirteen thousand, eight hundred and seventy two tons.
The total weekly losses of British ships for the war: approximately seventy-two thousand tons.
Mr Churchill, British Prime Minster, broadcast to the nation on the present war situation. 'DAMNED GOOD'.
On Monday February 10th, the RAF bombed Hanover and the Germans enter Rumania and Bulgaria, unresisted.

On the 16th I had leave and went out to Fyfield and spent the day hauling grains by tractor from Ongar station back to the farm.

Monday I returned to Kentish Town Police station for late turn duty at two pm There were no raids over London that night so I did a general inspection of bombsights. Japan threatened to attack Australia.

The following Thursday, four mines exploded near Ongar and shocked everybody!

On March 8th, London had its biggest air raid in eight weeks. Albany Street Barracks took a direct hit, Buckingham Palace was hit by a high explosive bomb. One policeman was killed. There were no bombs over Kentish Town district.

Total expenditure last week for the war effort was £95,600,000.
Total expenditure for the financial year to date £3,530,000,000

On March 11th, Mr George Kendall, British Minster arrived in Turkey for talks amd a bomb, planted under the floorboards of his hotel by the Gestapo, exploded killing his private secretary and several others. He was not injured.

War Weapons Week took place from March 14th. A collection was made throughout the country as an added contribution to the war effort. Herefordshire collected nine hundred and seventeen thousand pounds – Staunton-on-Wye contributed six hundred and sixty-four pounds.

Cost of Weapons.	£.
A bomber aircraft	20,000.
Fighter aircraft	5,000.
Barrage balloon	7,000.
Searchlight projector	2,000.
Battleship	8,000,000.
Aircraft carrier	3,300,000.
Cruiser	2,000,000.
Destroyer	320,000.
Submarine	350,000.
Heavy gun	6,000.
A.A. Gun	3,000.
One Torpedo	2,000.
One heavy A.A. shell	4.
One heavy machine gun	350.
Cost of equipping an infantry soldier	184.
Hand grenade	0. 4/-

Foot and mouth disease in cattle was rife throughout the country.

On March 16th there was a very heavy air raid on Clyde Side.

Germany has now lost five thousand, eight hundred and nine planes since May.

Public transport was having great difficulty in keeping to schedule resulting in long delays, I decided to buy a second hand motorbike, a Panther 600 with twin exhausts. With such limited time off it would take me to Essex and Hereford and back quicker, allowing me more time to rest.

On March 19th 1941 London had its heaviest air raid so far that year. Holloway Police Station had a direct hit and nine policemen were killed. A landmine in Albany Street did much damage. I volunteered assistance in rescuing survivors along with the ARP, LDV, WVS and the Police. I was standing on the wooden girders of a crumbled staircase with tiles and rubbish around me. I could hear someone moaning in pain. With the help of an ARP warden we made an entrance to the lower floor where we found, trapped by a heavy wooden beam, a man and woman covered in blood and severely injured. Another ARP warden shouted down to his colleague, "Hey Bill, alright?"

"No," said Bill. "We want two stretchers and an ambulance."

We were in luck. Because of a blocked road an ambulance was standing about thirty yards away loading two other casualties. The crew came to our assistance and with difficulty we extracted our two casualties, one unconscious, the other in great pain, onto the stretchers and carried them to the ambulance to be taken to Casualty.

A delayed action bomb was reported near the scene of the landmine. It was taken care of by Albany Street Police Station. I continued searching but nearly all civilians were now aware of the dangers of being killed or injured in their homes and went at night to air raid shelters or the underground railway stations.

On Thursday March 20th I had a few hours sleep before reporting at six am to the Station for early turn duty. Enemy planes had dropped a large D.A. bomb in Kentish Town Division during the night but it was safely defused. After going off duty at 2 pm I went for a spin on my motorbike.

On March 23rd I had time off so went on my motorbike to see Mother at Bushey, near Watford. I found the road fairly clear of bomb damage, in fact it was amazing how quickly the road could be repaired after a five hundred pound bomb had made a crater in the middle. There were no JCBs so most of the repairs were done manually.

I found Mum fairly well. She had been ill with influenza and was looking forward to warmer weather. I wished I'd had a home to invite her to.

I spent the morning of the 25th attending funerals and went out to Fyfield afterwards. Uncle George had bought a Ford V8 22 H.P. and in the afternoon the car arrived. I said, "That's a beauty, Uncle George!"

He replied, "She looks good".

Turning to Aunt Liz he continued, "Come on, we'll go to Ongar and collect that parcel. Jump in, Chris!"

I climbed into the back seat and Aunt Liz sat in the front with Uncle driving. We had gone about four miles when Auntie said, "George you are driving too near to the hedge". He pulled up, got out and went around to Auntie's side of the car. The front seat was a bench type, he said, "Move over". Without another word, Auntie proceeded to drive!

Yugoslavia overthrew her government and refused to allow Germany to enter the country, however the German way of doing things was to shoot first and then ask, but keep shooting. AN EVIL NATION.

Towards the end of March after finishing early duty I jumped on my bike and drove down the Western Avenue, around the Oxford Bypass, through Witney then via the A40 through Cheltenham and Ross-on-Wye to Hereford and on to Kilkington, a distance of one hundred and fifty four miles. It had taken three hours and thirty minutes and I'd used about two and a half gallons of petrol. On the Oxford Bypass I could cruise at ninety miles an hour!

On April 3rd the Nazi's order their Belgrade staff to evacuate then poured bombs on the city. It had been declared open and undefended yet the Nazi's bombed it unmercifully and machine-gunned the women and children. All lay in ruins. Thousands died, killed by the Nazi dogs that murdered them for the sake of murdering.

On Easter Monday afternoon I returned from early turn duty and took Dorothy Dale out to Whipsnade Zoo on the back of my bike. We thought what a problem it must be to feed all the different kinds of animals – elephants, lions, tigers, monkeys as well as the numerous birds and reptiles.

I spent my weekly leave out at Fyfield, rolling wheat and lucerne all day with the new Fordson tractor, returning to night duty on Wednesday 16th at ten o'clock. London received its heaviest air attack that night, the biggest raid of the war. Thousands were killed. Hundreds of land mines and delayed action bombs fell inflicting huge fires and enormous damage on the East End and Central London. I was busy all night helping with the flow of ambulances and fire engines. No Kentish Town police were killed.

There were no raids the next day but we were all on twenty-four hour shifts dealing with casualties. I was on traffic patrol helping ambulances through.

On the Saturday the East and North East of London received a second heavy raid, many of the bombs dropped were incendiaries and high explosive.

A big battle raged in Greece on April 21st.
Plymouth was bombed for the third successive night on Friday April 25th, there were many casualties.

The following Sunday our great Prime Minister, Winston Churchill, broadcast to the nation on the war situation. He spoke of the RAF Fighter Command and 'The Battle of Britain':

"NEVER WAS SO MUCH OWED BY SO MANY TO SO FEW".

He also said that the RAF were every night bombing Nazi strategic points adding:

"WE SHALL PERSERVERE UNTIL VICTORY IS WON".

On Saturday May 10th, from ten thirty in the evening until five the following morning the Germans inflicted the heaviest raid of the war, even heavier than April 16th. Loss of life and damage to buildings was immense and included Big Ben and the Houses of Parliament. One thousand four hundred and thirty six people were reported killed, one thousand seven hundred and ninety two injured. I was on late turn for three days, Sunday duty was two pm until ten pm but I assisted until two o'clock in the morning, diverting traffic. There were several delayed action bombs reported but this raid was so severe that it was difficult to pinpoint every D.A. bomb and reports could not establish accuracy. These bombs usually had a one-hour's delay before exploding.

On Thursday May 15th 1941 Grandad was eighty-nine years of age. I was on early turn until 2pm and, as it was a lovely day, I decided to go home for three day's leave that I had accumulated on my leave card. (Police are never paid overtime but given time off in lieu; i.e. if I attended Police Court in my own time or did extra duties, leave could be taken, where available). I left Camden Town around three. Traffic was light as it was a Thursday afternoon, although Western Avenue had many convoys of army vehicles. In fact, there were many army and air force transports on the whole journey but not enough to impede my progress. I did not wear a crash helmet as they were rarely used then and a cap was the favoured headgear. Of course when motor scooters became more popular, then accidents became more frequent and soon a law making crash helmets compulsory came into force.

It was about six pm and a lovely evening. On my way

through Hereford I had passed over Eign Street traffic lights and was travelling at about fifteen miles an hour approaching the Horse & Groom Inn. In front of me was an army convoy of about ten Land Rovers. I was passing them on the right hand side when, without any signal either by hand or indicator, the front Land Rover turned right. I was already accelerating to overtake quickly. I hit the bonnet of the vehicle, was airborne over the top and landed in the road. Rendered unconscious I came to my senses in the Victoria Ward of Hereford General Hospital. I had fractured my left foot, badly bruised my leg and had concussion, which gave me migraine and permanent head pain. I felt bloody sorry for myself.

Uncle Tom and Auntie Lula came to see me as did Jean and Father. Richard was now in training for No.3 Commando but obtained some leave and Alan, home on leave from the Shropshire Yeomanry, also came.

On May 22nd, Mr Moir Brown, my doctor, informed me that my fractured foot would heal satisfactorily and the bruising would go but it would take its time. I could expect headaches accompanied by nausea from my concussion but with plenty of rest they would also go eventually. I rested, helped by plenty of friends who came in to visit me!

My motorbike went in for repair with Wallis's in Hereford!

On May 24th 1941, the Nazi's sunk HMS *Hood* the largest battleship in the world. Only three men out of one thousand, one hundred and fifty were saved. Three days later on May 27th, a British submarine sank the German battleship *Bismark*.

Clothes were so scarce in Britain that rationing became necessary. Cloth was being woven in the Midlands but it all went into clothes for the forces and blankets. Women's tights were not yet on the manufacturing line. Silk and nylon stockings came with the American army. Lyle or wool stockings were worn before this. Knitting was never so popular! Jumpers and cardigans were unpicked and re-knitted several times.

At the end of May my injured foot was put into an iron. It

was very painful and I had an attack of nausea followed by migraine. I slept until noon the following day then got up 'with difficulty' in the afternoon and sat by the River Wye which flows past the hospital.

The next day Mr Brown came in to see me. He thought I was making good progress and recommended the quietness of the country for my migraines. Father came to take me home.

I rested my foot and showed improvement. A week later I went back to hospital and had the plaster removed and replaced with an elastic bandage. Although my leg was improving the headaches were still with me.

On June 22nd Germany declared war on Russia. Previously Russia had been Germany's ally but Hitler reversed this friendship. In his greed he had his eyes on Russia's oil fields and the large areas of wheat in the Ukraine. He thought a quick victory over Russia would give his forces the oil and wheat needed to finish off Britain and her Colonies followed by the last hurdle, America, and then world domination.

Russia however turned out to be a huge stumbling block. The winter was so severe that little progress was made. The Nazis gave 'their all' on the Eastern front, then Russia made some advances. The Germans tried to take Leningrad but the weather and the defences held them off.

By July 16th the Germans were within sixty-five miles of Leningrad but the Russian line held. Heavy losses were suffered on both sides.

There had been no air raids in Britain since May 12th. The Nazis were concentrating all their effort against Russia.

On August 6th I returned to London and Chigwell Hall Nursing Home where I was confined to bed. I was still having problems with my foot and bad headaches, especially at night.

Britain released a new 'night fighter', the Beaufighter. It had two forty horse power engines, a speed of three hundred and thirty miles per hour, took a crew of two, and had ten guns and cannons.

Dr. Jones C.M.O. visited Chigwell Hall and told me to continue resting as my headaches were persisting and my foot not healing.

On August 14th, Mr Churchill and Mr Roosevelt, America's President, met at sea.

At the end of August Uncle George collected me from the Nursing Home and I spent an enjoyable day at Fyfield with Mother and all the White family, returning later to Chigwell Hall.

In two years of war against the Luftwaffe, the Royal Airforce Command and anti-aircraft defences destroyed four and a half thousand planes. We lost fourteen hundred fighters, four hundred and fifty pilots being saved.

September 6th found America on the verge of war against Germany.

German Stuka bombers dive-bombed Leningrad. Many planes were lost but the Russians still held out.

On Monday September 8th 1941 it was the anniversary of the first big raid on London by German aircraft. British Bombers subjected Berlin to the heaviest bombing any German city had yet had. Germany squealed after the raid soon to be followed by many more.

On Wednesday September 10th I went to St. Thomas's Hospital and had my foot X-rayed and the following week I went to Lambeth to see Dr Jones. He told me that the X-ray did not show any improvement. My headaches had still not disappeared, he hoped for improvement otherwise I would have to leave the Police Force on medical grounds.

On Friday 19th Dr Jones cancelled the idea of my leaving and suggested we give my foot and head another chance! Two days later I was confined to bed with a sore throat and migraine.

A week later he visited again, found my foot and knee still improving but the migraine still persisting. The following month he sent me home for seventeen days sick leave and hoped my foot would get better in that time and the migraine disappear.

From October 25th until November 10th, I was at home in Kilkington resting my foot and head. The foot did not improve but the headaches were not as frequent. I returned to London on and went to see John Clements in 'Ships with Wings'. The next day I reported to the C.M.O. at Lambeth who, after a careful examination regretted that as my foot had not healed and the headaches still persisted I should return medically unfit. It was now six months since the accident.

I stayed at Camden House until November 20th and then left London. My services as a Police officer ceased on December 3rd 1941. I had seen and endured the bombing of London yet since my accident in May there had been no more air raids.

On November 14th torpedoes from a German submarine sank Britain's famous aircraft carrier Ark Royal, costing £3,250,000, with few casualties.
November 29th saw British troops fighting the Germans in Libya.

On December 9th I went to the County Hospital for an X-ray on my left foot and leg and consultation regarding the migraines. The X-ray showed a disposition of my third toe, my leg had healed, and the headaches were just a matter of time. As the accident took place whilst I was off duty I had no claim against the Police. At the end of the year I received twenty-nine pounds gratuity from the Metropolitan Police. I had been in the Police Force for over two years, much of that time during the Blitz, and had luckily survived a motorbike accident. I had a lot to thank God for.

By early February 1942 my headaches were improving, I had only had three so far that year, but my foot had not yet healed and I still walked with a limp. I decided to stay with Colin Parker on his farm at Bodenham near Hereford. He was an old friend with whom I had stayed on several occasions. A clever and progressive farmer, my duties with him would be lighter than at Kilkington.

On March 10th Japanese soldiers bayoneted to death fifty
British soldiers, officers and men, hands and feet tied,
they were prisoners in Hong Kong
Singapore fell into Japanese hands.
The Russians held German troops on the outskirts
of Leningrad. It was bitterly cold, minus ten degrees centi-
grade. Over a thousand British bombers attacked
Germany's munitions factory, Essen Krupps, the largest in
the world.

On March 14th Richard, now in No.3 Commando, was married to Miss Joy French in Brighton. I was confined to bed with a migraine and unable to travel. Towards the end of the month I went to Huntley Court, home of the Dale family, for tea. Dorothy was a nurse and she brought a friend home for the weekend, Miss Laurinda Johnston to whom I was very much attracted.

On the last day of March I sold my motorbike to Messrs. A Wallis & Co. Hereford for sixty-five pounds, I had bought it for thirty-eight.

Bombing of London was now 'hit and run'. In fact the only air raid to date was more of an incendiary attack than a bombing attack. However on April 27th, Bath was bombed very intensely. Many people were killed and the casualties enormous. This was the beginning of raids on the rest of the country. Hitler had decided to attack by air many English towns, Exeter and Cheltenham being just two and of no strategic importance.

The Japanese attack on the American Fleet in Pearl Harbour in December 1941 had brought the Americans into the war on our side. It took a long while to see any progress but without America's help things may have turned out differently. We had lost both the battleships *Prince of Wales* and *Repulse* to Japanese bombers. Tobruk had fallen into German hands and all was not going well with the 'Desert Rats'. Russia was yet to stop the German advance but Leningrad had cost the Germans hundreds of lives and they still failed to capture it.

On Sunday 3rd May Dorothy Dale and Laurinda Johnston came to Kilkington for tea. A fortnight later I went to visit Richard and Joy at Brighton. Linda came down a couple of days afterwards and we enjoyed rambling and picking bluebells. It was like having one's confidence restored. I had been sad losing an occupation I loved. Being a police officer during the blitz had given me a 'great feeling' for other people's suffering and loss of family. Now, during this break, I was falling in love for the first time. It gave me a renewed zest for life.

My headaches were becoming less frequent though my foot was still not better. I realised I had to get a light job. Farming did not come into this category, and I could not apply to the 'Services' as I was deemed medically unfit.

In the 1930s the Ministry of Agriculture, Fisheries and Food (MAFF) had formed The War Agricultural Service, Warag for short. Its purpose was to ensure that every available square yard of agricultural land was put to good use. Being a small island with a large population, Great Britain had relied on imports of food for many years. Tropical fruit, i.e. bananas, oranges and lemons, dried fruit; as well as hard wheat from Canada and a variety of processed tinned goods came from North and South America: corned beef, peaches and so on. It was very apparent that an island state needed to become self-sufficient. In 1940 parks and gardens were being transformed, we all 'dug for victory'. Cockerels and hens appeared where they had never been seen before!

Warag was developed to ensure that farmers produced as much cereal and vegetable as possible together with flax and linseed for use in armaments. Warag operated within a network of local committees. By the time I had returned from the police force Father was already on the committee of the Weobley and District branch of H.W.A.C. (Hereford War Agricultural Committee)

On July 6th 1942 a vacancy as cultivations officer in the Dore and District branch of the Warag became available. With my farming background and authoritative training I felt

I would be ideal for the post and so I attended a meeting with the H.W.A.C. to answer many questions as to my ability for the position. After a long interview I was accepted.

So I joined Warag and assisted farmers to fill in various forms stating their acreage under the plough and what crops were planned or sown. It was for me to visit the farmers and establish that the form had been accurately filled in and that the best husbandry was being implemented to ensure as good a yield as possible. All the men of service age had been conscripted and they were replaced by 'land girls', mostly town and city bred girls who had the choice of armaments or the land as their form of war work. When they first arrived on their allocated farms some had never seen a cow before, let alone milked one!

In 1942 the Women's Land Army had twenty thousand recruits to fill in wherever possible the vacancies left by men.

The Warag area that I helped to supervise is probably one of the most beautiful in the country. It lay on the borders between England and Wales, in the Wye valley, with the Black Mountains to the West and the River Wye to the East, from Hay on Wye to the North and Abergavenny to the South.

In August I was surveying land at Llanneynoe and Michaelchurch which meant a lot of walking which was good for my left foot. I had to inspect land suitable for ploughing and growing corn on and which was paid a Government subsidy of two pounds per acre. For wheat planted from 1942 there was a subsidy of three pounds.

Holding an executive position in the Agricultural industry, of importance to food production in the country in time of war, I felt sufficiently experienced in giving advice and in being able to judge the quality of a farm's output. The 'Dore' area had some very good quality farms, though the Black Mountain area was very marginal. The occupants needed advice and guidance so I tackled my new occupation with zeal and enjoyment. Living in the countryside again together with lighter duties could only help my recovery.

The ploughing and planting of old permanent pasture was well under way. Each county had its own directions and targets.

September had a low rainfall and plenty of sunshine. The Dore district was later in the season than the rest of Herefordshire because of the mountain's shadow which ran from the Sugar Loaf, that is close to Abergavenny, to Hay on Wye.

Harvesting was going ahead and farms on the Hereford boundary were finished by September 10th.

In October I finished surveying for the season and commenced certifying the acreage of cereals sown and the ploughing of old pasture in the autumn for wheat either sown or about to be, estimating the acreage of proposed crops for the coming year.

It was a cold wet December and except for looking after the stock there was little to do. I went to Brighton to spend Christmas with Richard and Joy, going to the theatre, dances and visits to the country and seaside. I was back in Herefordshire for the New Year and 1943. I do miss my visits to Fyfield!

The war, which I have not mentioned of late, was still as bitter as ever, but there were very few raids on this country and the situation abroad was looking brighter. The Russians were holding the German forces and Leningrad was still in Russian hands. Big British victories ensued for the eighth army led by General Montgomery in Libya. German and Italian troops retreated along the whole front from Alexandria to Tunis resulting in thousands of German and Italian Prisoners.

Church bells were ringing for the first time since 1939.

I decided that my Morris 8 was in need of an overhaul and as the roads used were very rough I decided on a larger second hand car. I contacted an old friend in London who put me in touch with a friend of his who knew of the whereabouts of a Hillman 10. I went up to London and met the owner of the car, living at Highgate. It was blue and in lovely condition: price, one hundred and forty pounds. I found both he and his wife very charming. I told them I had been on police duty close to their home two years previously. He introduced me to Mr J A Stone who dealt in fruit, vegetables and poultry. I spent quite some time with Mr Stone and agreed that in the October I would begin to supply him weekly with rabbits and would also arrange with farmers' wives the planning and rearing of their poultry, particularly the young cockerels for Christmas. We did not discuss prices at this stage as they would possibly increase by Christmas as all were in very short supply.

Whilst getting the car registered in my name, I went out to see the family. Mum was in Epping so unfortunately on this occasion I did not see her. I found the Watt White family in good fettle. Uncle George had just bought another cattle lorry to add to his fleet.

I returned to Highgate and collected the car and drove back to Kilkington.

The summer was soon with us. I became very busy surveying and certifying crops and visiting farmers in an advisory capacity. I enjoyed the work because it was interesting and my headaches were becoming less and less, my foot gave me little trouble and my leg was completely healed.

The war was now in our favour. The Germans were in full retreat in Tunisia. America was coming to our aid and American soldiers were now in training in this country.

I found Bill Griffiths, a partner with Griffiths and Hartland, Corn Merchants, Hereford to be very helpful with advice regarding fertilisers, prices of corn etc. I discovered that 'Holdfast' wheat was one of the best yielding wheats in the country.

I saw Linda several times when she was down at Huntley Court.

In October I starting collecting rabbits from different depots, the main one being Mr Morris, the Blacksmith, at Bredwardine. There were a lot of rabbits in this area, and quite a few rabbit 'catchers'. I bought a trailer for collecting them and made Wednesday my collection night from Mr Morris and Mrs Kinsey's, at Staunton-on-Wye. I tied the rabbits in bundles of ten and could then take them to

Hereford Railway Station early on Thursday morning to arrive Paddington by eleven am when Mr Stone would collect them.

The first consignment and all the following consignments were very successful. I paid the catchers the going price, between one shilling and sixpence and two shillings each cash. Mr Stone sent me a monthly cheque on receipt of my invoice. By December 31st I had sent him one thousand seven hundred and eighty-one rabbits and three hares!!

Christmas was near so I had to book the 'pluckers' for three days, 19th, 20th and 21st December. Mrs Handley was my commander in chief. She got the gang of pluckers together and supervised them whilst I went with the trailer to collect small consignments. Twenty birds and over, they delivered to Kilkington.

I would weigh and pay on collection or delivery. Prime young cockerels alive were £1 each, second grade, 18/- each, turkeys £2.10s. live geese £1.5s. (but too much work to dress). Poultry were very scarce and on the BLACK MARKET they would fetch double the price but the buyers would only want about three at a time. When all was finished and dressed they would be laid out on the slab tiles in the dairy.

On December 22nd I loaded the car and trailer with the dressed poultry and set off for London. There were fifty-two cockerels, twenty turkeys and ten geese. The car and trailer was heavily laden. I had arranged with Mr Stone to meet me with his van on Western Avenue. He was pleased with the poultry only there was not enough.

"Better luck next year!"

So 1944 arrived and with it a minimum wage for farm workers. Twenty-one years and over: sixty-five shillings a week, overtime one and seven pence per hour. Casual workers forty eight shillings a week. Health Insurance two shillings – one shilling employer and one shilling employee.

12

J une 6th, 1944 was an historic day as our troops landed
on the Normandy beaches.

On the Sunday I visited Linda at Huntley Court. I went to
London in middle of January and took Linda out to dinner
and a show. Although full air raid precautions were in force
people were treating the lull in air raids as if it was all over.
Children who had been evacuated were flocking back in
thousands.

On June 13th the Germans launched from platforms
along the coast of France the V2 bomb commonly called 'the
doodlebug'. It consisted of a H.E. bomb, about one thousand-
pounds of explosive, propelled by a paraffin fuelled engine
which cruised at about sixty-feet above the sea, at about
thirty miles an hour. When the fuel was exhausted there was
a deathly silence as the bomb nose-dived at whatever point it
had arrived, usually over the East-End of London. Of course
there were times when the engine would fail and the bomb
would drop either in the sea, or Essex or Kent

Eventually our planes could shoot them down, the RAF
heavily bombed these sites but the Germans kept making
new launching pads. The bombs just kept coming and there

was silence as the bomb made its way earthward, it was terrifying. A lot of lives were lost through these bombs to say nothing of the destruction of property.

The struggle to produce enough food still continued. The Warag became very efficient. The Dore and other branches like it throughout the country produced more and more food. Twenty thousand evacuees were returning to London daily, despite the V1 and V2 flying bombs. In Lambeth seventy-two flying bombs killed two hundred and sixty people, six hundred and forty-eight were seriously wounded. This was by July 1944. Of the six thousand, seven hundred and twenty five flying bombs in the period June 12th to September 5th, which approached the coast of England, three thousand, four hundred and sixty three were brought down either by fighter planes, A.A. guns or barrage balloons.

I continued surveying and certifying crops. The year's crops of both hay and corn were the heaviest produced since the start of the war.

In the middle of September, Mr Barber, manager of the Home Farm, Garnon's Estate, Byford, Herefordshire, decided to retire. Lt.Col. Sir Richard Cotterell Bt. asked Captain Hollis, to contact me and offer me the chance of filling the vacancy. I knew Sir Richard very well having helped him to form the Garnons troop of the Shropshire Yeomanry before the war. Also the Pantall's had been associated with the Cotterell's for three centuries.

Captain Hollis arranged to meet me when we discussed the position of Farm Manager. The farm was about six hundred acres with five employees, a free cottage, and salary negotiable.

I decided to accept the offer and take the position. I would live at Kilkington until Mr Barber vacated the cottage.

I found that planning the running of this farm very exciting as it had some of the most fertile land in the country. The oak trees in the park at the front of Garnons House were enormous, a sure sign of high fertility. This was a challenge. I wrote to Sir Richard who was commanding the Shropshire Yeomanry in Italy and thanked him. Alan my brother was with Sir Richard, now medium artillery.

The autumn, as usual, was very busy with corn planting, harvesting potatoes and threshing corn. I still kept Mr Stone supplied with rabbits.

In November I had a day's shooting at Kilkington with Mr Price from Scutmill farm. There were plenty of rabbits seemingly increasing each year. Alf decided that we should start with Portway so off we went starting at the bottom of Standsbank Wood. Mr Price stood about twenty yards out from the meadow hedge and I stood the same distance the other side. Alf put 'Popsy', his favourite ferret, into a hole leading down into the rabbit warren. It was a dry crisp morning, ideal for ferreting. Popsy found a rabbit and it bolted out my side and ran down the hedge into the wood, not a safe shot. Then another ran out Mr Price's side and across the meadow that he shot. We continued down the hedge, Popsy enjoying chasing the rabbits that were bolting. We shot twelve down the hedge and then went to Pool meadow and shot six more.

Alf then decided that we should go to Sedgepitt but first we approached the water with caution as it was a favourite place for mallard and snipe. We were lucky and bagged a brace of mallard and one snipe. These are very difficult to shoot as they fly fast and swerve from side to side. We ate our lunch with a bottle of ale.

It was now midday so we put the ferrets 'Tiny' and 'Jilly', into a fairly big warren and seven rabbits came out. From the next two warrens we bagged three. As it was now approaching dusk we called it a good sporting day.

Christmas came with its poultry season and once again I organised the purchase of live birds from the same suppliers, prices had increased and I paid two pence more per bird than the previous year. This year I borrowed a larger trailer to tow behind my car to Hereford railway station.

The weather was very cold which kept the poultry fresh. I put them on the passenger train at seven am. The road to Hereford was frosty with ice in places and, needing to go slow because of the restricted lighting, the journey took me two hours. However I accomplished the operation successfully. Mr Stone was delighted with the quality and I also managed to send one hundred and twenty rabbits that week too.

I was now Manager at Garnons Home Farm. I found the men very friendly and hardworking. The shepherd was Bob Jones who lived in a farm cottage about five hundred yards up the road. He had a lovely sheep dog, Lass, who was well trained and could bring the sheep to Bob very quietly even from two meadows away. Sheep get used to a friendly dog.

We had about one hundred and fifty Clun Forest ewes and lambing was expected early in February so Bob fed them with corn and hay. Bob was knowledgeable and loved his sheep. Next was Hugh Wadley the stockman, very knowledgeable and reliable. The farm carried a pedigree herd of Hereford cattle, fifty-two cows and heifers in which Sir Richard took a great interest. The wagoner was Bert Morris who, in his heyday, was a champion ploughman. The farm carried two tractors and he was one of the drivers as all ploughing was now done by tractor.

Robin Phillips was a tractor driver and general workman. Gilbert Hicks was also a 'general workman', a hell of a nice chap.

Christmas was a quiet time, I was unable to see Linda as she was on duty, but went to London early in the New Year when we went to a cinema show and a party given by one of her friends.

Early in the New Year Linda and Dorothy came home from London to Huntley where we had an engagement party for Linda and me. It was a happy occasion. I put an engagement ring on her finger.

The weather turned very cold in January with snow and a hard frost, the farm staff cleaning up buildings keeping under cover. On January 27th Mr & Mrs Barber moved out of the Home Farm.

Grandfather, Brook House, Eardisley had died the previous November aged 94, so his housekeeper, Mrs Pound, moved into the Home Farm as my housekeeper. It was very cold.

Linda came over for the day. We were busy planning the furnishing of the house and a wedding in early June.

In February we were busy threshing wheat and oats and sent to Griffiths and Hartland two hundred weight of wheat. I also sent sixty fat sheep to market. All fat stock was now graded and handled by the Ministry, payment by the pound in weight (kilos not yet used).

On March 1st we planted Epicure potatoes, Earlies, six acres in the Withens Field. Six land girls plus locals helped with the planting. Mr Davies, Secretary of Hereford Herd Book Society, came out and inspected the herd.

Friday March 23rd, Mother was taken ill and was admitted to St. Margarets Hospital, Epping. Linda and I went to see her and found her quite poorly. Poor Mum with no one to look after her. We stayed the night at Fyfield Hall and returned to Hereford on Saturday.

On March 28th I bought what was to be a great friend, a Ford 8 car, AVJ 390, for one hundred and five pounds. This car was to pull a trailer carrying hundreds of rabbits and poultry.

Mum was now well on the way to recovery.

On Sunday April 1st I went to morning service at the old church at Letton where I had been confirmed.

On Friday April 6th I bought five, two year old bullocks from Weyman Jones, a big farmer at Bodenham, these to summer graze then fatten in the yards during the winter, making good muck for the fields.

On April 17th, there was a bull sale at Hereford. I sent in "Garnon's Dragon", which sold for seventy guineas.

Linda's Mum and Dad, Mr & Mrs Johnston came with Linda for tea.

May 3rd 1945. The War at last coming to an end. Italians capitulate to unconditional surrender.

May 4th. Berlin captured by the Russians, Hamburg by the British, unconditional surrender.

May 2nd 1945, telephone put in the Home Farm –
Bridge Sollars 60

May 7th 1945 Germany Surrenders Unconditionally to the
Allies. The war in Europe is now over after five years, eight
months and four days.

About 306,984 of our troops have been killed –
59,793 civilians killed in air raids.

May 8th 1945, V.E DAY, HOLIDAY FOR ALL.

Prime Minister, Rt. Hon. Winston Churchill, made a speech
at three pm followed by the King at 9 pm

The War against Japan as bitter as ever. 400 Forts raid
Tokyo.

Our wedding was held on June 2nd 1945, at 1.30 pm It was decided to hold it at St. Mary's Church, Staunton-on-Wye, as Linda's home was in Cheshire.

The Rector, Rev. G.O. Lewis, married us. My Best Man was Arthur Dale from Huntley Court. Linda's Bridesmaids were Dorothy and Betty Dale. Linda's Father gave the bride away. The reception was held at Kilkington with over a hundred guests.

The Wedding was a big success. Members of the Young Farmers' Club, of which I was Chairman, formed an archway with hayforks and other agricultural tools for twenty yards outside the church and down the pathway. Sir Richard Cotterell made a speech and wished us a happy future. We said goodbye to all our guests after enjoying with them a fabulous reception, climbed into AVJ 390 and drove down to Torquay for our honeymoon.

When we returned from Torquay Linda set about putting Home Farm in order. At the end of the previous year we had attended the sale of household goods at Brook Farm and purchased linen and other essential requirements.

I now needed to attend to farm duties and, being June, it was a very busy time. Clover needed cutting, mangolds singling, the folds to be cleaned of manure that was put in Steps field in a large heap to convert into compost for autumn ploughing.

On June 16th we started haymaking by cutting clover and two days later the grass in Shortlands Meadow, the hay was ready before the clover. The weather was so beautiful and hot we started making a rick in Shortlands the hay being rowed into swathes and then by using a sweep attached to a tractor the hay was swept to an elevator and was dropped onto the rick.

The next big task was early potato rising, Thirty volunteers came from Hereford the first day and forty-six the second. All from Voluntary Land Corps and paid one shilling an hour. I railed from Moorhamton Station eleven tons of potatoes to Lancashire at eighteen pounds, five shillings per ton. This was one pound above local prices.

From June 19th until the end of the month, it was RAIN. Although just showers, it made haymaking impossible and ruined the clover in Hill field.

Linda and I went to Malvern on the Sunday afternoon. Malvern Hills on a sunny day is beautiful. We had tea in one of the many restaurants that were set up for summer entertainment for the many visitors.

Monday saw the veterinary testing for tuberculosis of the Home Farm herd. Known as the T.T. test, one hundred and sixty-five animals all proved negative.

V.J. Day, August 15th, this was a day to celebrate our victory in Japan and was followed by a public holiday on the 16th. Two great holidays. We all took part in the celebrations with children's sports on the cricket pitch at Garnons and by making use of the pavilion for the children's party. Food, because of rationing, was hard to come by so we all contributed what we could. This came out of the back of store cupboards!

By August 17th Harvesting was in full swing and the summer here at last. At the end of August Linda and I went to Huntley and spent an enjoyable evening there. We had finished harvesting.

September was a busy time but Linda and I found time to visit London, ruins of the bombing were everywhere – which was to be expected – but we had an enjoyable day and bought lots of things we required as there was more on offer than in the country.

We were so busy on the farm, there was sugar beet harvesting, ploughing and planting, threshing, potato lifting and the obtaining of extra labour to pick the potatoes. We managed to keep ahead.

I had entered our crop of mangolds, swedes, and sugar-beet in the competition for the counties' best crop and took first prize for Sir Richard.

On Sunday 7th Linda and I spent the day with Colin at Bodenham.

On the 13th I took part in Harewood End tractor plough-ing match. There were seventeen competitors. I did well but was not in the prize money. On the 20th Staunton-on-Wye Y.F.C, held a ploughing match at Kilkington.

The rest of October was busy, what with loading one hundred and twenty-three sacks of pedigree Juliana wheat at Credenhill for Milns of Chester, eighty sacks to Ratcliffe, corn Merchants, Hereford. Ploughing and sowing, we also loaded three more trucks of sugarbeet.

We were so short of labour that we used German Prisoners of War. The farm staff were against the idea but once they had arrived, six of them, we saw how hard they worked – sixty-three hours a week – and got used to them in a few days, even feeling sorry for them.

In early November, in spite of extra work, we managed to finish drilling wheat mainly 'Holdfast' variety.

On Sunday 2nd Linda and I went with Colin Parker to visit a farm in Berkshire which he was keen to obtain, it was four hundred acres. Later in the month Colin heard he had been successful.

I employed six more German prisoners of war to help with thrashing, one hundred and seventeen hours at one shilling and three pence, totalling £7. 6s. 3d.

Since October I had collected the rabbits, and this year more than ever before, over one thousand for the season. I also carried out the poultry collecting and dressing for Mr Stone. Seventy-five went by train on the 18th. The next day I had another load that I took by car and trailer to London. Richard came with me.

A couple of days later Linda and I went down to Brighton to spend a lovely Christmas with Mum, Richard and Joy.

So ended 1945 with Good Health and Happiness.

On Sunday January 6th Linda and I went to Colin's at Woodhouse, Bodenham, he was looking forward to taking over his new farm in Berkshire.

The Home Farm was proceeding very well. All seemed to go to a natural pattern with the four seasons being the directive part. It was now winter with snow, frosts and rain, the buying and selling of cattle, threshing corn and selling of wheat and oats. Rain and floods were everywhere.

Linda and her sister Mora went to Brighton for a break and to do some shopping.

Lambing season started in March and from twenty-two ewes we had forty-five lambs with a further one hundred and thirty to lamb.

Mr Bill Griffiths from Griffiths & Hartland, corn merchants, called to visit me and delivered three hundred weight of linseed for planting.

March 25th although getting late in the season for Earlies, the ground was still very wet, so we had a gang of women out from Hereford to plant and complete in three days.

Linda, Mora and I went up to the Elan Valley to Rhyder Reservoirs for a break. The Elan Valley joins the Wye Valley. The Resevoirs were full, supplying Birmingham, Coventry, Wolverhampton and numerous smaller towns with water. It is in the vicinity of Plymlimmon that the source of the River Wye and nearby the source of the River Severn are located. We had an excellent lunch at the 'Salmon', Builth Wells.

In April the staff was busy with cultivating, showers

caused a lot of delays but we kept all planting under control.

Sold J Davies of Bliss hall, Staunton-on-Wye, ninety hundred weights of wheat straw at three pounds per ton. It was Bliss Hall that Grandfather farmed as well as Old Letton Court.

The Lambing season finished with two hundred and twenty-five lambs from one hundred and twenty seven ewes, not as good as last year.

On Easter Monday we held a little party, The Dales, Pantalls etc. to congratulate Linda on expecting our first child. The sun shone for a change and we had eats on the lawn but rationing was still very tight.

On May 25th, Mansel Lacey Y.F.C, held their second annual great shearing match on the lawns at Garnons, there were fifty-two entries.

In June we started mowing nineteen acres amidst lovely hot weather and soon finished haymaking.

We played cricket, Garnons v Hinton Road on July 14th, they made thirty-eight, we made forty-six, declared. I made seventeen.

July 20th Y.F.C. held a rally on the lawns at Garnons, stock judging etc. Sheild won by Ross YFC. First rally to be held in Herefordshire.

Took Linda away for a break and went to Brighton, touring Sussex, then went to London for a little shopping and went to the Theatre. Returned to Home Farm ready for harvest.

August 3rd played cricket against Pontrilas and won. I made eleven not out.

Heavy storms and corn battered and down.

Collected two hundred and sixty four boltins from Bodcott.

Wet and stormy, cutting oats, as flat as the beer at the 'Nelson'.

This was the wettest harvest on record. There's some fine weather coming but its ever so far away. NFU predict seventy per cent of harvest has been lost.

September. The time is rapidly approaching for Linda to

produce our first born. She is extremely well and I have booked her into the maternity department of the Hereford General Hospital for approximately middle of October.

We battled with the harvest, it was hard work moving sheaves out to dry etc., we did get some help from woodmen from the forestry department of Sir Richard's estate. At this time I purchased privately some Cox's orange pippin, Bramleys and Newtons from the neighbouring farm, all bought on the trees and picked them myself with help from the locals. On Sunday October 13th, we picked three tons of apples, which I was able to get a friend to deliver to Hereford market and made a profit of sixty pounds. There was a great risk of wind before picking.

I took Linda to hospital at one am on Tuesday, Wednesday October 16th 1946. She gave birth to a baby girl, eight and a half pounds in weight, at one thirty pm. Both did very well. I was with Linda after the birth and stayed with her until the evening.

The farm was going fine, with the harvest finished we were now threshing Holdfast wheat. From eight acres, we produced twenty-one two hundred weight sacks per acre, the best cast I have ever seen.

I organised the farm so I could spend most of each day with Linda. We decided to call the baby Pamela. Linda and I 'organised' the christening. I bought her some magazines, all with recommendations on cooking, how to make one egg do what two would do, rationing was still so severe.

§

Newspapers were carrying many advertisements for berths on ships to all parts of the world and emigrating was becoming a 'fever'. Emigration offices in all Embassies were recruiting a lot more staff to cope. Linda and I did not talk about our emigrating at this time but talked a lot about the future.

Linda knew I did not want to be an employee and wanted to start something on my own, hence the little amount of money I had made on poultry and rabbits to Stone and from the fruit. I also bought and sold, after a polish up, a few second hand cars. One will always be in my memory. Bill Wootton in Byford had bought a new Ford 8 and was now selling his two-year old Morris 8, which was a wreck. I bought it for sixty pounds and put on two new front mudguards, new handles etc. With plenty of spit and polish it began to look like new and I sold it privately, advertising in the *Hereford Times* for two hundred and ten pounds.

I brought Linda and Pamela home on Sunday October 27th having spent every afternoon with them. Pamela soon acquired the name of 'Puffer' as she always puffed, and was as healthy as any baby could be. She had a lovely cot, pram, and a devoted, clever Mum.

The farm was as busy as ever with ploughing and planting. We thrashed one hundred and fifty-eight sacks of oats, this was possibly the last year for the thrashing box as we had ordered a combine harvester for next season. In addition we had acquired a new tractor on rubbers to haul the sugarbeet to Moorhampton Station.

Amid plenty of rain and so much work on the farm, we finished the corn planting, it was very cold with hard frosts. I had already organised the poultry for Christmas, collecting rabbits from a further depot at Letton, all this amidst the farming, bailing hay and looking after stock. It was a cold December and Christmas soon came. The poultry for Stone were plucked at Kilkington. I sent to him one hundred and twenty five cockerels, fourteen ducks, forty Turkeys and seven geese.

Prices each: *Ducks £2.10s. Geese £3.10s.*
                            Turkeys £4.10s. Chickens £3.00

Christmas was very cold. We all went to Huntley Court. Linda was now completely recovered from the baby's birth and Pamela was so good she stole the show!

We saw the New Year in at home it was bitterly cold. I went rabbit shooting at Kilkington and had a good day's sport. Although it is January we are still hauling sugarbeet.

On January 19th, 1947, the Rev. G.O. Lewis christened Pamela at Tupsley Church, Hereford. She weighed twelve pounds eight ounces. Her Godfather was Mr J Dale, and Godmothers Mrs Dale and Auntie Bee.

January 22nd 1947 was the beginning of a long spell of very cold weather never before experienced by anyone in this country, fifteen degrees below zero. Snow everyday. Minister of fuel reports all electricity and gas is to be cut off.

Conditions were very bad and food was scarce. I sent a tractor and trailer to Hereford, conveying housewives from the farm and estate to do their shopping.

§

I talked to Linda seriously about getting out to a new country. We were young and I was used to working hard. We liked Australia but thousands were going there, Canada too cold, Rhodesia and South Africa, YES but we would wait a while before making a final decision.

On the farm it was all hands to feeding stock. Snow was six feet deep in places and freezing hard every night.

On the 21st heavy snow again and for twenty-four days the temperatures has been freezing.

We now come to March and it was still snowing with freezing snowdrifts up to ten feet deep.

On March 9th the heavy snow all over England started to thaw but it began snowing again that night. We had the first warm day for two months on the 15th and it turned to rain.

On the 16th the weather turned to thaw and a gale blew down the whole of 'Steps Orchard', about thirty trees. All telephone communications were down and there were floods all over England. It was the first time the River Wye with Maddle Brook had flooded as far as Portway, there now being NO ENTRY. Winds reached one hundred and five miles per hour causing havoc, roads everywhere were blocked.

Sunday March 23rd and Pamela continuing to grow. I talked to Linda seriously about emigrating and told her that we would be better off in South Africa. General Smuts was the Prime Minister of the United Party and one pound was the same value there as here. She agreed and after a further discussion we planned for me to go to London the coming Friday, March 28th, which I did going to South Africa House, Princess Gate. I met Mr Brendon Quinn of the 1820 Settlers Association, he remarked that, with my farming experience, I would be an asset to South Africa. I told him I wanted a position of farm manager with a house so that my wife and daughter could join me as soon as possible, I knew there were vacancies for grooms and stockmen on some boats where I could work my passage. He advised me to contact the Union Castle Steamship Company, freight depot, or better still 'go to see them'. That's just what I did. I met Mr R R Brown who was in charge of Livestock and gave him details of my experience. He informed me that he had several consignments of horses and cattle to go in due course but I must be prepared to join the ship at very short notice to which I agreed.

I returned home and told Linda all about it, she was naturally a bit anxious as neither of us knew anything about South Africa.

That night I went up to Garnons to see Sir Richard telling him of my plans to go to South Africa. He was very nice about me leaving and wished us well.

A week later Mr Brown had a consignment of horses on another shipping line that was going to South Australia the next week, I explained it was a bit too soon.

On April 11th Linda was taken ill with appendicitis and operated on at Hereford General Hospital. Pamela was being looked-after by Mrs Dale at Huntley Court.

Both Pamela and Linda progressed well with Pamela now on 'Cow and Gate' milk. I went to visit Linda most of the days she was in hospital and, before I took Linda to Huntley for a week to get over her operation and to rejoin Pamela, we were both inoculated for Yellow Fever, ready for emigrating.

Things were now quite hectic we had told our friends and relations of our plans, they thought it a big step to take.

Work on the farm was progressing well and the weather was good.

On Sunday May 25th, we took all our furniture to the Assembly Rooms in Hereford ready for our sale on the following Wednesday.

On June 7th I completed my services at Home Farm for Sir Richard.

We left Herefordshire on Sunday with a car and small caravan, complete with Pamela – 'Puffer' – and stayed the night at Auntie Bee's Wooton-under-Edge, Glos, setting off the following day and reaching Babbacome. We stocked up on provisions and travelled through Cockington village and out to Dartmouth where I fished for salmon on the River Dart, but caught nothing. We reached Penzance and at Boscastle Hill, found our car could not reach the peak so we had to unload and then succeeded. It was lovely weather. On to St. Ives, Lands End and Tintagel, visiting King Arthur's Castle before visiting Ilfracombe. From Bristol on the ferry across to Chepstow costing fifteen shillings and sixpence then Tintern Abbey and home having covered six hundred and ninety seven miles. On Tuesday 16th we took the caravan back.

On Thursday Linda and I, along with three trunks, went to London staying the night with friends. We planned that she and Pamela were to stay at Huntley, joining me as soon as I found accommodation.

At three pm on the 20th June 1947 I boarded S.S. *Umtata*, ready to sail to Durban, South Africa. I had signed on board as cattleman, working my passage and being paid one shilling. I said goodbye to my darling who kissed me farewell before she left for her journey back to Hereford.

SO MY BIGGEST ENTERPRISE YET.
'NOTHING VENTURED NOTHING GAINED'.

PART IV

THE PIONEER YEARS

13

On Saturday June 21st, 1947 at ten past three in the afternoon, loaded with seven thousand tons of cargo, including vehicles, flour, oil etc, anchors were drawn. With a couple of toots from the ship's siren and a low muffled noise from the engines we commenced our journey from the Royal Albert Docks, down the River Thames past Tilbury, Gravesend and Margate and out into the Dover Straights. The sea was calm and I was surprised at the amount of shipping using the English Channel from barges to passenger liners.

The next day as we approached Southampton I had a wonderful view of the *Queen Mary*, the *Queen Elizabeth* and the *Aquitania*. Southampton Docks were very impressive with a workforce on every ship. It seemed as if every berth had been taken.

The *Umtata* docked, hatches opened up and without delay huge cranes lifted all sorts of goods, agricultural machinery, cars etc. to be safely secured in the holds. I made my way off the ship for a tour of the dockland which had received heavy bombing only a few years before and I was amazed at how quickly it had been made operational again. Not so the housing, the most severely damaged would have to be completely rebuilt again. Considering the state of their homes people were very friendly and cheerful.

I did not have any meals on shore, rationing was still severe. I could have all my meals on board and very good they were too. As telephone boxes were 'non operational' I could not telephone Linda. The telephone exchange was being rebuilt as it had received a direct hit with many casualties.

It was a beautiful day and being fond of tennis and cricket I was pleased to see both tennis courts as well as cricket pitches being repaired. I was told that the planning department had authorised new courts and an extension to the playing fields. It was nearly dusk upon my return to the *Umtata* the cranes having ceased work for the day.

Next day I assisted with the loading of thirty-eight Pedigree Jersey cows, heifers and one bull. Each animal had a 'sling' placed around its body and was hoisted on board by a crane. I was in charge of supervising the animals having them placed in stalls, a smaller animal next to a larger one and making sure they had plenty of room to lie down. Three of the cows were in milk so I had them put together at the top end of the section making it easier for me to milk as well as giving us fresh rich milk daily. The bull was placed in a stall at the bottom of the section. Then came ten tons of hay, eight tons of straw, two tons of feed and water. This was stored under cover at the stern of the ship and organised by the stevedore. All the other cargo had already been loaded. The thirty-six passengers were all on board and we were ready to set sail. A voice called out, "Stevedore, make way!"

"Aye aye sir!" a reply came back.

On Monday June 23rd 1947 at four in the afternoon on a beautiful hot cloudless summer's day, amid waving, cheering and shouts of 'bon voyage' from the passengers, the bow of the *Umtata* slid gently into the sea. She sailed down the Southampton water out into the Solent and the English Channel.

Now my work started, the cattle were thirsty. The water was kept in a large drum continually fed by a ball valve.

Carrying two at a time thirty-nine bucketsful were required in total! I fed the cattle a portion of hay, chewing would help them settle. Milking was an effort because, although the sea was calm, the slightest roll of the ship caused the milk to spill. Sitting on a stool which was too low for me, I tried to hold the bucket between my legs. By the time I had fed the animals more hay and finally finished my chores we were well out into the channel.

Tuesday was Midsummer Day, the channel was calm and the cattle were settling down as if to say that they had better make the best of it. I had a little cabin with a bunk and washbasin. I took my meals with the ship's crew – the night was starry and beautiful. We had soup, followed by roast lamb and vegetables, ice cream and strawberries, all washed down with a bottle of beer.

Next day we entered the Bay of Biscay encountering slight rollers, the cattle were getting used to the conditions but I found that milking and carrying the water was a task that called for 'rhythm'. The cattle had settled down and so had I. We sailed out of the Bay of Biscay into a calm sea where I saw quite a few flying fish, it was a far cry from being on the farm. I made a plan of procedure for my daily routine.

7 am	*milk three cows and hand the milk to the chef. Water and feed cattle*
8.30	*breakfast consisting of bacon, two eggs and sausage etc (on land it would be one egg if I was lucky) plenty of toast, butter and marmalade*
11 until noon	*Coffee break*
12 noon	*Feed and water the animals followed by lunch and siesta.*
5 until 6	*Feed and water. Shut shop.*
7 pm	*Dinner – the food was very good.*

On the 27th we arrived at Las Palmas, Canary Islands, docking for six hours, loading and unloading cargo. In my diary I made the following remarks about the citizens,

'...the citizens were charming.' The *Umtata* sailed out in a calm sea and warm weather. Three days later we were off the coast of Freemantle, it was getting warmer. On July 2nd at nine pm we passed over the equator, conditions were warm with a strong wind but the following day we encountered strong winds and heavy seas. Meals for today were:

Breakfast.	*Porridge, fish, followed by bacon & egg, rolls, butter, toast, marmalade, coffee, oranges.*
Lunch.	*Fish, cold meat and salad, cherries and cream. Tea and cakes at 4pm*
Dinner	*Soup, roast duck, fish or cold meat, ice cream, grapes, coffee.*

Cigarettes on board cost 2/6d for 50 Players, 2/9d for Churchmans No.1 and 2/-d for Waverleys. A can of beer cost 10d.

Each morning the captain did a tour of the cattle and their provisions with me. I found him to be a very nice gentleman.

On July 4th we arrived at Ascension Island and had to unload the cargo at sea. This was a very difficult operation as the sea was rough but the crew was used to taking provisions aboard under such circumstances.

We arrived at St Helena Island on Sunday 6th, dropping anchor outside port and going ashore by small boat to tour the Island. We visited the tomb of the French Emperor, Napoleon Bonaparte, who was interned here by the British Government and who died in exile on the island on May 5th 1821.

We left the island at ten in the evening in calm seas and fair weather. The cattle had now adjusted to life on board. Next stop was Cape Town.

On the 8th and 9th we sailed into very rough seas and the following day at eleven o'clock in the morning we ran into a strong gale. One minute the bow of the Umtata would be pointing skyward and the next dipping into the sea with the stern out of the water. Great waves crashed over the deck soaking the cattle and myself. At two in the afternoon, looking like a drowned rat, the captain appeared on the upper deck and waved me to join him. We stood on the steps leading to the ships quarters, holding the rails for support. "I'm sorry to tell you that I may be forced to jettison the cargo." Clearly, the captain was including the cattle!

At that moment the ship gave a shudder making the situation even worse, "No! Please don't destroy those lovely animals, can we leave it another hour before making such a decision?" I begged.

Suddenly, in answer to my prayers, we saw a glimmer of sunshine through the clouds. The captain said, "Let's hope that means a break in the storm!" More sunshine appeared and although there was no break in the fury of the storm it did not get any worse. At four o'clock there was a break and an hour later we had ploughed through it. By six o'clock we were beyond the storm.

Now I was busy watering the cattle, thirsty from the seawater. The boat, still rolling, made it very difficult to carry the two buckets of fresh water given to each cow (a total of 60 buckets) and I just hoped there would be enough fresh water left to get us to Cape Town.

Next day was beautiful with a cloudless sky and calmer seas although a nip in the air. There was a lot of cleaning up after the storm but the animals appeared none the worse for their adventure, their milk yield unaffected. The passengers and crew were grateful to have fresh milk each day.

The coastline of the Cape of Good Hope was now visible with mountains in the background the scenery was very picturesque. The sea here was different to the rest of our voyage although we were now encountering rollers – long heavy waves – the water was very clear with visibility to a depth of about twenty feet.

We arrived at Cape Town docks at half past five in the afternoon. After attending to the cattle I joined the crew for an uptown visit of Cape Town. It was wintertime so although the air was cool to cold, it was lovely and fresh. We made our way to the Delmonica at the Grand Hotel where the first thing we did was to order fish and chips. Although the fish was fresh and tasty the chips were not the King Edward variety!

A popular drink was 'Lion' beer at elevenpence per bottle. Spirits were quite cheap and the wine, for which South Africa is noted, very plentiful. On the outskirts of Cape Town at Stellenbosch, the main grape growing area, there are hundreds of acres of vineyards.

Whilst most of the crew drank beer I settled for Cape brandy and ginger ale. However I was not aware that it was very potent and had the 'kick of a mule'.

My look around Cape Town did not materialise for I went no further than the Delmonica. After four of these brandies I was 'out for the count' and had to be taken back aboard the *Umtata* by a member of the crew where I was thrown on my bunk to sober up, several hours later. It was the first and last time I had ever been drunk. I managed to get through my chores the next day despite a sore head.

Later, on the Friday, I went with Charlie, an assistant chef, on a tour of Cape Town and visited Table Mountain. The weather had turned to rain and was quite cold.

Upon my return to the ship I met two farmers who were inspecting the cattle. They were quite impressed at the quality of the herd and although I could not help them with details of pedigree I could give them details of how well bred they were. The farmers were from 'George' and had a small herd of Jerseys themselves. There was quite a write up in the local press on the arrival of such a valuable herd of Jersey cattle, worth eleven thousand pounds.

On Sunday 13th the off-loading and loading of the ship was complete. The cattle received a top up of water, some new hay and fresh straw. We left Cape Town at four in the afternoon en- route for East London in South Africa. We ran into gale force winds and stormy weather. The following day in very rough seas we passed the Cape of Good Hope. It rained all day but the cattle were fine. We arrived at East London on St. Swithens day, July 15th.

The ship's first officer, who I had got to know, told me that if I wanted to buy a car East London was the place as cars were much cheaper there particularly if it was a Ford. He understood the Ford Motor Company had an assembly plant in East London. As soon as I could I went to see the secretary of the 1820 Settlers Association, a Mrs Creswell, for advice on how to go about it. My plan was to buy a car then motor to Durban, about two hundred miles away after first attending to the cattle. Mrs Creswell knew the manager of Dominion Motors, Mr Anderson. I found him to be very helpful, he offered me a second hand (as new) 1947 Ford V8 de-luxe with only four thousand one hundred and forty-six miles on the clock, with licence and insurance thrown in for four hundred and fifty pounds!

I had to change my English driving licence for a South African 'Life' driving licence, photograph required, issued by the Licencing Authority. I still use this today. The licence number is 98489 and stamped East London, dated 18.7.47. It has no endorsements.

I drove the car back to the *Umtata* with the idea of seeing the captain and to ask permission to drive the car to Durban. However, the captain had been waiting for me for two hours. I'd heard several bursts from a ship's siren earlier, unaware that in fact these bursts had been calling me!

I quickly explained, offering to attend to my duties before driving to Durban but the captain would not hear of it. He informed me that he would have the car strapped down on the fore deck and conveyed on to Durban, which was our last stop. This would enable me to carry out my chores with the cattle at sea. Whilst he was annoyed at being delayed from sailing by a member of the crew, the captain was very understanding and forgave me.

The car was immediately hoisted on board, strapped down and the *Umtata* then made her way to complete the voyage to Durban. The sea was smooth and the weather beautiful as we passed St. Johns and Margate, enabling me to give the cattle stalls a good clean.

We arrived at Durban the following day, Saturday July

19th 1947 at seven am, having left Southampton on Monday June 23rd. We had a slight delay in entering the harbour having to lie at anchor waiting for the pilot to escort us to the docks. The sea was calm but was not without a heavy swell. Having escorted several other ships in it was now our turn to be approached by the pilot boat. The pilot climbed aboard and navigated the Umtata over the bar.

We were soon tied up alongside and the gangway hoisted for exit. 'Hey presto' ALL HAD MADE IT including the cattle! The passengers bid us farewell before collecting their luggage and going through customs.

Mr H G Conrad, the owner of the cattle, was the first person to approach me where I stood by the bull. He was carrying a silver mounted walking stick and a folder containing details of the cattle. After asking questions and making a careful inspection of each and every animal he seemed pleased at the end of his tour with the condition and contentment of the cattle. "Thank you very much for looking after my cattle so well, if you go up to Smith Street to Parry Leon and Hayhoe, you'll find a bonsella (gift) there for you to collect."

An Afrikaner farmer, who was looking at the cattle, greeted me with, "Goie Mora mannear Ooh Gandit." Realising I did not understand the Afrikaans language he broke off into English which he spoke fluently. After a brief conversation I asked to be excused as I wanted to see my car off loaded, parking it in a wide space close to the *Umtata*.

It was warm and whilst giving the cattle water I was approached by a gentleman who spoke to me, "My name is Bert Ellet, I also import Jersey cattle and have a small herd on my farm about thirty miles from here."

"Pleased to meet you," I replied, "I'm Chris Pantall, a farmer by trade. I worked my passage here and want to find a job as a farm manager as soon as possible. I've a wife and eight-month old daughter waiting for me to find accommodation so they can come and join me. Can you help?"

He replied, "I live on my farm at Cato Ridge. Come and stay with my family and we'll discuss your future. This is a wonderful country badly in need of more immigrants from England. I'm from Jersey myself, emigrated here several years ago. Very pleased to make your acquaintance!"

We agreed that after I had signed off and said my good byes I would follow his Chev pickup to Parry, Leon and Hayhoe's to collect my bonsella.

I found the captain and thanked him for a wonderful journey, congratulating him for pulling the *Umtata* through the awful storm.

"You looked after those cattle so well," he replied, adding "I wish you the very best of health and good luck in South Africa."

I found the other members of the crew and bid them goodbye, thanking the chef particularly for feeding me like royalty.

Mr Conrad had his own cattleman so, my duties completed, I departed following Mr Bert Ellett in my car. I was amazed at the lovely office buildings and wonderful shops set in the widest streets I had ever seen.

Later, Mr Joubert of Parry, Leon and Hayhoe explained that when the authorities built Smith Street they made it wide enough for a span of oxen, twelve, pulling an ox wagon, to turn around in the road. The whole of Durban was less than a hundred years old.

I opened the envelope from Mr Conrad. A note inside said 'thank you' and attached to it, twenty-five pounds in notes.

Throughout the voyage I had written regularly to Linda keeping her up to date with my experiences. I now wanted to send her a telegram letting her know I had arrived safely. There were no cablegrams, it was only in the last few years that a telegram could be sent: Morse code was used before this. I explained the position to Mr Ellett, following him to the general post office.

We left Durban and I saw a signpost for Pietermaritzburg, Johannesburg. We kept on this road, motoring on through Pinetown a little village on the outskirts. Some parts of the road we travelled along were untarred and made of dirt. We were also passing through Zululand it was very mountainous and called 'The Valley of the Thousand Hills.' Occasionally, when able to do so, we were able to look down and see the sea along with hundreds of mud huts, goats and sheep. In the distance was the Umgeni River. It all reminded me, in a way, of the Black Mountains. We were climbing the whole journey, now through Hillerest, possibly two thousand feet above sea level. This was the Natal Province. Travelling along a continuous tarred road we passed through Hammarsdale the road here was no longer steep but, like the rest of the journey, winding. There was very little traffic, we only met a dozen cars in total.

We came to a narrow dirt road ahead on the right, sign posted B W Ellett – Pembroke Farm. I followed behind as we drew up in the courtyard of an elegant looking farmhouse. Ten Jersey cows grazed in a paddock at the rear of some cowsheds surrounded by numerous tall gum trees. As we parked the cars a lady came out of the house, waving our arrival. Mr Ellett said, "Meet my wife Lucille and please, call me Bert."

I introduced myself and we shook hands, "How kind of you to invite me to stay for a few days to sort myself out."

"It's our pleasure," she smiled. "It's lovely to have someone from the old country to visit us, come in and have a cup of tea, you can bring your baggage in later."

Bert and Lucille had emigrated from Jersey a few years earlier setting up a small farm of imported Jersey cattle. He had recently imported three heifers and a bull, some of the cattle I had accompanied were related to his pedigreed stock.

We had a walk around the farm it was ideal for the purpose of importing Jerseys then selling to South African farmers. Seeing two bulls in an enclosed shed I remarked, "Jersey bulls are not docile."

"Those two are dangerous and aggressive," Bert replied, "but with a ring through the nose and a long stick with a hook at the end fastened to the ring, they're safe enough to lead!"

It was now seven in the evening. Suddenly Bert said, "It's Sundowner Time!"

This was part of the South African way of life, to sit down after a hot day, relax and have a chat over either a beer or a glass of wine. Spirits were not so popular.

"So, to your future Chris, what can we do for you?" Bert asked.

"I think this country has opportunities for farming Bert. My first priority is to get myself a farm manager's job, with a house, so that I can bring Linda and Pamela out to join me. But where! I know Natal is the most English of the five provinces." (The others being, The Transvaal, Northern Transvaal, Orange Free State and the Cape).

"Chris, when you say the 'most English', the Afrikaner population is only a few thousand and they fought the English and the Zulu Tribe at Blood River. They're chiefly farmers, the word Boer means farmer." Bert explained.

"I think I prefer Natal." I replied.

"I love Natal." Lucille said, "We often pop down to Durban, it's very English. We have two daughters who aren't here at the moment, they're staying with friends but they'll be here at the weekend. Come on, suppers ready!"

We continued our conversation on job hunting over supper. Bert said, "I want to go down to Transkei, I sold a bull to a farmer at Eliottdale, he's interested in a couple of cows. There's also a farmer in Kokstad, which is East Grigualand, who is starting a herd of Jerseys. It's a lovely part of the country near to Port St. John and the Indian Ocean. I take the Farmers Weekly – we can look for any farming vacancies."

After supper we went to feed the bulls, the cows had already been milked by an African worker and we went to see if they were OK.

Later we looked through the Farmers Weekly, finding nothing. Bert said, "You know Chris, there's a lovely little poultry farm by the railway line at Cato Ridge, only three miles from here!"

"I can't afford to buy it. I've very little money, that's why I was working my passage." I explained.

"Tommy Dart came from England many years ago," said

Lucille. "He built it up then sold it to a Mr Stowe. He's only
been there a few years and now wants to sell. Tommy retired
to Pietermaritzburg. I'd like you to meet Tommy. I know
he'd like to meet you. He likes to keep in touch with the old
country. Whilst you and Bert have gone cattle hunting I'll try
and organise a meeting!"

"Lucille that's so kind of you," I replied. "I'll look forward
to meeting Mr Dart. Does he have any knowledge of farming?"

Bert chimed in, "Tommy made his money hauling
munitions for the British army during the Boer War. All the
way from Ladysmith to Pretoria with a span of oxen! He's a
great man. He'll tell you all about it. He came to Cato Ridge
and built the poultry farm which he called Sunnyside Egg
Farm."

I told Bert I was looking forward to our trip to East
Grigualand explaining that I was near there whilst visiting
East London and had met a farmer on my arrival who had
introduced himself as Johannes van den Berg. He'd told me
that he was not a buyer but was interested in the cattle on
board. He had given me his address telling me to contact him
if I wanted to settle in his wonderful part of South Africa. As I
had been anxious to buy a car I did not pursue the matter.

Bert said that he did not think I would want to settle
there as it was too near Basutoland which had too many
African townships.

We set off early the next day for our trip to East
Grigualand. As it was a long journey I offered to take my car
for which Bert was pleased.

"The people you want to visit may not be there." I said.

"The post is so slow it could take three weeks to get
there." Bert answered.

We set off travelling through Pietermaritzburg, capital of
Natal, and took the road to Kokstad. When the surface was
hard, it was a dirt road and very dusty particularly when
following another vehicle. The countryside was very bare with
only the occasional gum tree plantation. A lot of maize was
grown and was known as mealies. Bert said, "We'll call at

154

Kokstad on the way back but first we'll go to Butterworth. There's a Mr Phillips I'd like you to meet, he has a farm two miles from there.

It was still early. Bert was driving and I was able to view the countryside. He said that it was a lovely car to drive. We were now travelling through the township of Libode, thousands of acres, chiefly cattle, all belonging to the Africans. Bert told me they were all crossbred. There were no fences along the roadside making it hazardous for the motorist.

We were now approaching the small town of Umtata. All of a sudden a half-grown heifer galloped in our pathway. Bert immediately applied the brakes but we collided with the animal, injuring it and severely damaging the near side front wing of the car. As if by magic one hundred and one Africans appeared, none speaking a word of English and Bert only a splatter of Zulu. We hobbled into Umtata and found a garage. The proprietor was very helpful and undertook repair of the damage, telephoning Dominion Motors at East London, where I had bought the car and arranging for spare parts to be delivered next day. As the car had comprehensive insurance I telephoned them receiving permission to proceed having already informed the police.

We stayed the night at a local hotel and hired a car – something unheard of in those days – belonging to Mr Smith the garage proprietor. After breakfast the following morning we set off for Butterworth enlisting the assistance of a local police officer when we arrived. The officer knew Mr Phillips and fortunately we found him at home.

I left Bert to discuss his business and wandered off to look at a vineyard nearby. A six-foot high meshed wire fence totally surrounded the one block of about thirty acres there were no fences anywhere only strands of wire dividing paddocks.

I made my way back to find that Bert had concluded his business. Before we left Mr Phillips kindly telephoned Mr Smith at Umtata and was informed that the parts had arrived and the car would be completed by nightfall.

Upon our arrival back at Umtata, Bert and I made our way to the police station to make a statement concerning the accident. I paid Mr Smith five pounds for the hire of his car; mine was now completely roadworthy.

Money by the way was exactly the same currency here as in England only it had South African Reserve Bank and other jargon printed on both sides.

Early the next morning we left our hotel and drove to Rietvlei, commonly known as a dorp, a few miles from Kokstad and found the farm following Mr van der Merwee's instructions. He lived in a very attractive Dutch style type of house popular in South Africa. Mr van der Merwee owned about one hundred acres and grew lucerne as well as mealies. Before concluding business with him, Bert took an order for one of his two Jersey bulls wishing him 'Tot Seins' (goodbye) before we drove back to Cato Ridge. He thought our journey had been very satisfactory.

True to her word, Lucille had contacted Tommy Dart. "He would like to meet you in about a fortnight's time," she said.

"Thank you Lucille, I'll go and have a look at farms in the Mooi River area. I want to visit a Mr Phipps then go on to Val, a small village near Standerton, to see Sydney Reynolds about the prospects of employment.

I drove up to Mooi River and visited the farm owned by Mr J G Phipps. I had been given an introduction through Mrs Cresswell of the 1820 Settlers Association who had helped me buy my car back at East London. She had telephoned Mr Phipps advising him to expect me and asking for his help.

In addition to owning a large farm he had a large whattle tree plantation, the bark of whattle trees was used for tanning leather and about thirty-acres of gum trees. These trees grew as straight as a gun barrel to about thirty to forty feet. When felled they were cut into different lengths and used for props in the mines. In the ever-expanding gold mining industry there was a never-ending demand for these props.

Mr Phipps had a herd of Tamworth pigs. He took me in his pick-up to the Estcourt bacon factory close by. I found the factory very interesting, the demand for bacon, sausages and hams far exceeding the supply. Many farmers in the area produced 'baconers' as a sideline to growing mealies.

Although interested, I was no nearer my goal of finding employment. Over a glass of beer Mr Phipps suggested that I could join a growing company like Hulletts on the coast, sugar planting, or one of the large farms in the Transvaal such as Sydney Reynolds at Val.

I explained that what I really wanted was employment as a farm manager on a mixed farm, visiting a few would give me an idea of where I would like to live.

Mr Phipps was keen to help, "There are a lot of big dairy farms around here, we'll go and visit Nestlés milk factory, it's close by.

We drove to the factory where Mr Phipps knew the manager. He was delighted to show us how they processed the milk but I felt that I was wasting my time as I had no desire to be involved with cattle. I wanted to supervise the planting and harvesting of mealies, corn, lucerne and other crops.

"The big farms such as Hulletts have so many indians as foremen that white managers are few and far between but they do have senior staff, continued Mr Phipps. "The Free States have big farms but again nearly all the managers are Afrikaners.".

"I'm seeing something of the country," I answered gratefully, "I'm sure I'll find what I'm looking for in the right place. Thank you for your time and hospitality."

I bid him good day and set off heading for the Transvaal. Although the dirt roads were fairly wide they were rough and uneven and bumps in the road made driving over forty miles an hour impossible. I passed over the Val River and made my way to Mr Reynold's farm, Val is a small dorp not far from Standerton. Sydney Reynolds was well known to the Secretary of the Hereford Herd Book Society having bought Herefords from the Vern, a well-established Hereford farm. A 'Vern Robert' bull was recognised throughout the whole of the Hereford cattle world.

I found Mr Reynolds to be a charming man. He and his family had settled on the farm, descendents from the eighteen-twenty settlers. As Mr Reynolds said, "It's a story in itself!"

It was suggested that I should visit Mr H G Crooks of Platrand Farm, near Standerton. Mr Crooks had a big farm and may be interested in employing me as his general manager.

I made my way to Platrand Farm, it was now winter time and the nights were cold and freezing. The usual weather pattern was, no rain for the months of May, June, July and August. At present they were harvesting mealies. The farm grew a lot of pumpkins fed to their large herd of pigs. Unfortunately Mr Crooks was not at home having gone to Durban.

I had the names of quite a few farmers in the Transvaal, Southern Rhodesia and Natal. Cape Province was more of a wine-producing region so I thought I could try there if all else failed.

I stayed at a small hotel in Standerton where the food was quite good. A noticeable factor was their three-course dinner, beef with horseradish sauce, lamb with mint sauce, or pork with applesauce one could help oneself to vegetables, chiefly pumpkin. I suspected all the meat 'belonged to the same animal,' it was left to the imagination what animal that was.... I paid twenty-five shillings for bed, full English breakfast and dinner.

At six am on Thursday July 31st I was on my way back to Cato Ridge, four hundred miles away. It was light at six am and dark at seven pm There was only two hours difference between summer and winter. On the way back through Howick in Natal I decided to stop, there had been very little traffic and I had made very good time. The only holdups on the road had been cattle and I had often passed a span of oxen pulling a wagon of mealies or other agricultural merchandise. The winter countryside looked so bleak and uninviting I was glad to leave it behind. Natal was much more my scene. After a cup of tea and a sandwich I walked over to the Howick Falls over a hundred metres in height. Water tumbled over rugged rocks roaring as it reached the bottom. I said "Good afternoon," to others sight seeing.

"Sorry, we Afrikaners, No speakey Engleesh. We from the Cape."

"Sorry," I replied.

I arrived back in Cato Ridge early in the evening and saw Lucille waiting for me to open the car door. "Hi there! Lucille."

She threw her arms around me saying, "Welcome home Chris. Before we have a natter I'll put the kettle on. Would you go over to the bull shed and give Bert a hand to take Herman (the bull) out to graze please?"

I found Bert mixing the bulls feed, "Welcome home Chris," he called. "You've come just in time. I can't fasten the clip onto Herman's nose ring!"

I took the rod holding the clip with my right hand using my left hand to grasp the ring holding it up along with the bull's head. I fastened the clip onto the ring with my right hand, now Herman was a prisoner and could be led out of his box into a paddock and I could relax my hold enabling him to graze.

Bert said, "I always have trouble with him."

I replied, "I'm that bit longer in the arm so can reach further. What about Ferdi." I suddenly remembered Ferdinand, the other bull.

"I can manage him." Bert replied. "As Herman is the better pedigree I think I'll send him to van der Merwee. I grazed Herman for about twenty minutes before putting him back in his box, which Bert had cleaned out, adding fresh litter, feed and hay. Walking side by side we went into the house for a 'sundowner' which took the form of a cup of tea.

"Tommy is looking forward to meeting you Chris, he really regrets selling the poultry farm to the man that bought it," said Lucille.

"I can't afford to buy a farm." I said quickly. "But I'm looking forward to meeting Tommy; out of curiosity as to why he's so keen to meet me."

"Well Chris, he's over eighty years of age and has had a hard life. Imagine driving a span of oxen over the rugged countryside between Ladysmith and Pretoria. He had to cross two rivers, the oxen pulling a wagon loaded with ammunition collected from a train at Ladysmith – the railway line didn't go any further – to a depot at Pretoria for the British army to use during the Boer War.

That's how the story goes but Tommy says very little about it. He did enjoy building Sunnyside egg farm."

"Another cup please," chimed in Bert. "How did you get on during your visit to Northern Natal and the Transvaal?" Bert enquired.

"Well," I replied, "I was made welcome by some enterprising people but to cut a long story short I personally would not fancy living beyond Natal."

"Yes," said Bert. "We prefer Natal."

Lucille said, "Chris, you've had a long journey, may I suggest that tomorrow you and I pop into Maritzburg before we all go down to Durban for the day. Bert can do all the jobs he needs to do and we'll pick him up on our way back."

14

Off we went the following day, a tarred road taking us all the way into Pietermaritzburg. A Town Hall, surrounded by flowerbeds and dominated by a large clock, was very impressive. Although winter it was quite mild. Bougainvillaea, growing on fences, was not yet in season its dark red flower yet to bloom. We drove down a side street to a corn merchant depot filling up the boot with feed for the cattle. Lucille also bought groceries before we drove up Longmarket Street. It was plain to see the whole town was steeped in history.

We called at the home of Tommy Dart, a lovely little house, being met by his daughter who told us that Tommy was away for a couple of days but would be there for us to meet the following Thursday. "I'll have the kettle boiling for three o'clock on the 7th of August," she promised.

"I think we should wait until your father comes home before we make a definite appointment," I suggested.

On the way home I said to Lucille, "I think Sunnyside egg farm might be worth a visit, let's ring Mr Stowe to make an appointment!" When we got back to Cato Ridge Lucille spoke to Mr Stowe, "Just a quick visit," she told him.

"How about next Wednesday at eleven am" Mr Stowe

suggested.

Lucille looked across at me for confirmation and I nodded O.K.

The three of us set off for Durban, all downhill. This was the Hillcrest area through plantations of gum and wattle trees, thousands of acres, piles of sawn up ten-foot lengths of gum trees ready for transportation to mines. Arriving at the sea front we decided to visit a snack bar. There was such a variety of fish to choose from, mine was very tasty. After a visit to the aquarium we went down town to the shopping area. Some of the big shops here were twice the size of those in Hereford and merchandise was a lot cheaper than in England. Although it was wintertime and very cold in the Transvaal, here in Durban it was lovely and warm.

We motored back to Cato Ridge where I found a letter waiting from Linda. I had posted one to her explaining how hard I was trying to find something suitable, how large the country was and, although I had not seen an advertisement for a farm manager, I was sure something would come up shortly. Linda's letter was full of doom and gloom. She had got herself a job as a 'live-in' nanny. It was company for Pamela who was well and thriving but the situation was not what she had expected by marrying me. She had married for better or for worse, and this was definitely worse so I had better hurry up and find accommodation.

On reflection I had to admit that it was not fair to keep Linda waiting from June until August without having my sights set on a target. But I was trying and it was important to know just where we should settle and what kind of work I should do – farming yes, but here white farm managers were not needed when Indians in most cases were able to take charge. Indeed many Africans fell into that category. I had to put my thinking cap on, considering other types of employment. No other country in the world was richer in minerals than South Africa. It was a very young country with lots of opportunities but I only had one thousand four hundred pounds – earned from my rabbit and poultry sales plus the sale of a couple of cars, thank God I had that!

I had received nothing from father but I had good health and was not afraid of hard work. Not being a believer in 'something will turn up' I knew I must go out and find it.

Politically and under General Smuts the Prime Minister of the United Party the future was unstable. The opposition, being Afrikaners, were 'knocking at the door'. They had different ideas of running the country and would push for Apartheid: segregation of the blacks from the whites, making existing black city dwellers move into black townships. These townships were already established on the outskirts of cities but were not compulsory. Compared to living in city accommodation living in townships was cheap.

The country's mineral wealth was great with deposits of iron ore to be found all over South Africa, Iscor State owned steelworks producing several million tons of steel each year. There were enormous reserves of coal, seams were very near the surface and mining coal was quite cheap. The Boksburg area produced the most coal, oil from coal known as Sasol was still in its infancy having many teething problems.

Gold deposits are numerous in South Africa. In the Johannesburg area piles and piles of mine dumps can be seen: waste from digging ground hundreds of feet below the surface, when surfaced the gold is extracted. Big gold deposits are being mined in the Orange Free State Area. Numerous diamond mines are to be found here and in the North West Cape. Kimberley is well known for its diamond mines and boasts of having produced the largest diamond in the world.

Sir Ernest Oppenheimer was one of the pioneers in the diamond world, de Beers being a well-known Blue Chip on the stock market. But Gold stabilised the economy of South Africa.

The Africans have a long line of history, belonging to many tribes, not only in South Africa but also in Southern and Northern Rhodesia, the Congo, Uganda, Kenya, South West Africa, Bechuanaland, Mozambique and Portugese East Africa. Many Africans have two wives, according to their wealth. This is not monetary wealth but is dependent upon land, how many head of cattle, goats, sheep and pigs they own. In some parts of South Africa, Africans live on white owned farms. It is a kind of labour-tenant agreement. They are given a plot of land for their own use and in return all the family work for a specified period. A small wage is paid and a ration of mealies and meat. This is a method of getting labour for the farm and is mostly used by the Afrikaner farmers.

The Indian population is spread throughout the whole of Africa. Throughout South Africa an Indian store will be found in every village, dorp, run and owned by Indians. After the 1820 settlers came from England Indians were imported from India, under a government scheme, to work on the Natal sugar farms and Durban became their settling ground.

South Africa has many diseases not known in England. Bilhavzia was a common disease picked up from streams, rivers and dams. It is a small parasite that burrows its way into the skin of human beings and settles in the blood stream. It is rarely fatal but causes weariness and other complications.

Dysentery is also very common in the African community.

§

I decided that I must see if the sugar cane industry held any opportunities for me. I went to Durban travelling up the north coast. If it held nothing else it certainly was very beautiful. I made my way to Umhlali, driving through Tongaat. All the land leading down to the sea was planted with sugar cane.

I was informed that all the sugar cane was grown from the Mozambique to the Cape, the largest sugar cane factory being Hulletts at Umhlali. I had telephoned Mr Hullett requesting an interview so he was expecting me.

At the entrance to his home was a signboard, 'R S L Hullett – Sheffield Farm, Umhlali.' It was a magnificent dutch style residence, each end at the front having a large white gable. Mr Hullett was waiting as I pulled up, "A pleasure to meet you," I told him smiling.

"And you to," he replied

"What a beautiful day," I said.

"Every day is like this, that's why no one says, nice day."

I asked him why his farm was called *Sheffield*.

"My Grandfather came from Sheffield here to Umhlali. Come on in. Over the years Hullett's has acquired a good deal of sugar growing land and we also established the first modern sugar-extraction factory. It has expanded over time and we now buy hundreds of tons of sugar cane from farmers."

We had a general chat over a flagon of Lion ale and I asked him what the prospects were like in the sugar cane industry for a settler such as myself.

He replied, "Unless you have a knowledge of the industry, marketing, engineering or other skills, I'm afraid, none. Indians and their families are our work force and make good supervisors. Come on we'll take a jaunt over to the mill."

I jumped into a Chev pickup and in a cloud of dust we made our way to the Mill, about five minutes away. Sugar cane was both stacked and in truckloads.

"The stacks are our cane," explained Mr Hullett, "and the trucks are from the farmers."

The extraction of the sugar from the cane was very interesting. I could quite see why sugar from cane was superior from sugar beet grown in England. This sugar when dried was of a soft texture whilst our sugar was course.

We then drove up the Umgeni valley. The River Umgeni was very low waiting for the 'rainy' season. Mr Hullett said, "Years ago this River had crocodiles. In recent years they have been exterminated but not many miles away from here, in Richards Bay, there are plenty."

There were thousands of acres of sugar cane that seemed to thrive in a dry and hot climate. I doubted if anything else would grow in this undulating countryside. He drove us to a part of a sugar plantation. "We have to divide the whole area into three because every three years we replant one area, it takes a lot of labour but no doubt in the future we shall have all this done my mechanical means."

Whilst I found this interesting I couldn't see any opportunity for me in this industry and I knew I must press on. We returned to 'Sheffield' and after a cup of tea and a biscuit I bid my host good day with 'tot seins'. He laughed and said, "Good luck."

I'd noticed during my journey down the South Coast that inland from Amazimtoti in the Richmond area there were quite a few farms that had bullocks in contained areas. For example, twenty bullocks would be in one small area with feeding troughs, fed with hay and a cereal ration placed in the troughs. With this type of feeding a heavy two-year old bullock could become prime quality beef within a few months. I was interested and called in at one such farm, introducing myself but being careful not to say I was interested in carrying out a similar venture myself. However, Mr Gibson was very friendly and I told him that we fattened not only bullocks but heifers in about three months, in stalls, chiefly Hereford Cross Shorthorns. Mr Gibson said, "This is a free market, there's a great demand from the butcher for top quality disease free beef. Ninety-five percent of the beef produced in South Africa were Afrikaners, commonly known as 'Trek Ox'. Top class hotels buy my beef through my butcher but neither I nor the other farmers using this method can ever meet the demand."

As I'd guessed two year old bullocks were fed a special high protein ration, in this case lucerne, in place of hay. The bullocks were bought from markets in various places, his from Richmond market, Afrikaner Cross Friesians were popular.

I could see a future for this type of farming and in my mind delved into this. I chatted with Mr Gibson and he introduced me to his wife and daughter insisting that I had a meal with them. As I had not eaten since breakfast and it was now five pm I was glad of the invitation deciding that I would stay the night at a hotel at Richmond.

We continued to chat, his wife joining in. I said, "Mrs Gibson you are obviously part and parcel of this operation, what exactly do you do?"

She replied, "We've over five hundred acres and, whilst Roland is either at the market or looking after the rest of the farm, I attend to the bullocks. The water is automatic from a bore hole and I have to feed the lucerne and cereals by hand three times a day but I do have two good Africans who help me. We've over a hundred fatteners, sending out about ten weekly and these have to be replaced. I also mix the feed that we have delivered."

Suppertime came, sausages and mashed potato washed down with ale. The bread was homemade but very coarse. After the meal I thanked them both for their hospitality and promised to keep in touch.

With a lot of 'food for thought' I made my way to Richmond, the town I had seen earlier, booking in at the local hotel. I gave Lucille a ring telling her of my new find. She was very interested, "Chris, you must go to the bank and apply for a loan."

I replied, "I'll be home tomorrow."

I returned to Cato Ridge to find that Bert had gone to see a customer at Ladysmith and would be back that night. I helped Lucille to feed the cattle and was glad to hear that Herman had been collected. We had a little natter then Bert arrived.

Over dinner I told of my experiences saying that it would possibly be too costly depending on what the bank would loan. I would need a small farm with a house, at least twenty bullocks, fattening equipment, water supply was important and whilst I was building the business up we would have to live.

At a rough estimate I thought I would need at least fifteen thousand pounds!

The telephone rang it was Mr Stowe. He had cancelled our previous meeting and wanted to organise another for the following day at three in the afternoon.

Tommy Dart would be there too. I thanked him and told him yes. The three of us went back to the bullock proposition. I said, "I'll bet there's no beef producer in this country that blood tests for T.B. (tuberculosis) a disease that must be carried by cattle including milk herds. Just before I left England the Ministry of Agriculture had blood tested every animal on the Home Farm, all had tested negative. If I went into beef production I'd blood test all the bullocks I bought putting any that tested positive back in the market. I could then guarantee my beef cattle free of TB this would be such a good selling point for the butcher – DISEASE FREE BEEF. It would soon catch on, good news for the butcher's customers and my cattle."

"Well Chris, it sounds good, but it all depends on the bank giving you a mortgage to buy. Land is not let in South Africa."

The next day, Saturday August 16th, I went to Sunnyside egg farm and met Mr Stowe, Tommy had not yet arrived. Whilst we were waiting I said, "Mr Stowe, why are you selling?"

"I'm not a farmer Chris," he replied, "I'd like to return to running a chemist shop."

Just then Tommy arrived. We made our introductions and he asked, "What part of England are you from?"

"Herefordshire," I replied.

"Well I never – I was born at Hay on Wye!" he exclaimed.

"I know it well, father used to buy our breeding ewes at Hay market."

"Is Morgan Jones still at Sugwas?" Tommy enquired.

"Yes, but he would be the son of the man you knew. Who else did you know?"

"Parry (The Stowe), Andrews (Stretton Sugwas) and Rudge of Baysham..."

"Yes, those families are all still there and, like my family at Kilkington, date back from the seventeenth century."

Over a cup of tea he said, "I built this little farm after I retired, when I couldn't run it any longer, I sold it to Mr Stowe and, not being a farmer, he wants to sell. I wondered if you would be interested in buying as you are a farmer?"

After a few seconds I replied, "Mr Dart, even if I wanted to, what would I buy it with, washers? I have very little money and in any case I haven't seen the place yet!"

Tommy turned to Mr Stowe. "Can we take a walk around?"

"Yes, certainly," replied Mr Stowe.

Tommy and I walked down the pathway leading to the piggery. There were four pigsties holding ten pigs. Sties were used for fattening up the pigs, infertile eggs from incubators being part of their feed. We then inspected five large poultry houses each containing about two hundred fowls before looking at smaller houses all containing different breeds but all pure breds: white Leghorn, Rhode Island reds and black Australorps, all the birds looked well. We met an African who was collecting eggs who told me, in broken English, that his name was 'Induna'. I later learned that this meant, 'boss of the African staff'. I thought the ten-acre farm was well situated. The brooder house came next – this was a building containing twenty partitioned pens suitable for small chicks. Almost empty, most of the young stock were outside in wire pens in small houses, called the orchard.

Next on our tour was the incubators and store rooms but Tommy said, I'll leave Stowe to show you around those later, let's sit down and have a chat."

We found a nearby bench under a peach tree, "I love this little farm," said Tommy affectionately, "but since Stowe decided to sell he's neglected it. I would like to see a young man like you put it in order again. Would you be interested?" he asked, looking at me.

I replied, "I'm not a poultry farmer and, in any case, I couldn't afford to buy."

I went on to tell him about my visit and interest in beef production.

Tommy said, "No bank will lend you the money for such a venture, banks are not farming minded." He then asked, "How much money have you got?"

"One and a half thousand pounds, maybe a little more with help from my wife." I replied.

"Look," said Tommy, "If you can raise three thousand, I'll give you a bond for another three thousand." As Tommy said the word *Look* I was reminded that he originated from Herefordshire.

"Thank you for the offer and your interest but I know Mr Stowe will not take less than six thousand.... he mentioned earlier that someone else from Maritzburg would give him that!"

"That's true," said Tommy, "but he's no farmer either, that's why I want you to buy it. Come and have a good look around then if you're still interested laddy I'll ask you to give the Standard Bank the cash you have and I'll stand security for say a thousand pounds for your general expenses plus a bond for the three thousand pounds. Let me know your decision after you've carefully thought it through and, if you want my help, meet me outside the Standard Bank at ten o'clock next Wednesday and I'll introduce you to Mr Kettle, the manager.

As we walked back to the house we passed through a lovely peach orchard not in fruit as it was winter but, like the bougainvillea, on the other side of the house still green and not in flower. Tommy bade us good day, waving as he drove off in his Chevrolet, turning to Mr Stowe I said, "I'd like to have a look at the books to see what the future looks like for day old chicks."

"I sell over twenty thousand and never advertise. That's about two thousand pounds turnover, with another five hundred on pigs!" he replied.

All sorts of plans were now racing through my head. I could work hard and possibly expand. Although short of cash here was an opportunity to have a house for Linda and Pamela. My first priority was my family, although barely two months had passed since I had left them in England, I had not so far made any headway in securing a farm manager's job. Now two possibilities had arisen. The possibility of buying a small farm and fattening up bullocks, requiring fifteen-thousand pounds but, as yet, no backer; and now running a poultry farm costing six thousand pounds and a backer in Mr Tommy Dart to the tune of a three thousand pound bond loan repayable in five years.

I realised Tommy Dart's offer was too good an opportunity to miss but where was the three thousand pounds to come from? I wrote a long letter to Linda telling her that I thought this was an opportunity far and above a farm manager's job. I explained my plans to expand the breeding side of the business by buying fertile eggs from disease free hens but, more importantly, here was a home for the three of us. Who was there I could borrow two thousand pounds from, my father? I had worked for him for fourteen years with no payment. I knew it would be a waste of time asking him. He had never been on my side with anything I had done and certainly not when it involved money. I wrote to Uncle Tom but, as expected, his reply was not in favour of such an enterprise suggesting I should come back and find a job if unable to get one in Africa. So, none of my own (Pantall) family came to my aid. But this did not put me off when a practical stranger was standing by me and loaning me – at no cost – half the expenses. Linda wrote to me, telling me she could raise one thousand pounds, selling shares she had in the stock market. This made the deal possible, with her thousand, my fifteen hundred, Tommy's three thousand pounds bond and the sale of my car to Mr Stowe, as a trade in for his Chev pickup we could meet it! Mr Stowe had knocked the purchase price down by two hundred and forty pounds giving me two hundred and sixty pounds difference to make a total of five thousand, seven hundred and sixty pounds.

As arranged, on Wednesday August 20th 1947 I met Tommy at the Bank and was introduced to Mr Kettle the manager of the Pietermaritzburgh branch of the Standard Bank of South Africa. Tommy and Mr Kettle were great friends so we were able to proceed with the financial side leaving Tommy's solicitors to 'tie the deal up'. I gave my address as c/o Albert Ellett, Pembroke Farm, Cato Ridge, Natal. I could not thank Tommy enough for all his help assuring him how very much it was appreciated. His loan, or bond, was for five years, at the normal bond rate it was repayable on or before September 1952.

Mr Kettle opened an account for me, into which I paid fifteen hundred pounds to be blocked, along with the two hundred and sixty pounds for the car, from the final purchase price on the sale day. Mr Kettle also agreed to give me overdraft facilities up to one thousand. Feeling nervous yet very happy at the prospect of working for myself, I'd already made plans for the future. I called in at Sunnyside to give Mr Stowe the news and he seemed quite pleased. His wife said, "Mr Pantall, if my husband agrees, whilst the deal is being completed, you could stay here with us. We have a spare bed."

Mr Stowe said, "Yes, as soon as I hear from my solicitors, you will be most welcome."

"Thank you so much, I'm very grateful. Would it be in order to visit Sunnyside tomorrow, there's so much I have to learn about poultry and incubation?"

"Please, wait a couple of days until my solicitors give us the OK to proceed." Mr Stowe replied.

"Thank you both, I'm looking forward to living at Sunnyside. I'm off to Camperdown to send my wife a telegram." There wasn't a Post Office at Cato Ridge.

I let Linda know the good news, as soon as the deal was signed she would be on her way to join me. I thanked her so much for her contribution that had been so crucial in sealing the deal, letting her know how much I looked forward to our reunion.

As I drove back to Cato Ridge I realised how much work there would be getting Sunnyside clean and tidy but first and foremost I had to learn about poultry diseases.

The main hatching season was from April to September and I now needed to plan how much breeding stock I would need. I also had to investigate Mr Stowe's present egg supplier from whom he bought one hundred and eighty pounds worth of eggs. However my immediate concern was to plan a visit to the nearest poultry laboratory for help and information as I intended that my chickens, when sold, would be from disease-free stock.

On my arrival back I met Lucille, saying, "all eggs half price!"

She laughed, "You made a deal then!"

I replied, "I have been very lucky meeting all of you and Tommy is a honey!"

Bert now joined us and I went on, "There's such a lot to learn and much work ahead but I'm so pleased with the deal."

"Glad to hear it Chris, it will be so much better than working for some farmer!"

Bert said.

Later I wrote a long letter to Linda, telling her of our plans and suggesting that as soon as I knew when the house would be vacant she should book a passage on a Union Castle boat.

I spent the next few days helping Bert to repair the bull shed that Herman had damaged and studying a few books obtained from the local vet at Hillcrest. Mr McDonald was a keen poultry keeper himself albeit only as a hobby. I paid him a visit one afternoon and he gave me lots of useful information.

"Make sure you blood test all your breeding stock and eliminate all reactors to the antigen test!"

"What test is that?" I asked.

"BWD, it stands for Bacillary White Diarrhoea, it's a germ which passes into the egg from the body of the hen that laid it. Fortunately the blood stream of the hen carries a reactor that shows up in an antigen test. The antigen is in liquid form a few drops are put onto a plate with twelve inspection sections. Blood is taken from the hen by piercing the main blood-vein in the wing. An instrument with a loop at one end and a needle at the other enables the operator to gather blood in the loop and mix it in the antigen. If the bird is a carrier of BWD the antigen will curdle. If the bird is not tested the BWD germ will pass into the chick and infect all the other chicks as it is highly infectious and the mortality high, at least fifty percent deaths. The reason for twelve tests on a plate is so that twelve birds can be tested in one operation."

"How often should the tests carried out?" I inquired.

"Once per year but, with big flocks, it is hard work and time consuming. Usually testing is done in the New Year before the hatching season starts in February or March."

I asked him about other diseases, he replied, "There is one that we always seem to have in wet damp weather, Coccidiosis, this is also a killer and must be treated at the very first sign of the young bird becoming listless with drooping wings. It's a disease confined to between four and ten week olds and it's fatal if not treated with a Coccidiostat. If you go and see the chief veterinary officer at the laboratory in Pietermaritzburg, he'll tell you how to set about testing and supply the antigen. He'll also help you with information on other diseases and poultry welfare."

I had a look around Mr McDonald's poultry pens before I left, impressed at the tidiness and how healthy the poultry looked.

He said, "A backyard poultry farm but it's surprising how much a vet has to learn in poultry today."

As I took my leave Mr McDonald insisted on loaning me a very interesting book 'The Management of Poultry'. I shook his hand and thanked him for his help promising to return his book as soon as I'd digested the contents.

"I hope it will bring you the very best of luck," he replied.

On the way back to Pembroke Farm I called in at 'The Valley of the Thousand Hills Hotel' for a quick cup of tea and a look at the quite breathtaking view.

At suppertime, I said, "I must make a plan of what type of poultry to keep and I must arrange to see Mrs Galtry." Mrs Galtry owned one of the largest poultry farms in the district.

"Time will soon pass Chris, before you know it you'll be installed in Sunnyside. I'm sure you've made the right decision!" Lucille said.

Bert joined in. "Chicken farming will prove to be a lot more lucrative than Jersey farming, it takes a lot of capital to buy bulls and heifers."

I stayed up late reading poultry books spending time

looking through the book that Mr McDonald had loaned to me and making notes for future reference. An advert caught my eye as I read through the poultry section of The Farmers Weekly. Dundarach poultry farm in the Cape were advertising: 'day old Black Australorp unsexed, BWD tested and CRD free'. I looked up CRD and found it stood for Chronic Respiratory Disease, making a mental note that some new Australorp and Rhode Island Red blood was needed, the latter having to wait. I knew that it was no good buying in new stock for Sunnyside until I'd cleaned the place up. First I wanted to visit Mrs Galtry.

15

Mr & Mrs Galtry lived at Kloof farm about half a mile from Cato Ridge and the next morning I set off along the dirt road, turning off and driving up a small drive to a very nice English type house with a corrugated iron roof. Finding them in the egg shed adjoining the farm, I apologised for turning up without an appointment and introduced myself.

Mrs Galtry said, "That's alright we're pleased to meet you!"

Mr Galtry who had come over to join us exclaimed, "My wife will show you our poultry."

We walked around to the poultry section of what appeared to be a large farm growing a lot of mealies. I liked the position of the farm, standing quite high with plenty of ventilation. The poultry section was in separate pens of wire netting, the sides of each pen being about two-foot high and built of concrete.

The poultry houses were fully equipped with laying boxes and perches having a separate door for entry into each house. A water trough provided the birds with water. Being disease conscious everyone had to place their feet in a trough holding disinfectant before passing through. There were three Africans working on the poultry section and Mrs Galtry informed me that all the natives were called 'boys' throughout South Africa.

"On our way back Mrs Galtry said, "Like most farmer's wives I like to keep a few hens to produce eggs for sale at the local store, the cash buys the family groceries. But as I've been supplying breeding eggs to Mr Stowe I get a little more than market price for them."

When we returned to the egg house-cum-office I said, "Mrs Galtry I have a proposition to put to you!"

"Let's go into the house and have a cup of tea," she suggested.

Mr Galtry joined us and I said. "Congratulations on having such a tidy poultry farm and healthy stock!"

Thanks to the vet's books I think they thought I had a great knowledge of poultry! I explained that I would shortly be taking over Sunnyside egg farm.

"It's my plan to change the name to Sunnyside Poultry Farm and, as from next March, increase the stock numbers adding another incubator. I intend to advertise day old chicks, blood test every bird and sell quality disease free stock."

"All my poultry comes from Sunnyside." Mrs Galtry said.

"I think we need some new blood lines," I continued, "I have plans for Black Australorps and Rhode Island Reds. Leghornes I've yet to plan."

Mrs Galtry asked, "Do you want me to keep on supplying breeding eggs?"

"Yes please," I replied, "I'd like you to keep Black Australorps. I've noticed that Dundarach in the Cape are offering day old Black Australorps, unsexed, for sale. [Sexing of chickens had not yet come to South Africa] We could select the best cockerels for breeding into our stock."

Mrs Galtry was in agreement so I went on, "If I bought three hundred unsexed would you rear them here, they need to be purchased now as Sunnyside will not be ready due to the season being nearly over. It seems such a pity to lose a season when the new stock would be matured by next April."

Mrs Galtry said, "I think it's an excellent idea, as I'm sure we trust each other. I'll get the brooders ready and you go ahead and get the chickens. I know of Dundarach, they won several prizes at the Rand Easter Show a couple of years ago."

Mr Galtry said, "We'll need to expand and build more houses, we're not in the business of hatching and will be happy to supply you with eggs. I'm always very busy on the farm and leave the poultry to my wife. How many fowls do you want us to keep?"

"About one thousand laying hens would give me about three thousand eggs per week." I answered.

"I'll have to think about that," he said slowly, "it would mean building quite a few more houses."

"I like the idea," Mrs Galtry said, "We'll keep at least one thousand hens as long as you do the BWD and CRD blood testing. I think they call CRD, PPLO but I don't know what it stands for"

Fortunately I knew, "It's a veterinary term, P.P.L.O, Pluro pneumonia-like organism referred to as CRD." I said, getting up from my chair and shaking hands with Mr & Mrs Galtry. "Thank you both for such an enjoyable morning. I've a lot of work ahead of me bringing Sunnyside up to your standard but I'm sure this meeting will be the beginning of a great partnership."

§

I returned to Pembroke Farm just in time to help Bert place the leading hook on to Fergi's nose ring before leading him out to pasture. Jersey bulls are known for their aggressive nature well suited to the bull rings in Spain. Fergi was very docile however when released to graze with the cows.

Bert had to go to Camperdown and I returned to my books mulling over my visit to Mrs Galtry. Whilst Sunnyside would be the home of pedigree stock and the main supplier of eggs I hoped I would need more eggs. A Mr Leroyd, who lived near Pietermaritzburg, also supplied Sunnyside with eggs so I thought about a visit.

Next day I went to see his poultry farm and, having telephoned earlier, he was expecting me. A short tarred drive led from the main road up to his home hidden from view by evergreens, the lovely house only coming into view when turning into the circular drive. Mr Leroyd was waiting to meet me. "Welcome! Both here and to South Africa," he said.

"Thank you so much." I replied.

Mr Leroyd's poultry farm was small, very well kept and stocked with mostly Leghorns, this meant I would only have Rhode Island Red new blood lines to worry about. I also had to consider theft and the possibility of disease hitting Sunnyside. Using Mr Leroyd would ensure that 'all my eggs would not be in one basket', still having the nucleus in Sunnyside's breeding.

"I've always bought my chickens from Sunnyside," he told me, "always Leghorns. I'm retired and poultry is a hobby which keeps me very busy. I love looking after them."

Mr Leroyd confirmed that he would like to continue supplying eggs to Sunnyside. He had eight hundred unsexed Leghorns last July giving him plus minus three hundred and seventy pullets for the next year replacing two hundred three year olds. Unfortunately we had to cut our meeting short as Mr Leroyd had forgotten a meeting he had to attend at four o'clock. "I'm on the local council," he informed me.

I congratulated him on having the best-kept poultry I'd ever seen and advised him that I intended to blood test all the stock.

"Thank you," he replied, "I'd hoped you would do that job!"

I was now 'ready to go', but the powers that be take a little time. It was now the end of August and the bank manager thought I would be able to take possession in early November and I wondered why so long. He advised me that because a mortgage was involved it would take longer.

I had managed to get the eight hundred chicks from Dundarach Special Pen A. informing the bank manager as they cost seven pounds per hundred, amounting to fifty-six pounds. The cost of ordinary pens was six pounds per hundred but I had wanted the best for breeding and paid an extra one pound per hundred.

On Monday September 1st 1947, I said goodbye to Lucille and Bert going to stay with the Stowe's at Sunnyside. As I was purchasing the farm they had agreed that I should be their guest at no charge for my keep but I could not start doing any alterations to the farm before taking over.

I wrote to Linda and asked her to book her passage ready to arrive in early November. It would take five weeks from Southampton to Durban so if she sailed early October she would arrive in Durban the first week in November. I couldn't wait. I was due to take over Sunnyside on the first of November so we would be able to pioneer the project together. I also told her of my plans to increase the incubation and advertising and how much work there was to be done on the farm.

I received details from our Solicitors regarding the contract to purchase Sunnyside egg farm, described on the documentation as 'Sub Division 'C' of Lot 20 of 'Uitkoomit' and 'Doornrug' No 852 County of Pietermaritzburg, ten acres. A search was being made, slow because it had to be registered in Pretoria.

I decided to make some enquiries from the veterinary department at Pietermaritzburg on diseases in poultry and what was the best method of eradicating both BWD and CRD. I found the staff of the poultry section in the veterinary department very helpful. They explained that they have two members in the field who visit various poultry farms and that once tested free of reactors, confirmed by a second check, the owners are issued with a BWD free certificate. A Mr du Plessis confirmed that there was no record of a certificate issued for Sunnyside Egg farm.

They supplied me with antigen, plates and a needle explaining that if any reactors are found they must be destroyed immediately burning the carcass if possible. I was advised to be careful when taking the blood sample ensuring it was well mixed in the antigen. Each bird must be kept in a separate compartment so that should there be a reactor it can be identified. Having completed the testing of twelve birds with no sign of any change in the colour of the antigen then these birds can be placed in a separate pen before continuing with a further twelve.

I told them I had two suppliers of fertile eggs and nine hundred young birds not yet matured. The chief said to me, "To get a certificate you have to use only certified BWD free stock so the two suppliers would have to obtain a certificate. A test for CRD would come later," adding, "I cannot stress too strongly that on no account use eggs other than from the two suppliers you have told me about. We will, of course, make a very careful inspection of these two farms in case there is any malpractice of sending eggs from another source to the hatchery. We don't like issuing certificates other than to bon-a-fide poultry farms who only use eggs and incubators from the specified farm."

I thanked him for his advice and help, "I hope you won't mind if I keep in touch for advice from time to time?" I asked.

"We shall be pleased to help you," he replied.

I made my way to Mrs Galtry's farm to let her know what had transpired. If it would not be an inconvenience I would have liked to commenced testing her stock before taking over Sunnyside.

"It would mean we would get your stock tested before I get too busy at Sunnyside." I explained.

Mrs Galtry agreed, adding, "I have the crates from the last test and you can have the help of the two boys that know how the testing is done."

"Thanks so much for your help, we'll have the best disease free stock in the country before too long," I promised.

"Did you know that your chickens had arrived from Dundarach. My husband was at Cato Ridge yesterday and saw the chicken boxes addressed to you. The stationmaster agreed that he could bring them here. I put them straight under the brooder. Only two were dead and none since, they only gave us the eight hundred, no extra."

Upon inspection I said, "they certainly look a healthy uniform bunch." Mrs Galtry was pleased with them too. I was glad I had enlisted her help getting the chickens.

I received a long letter from Linda. She was getting fed up with her life and anxious to join me. I could well appreciate this, as I was keen for her to join me as soon after the first of November as possible.

Although I was staying with Mr & Mrs Stowe I did not tell them of my plans, I knew as much about poultry farming as he did. I was longing for the beginning of November when I took over.

There were four cows included in the stock, all in milk, two heifers and ten pigs. I thought of making the pig herd all sows, produce piglets and sell them as weaners. It would need a well-bred Tamworth boar so that I could cross him with Large White sows. I could dispose of the infertile eggs with the pigs but there was no room for a dairy herd so I thought I would sell the stock with the exception of one cow in milk keeping her until the end of her milking time. We could then get our milk delivered by a neighbouring farmer, Mr Colin Buchanan who lived with his mother and father on a farm adjoining Sunnyside.

I spent the remainder of September blood testing all Mrs Galtry's stock. Every bird proved negative of BWD. A good many of the birds were too young to be tested and would be done the following March. I was very pleased with the result, their health and management.

It was then time to test Mr Leroyd's birds. I found him to be a very nice gentleman who insisted on my calling him by his christian name of Les. We got on famously, him calling me Chris. His poultry farm was a picture, all 'his boys' were happy. The birds were very quiet, Leghorns usually are known to be a flighty breed. The tests went through taking several days, all negative. Mr Leroyd had about six hundred young birds too young to be tested until next March. I suggested we bought two hundred unsexed Leghorns from Dundarach next April, using the cockerels would give us some new blood in a couple of years time.

I was by now gaining a lot of experience in the poultry world and still studied the books loaned to me by the vet, Mr McDonald. I'd since learned that he was a very good vet, experienced and popular.

We were now at the end of October the weather was becoming warmer, leaves appearing on trees. Spring had arrived.

Linda was now on the *Carnarvon Castle* and I hoped the boat would not encounter a gale like the *Umtata* had.

On Monday 3rd November 1947, with Tommy Dart present, I took possession of Sunnyside egg farm, immediately changing its name to Sunnyside Poultry farm. I told Tommy of my plans and what I'd been doing the past two months. I think he was impressed saying, "Well done Chris, you have a bit of tidying up to do and I have no doubt you'll work hard to do it. I'll be off now, leave you to prepare the way for your good lady and baby daughter. The best of health and good luck.' He drove away, waving out of the window as he did so.

The Stowe's had left earlier leaving me with a couple of beds, some crockery and saucepans for the 'Welcome Dover' coal-stove. I set about tidying up with a broom. Mary, the house-girl, helped me. She could speak very little English as the previous madam could speak Zulu, her language. I had got to know the four boys on the farm and, of course, Induna, who was a gem. I inspected the farm and poultry houses feeling very pleased with the prospects it offered, so much more than I could ever have imagined on leaving the *Umtata*. I now possessed a Chev. pickup instead of a car much more suitable for my purpose.

Time went by very quickly and on the Friday I drove down to Durban docks waiting on the quayside as the *Carnarvon Castle* came in. There was Linda with Pamela in her arms waving from one of the lower decks. As soon as the gangplank was lowered I went on board finding Linda and Pamela. Big hugs and so many kisses for them both, Pamela had grown so much since July. After our reunion Linda showed me her cramped quarters, the Union Castle had done away with cabins to make the accommodation like that of a troop carrier. It had been a terrible journey. The other passengers in this section had lots of children all noisy and uncontrollable. She had had little sleep throughout the journey.

I carried Pamela whilst Linda and I shared the luggage. Our first call was immigration and passport control, then on to collect our luggage which included a pushchair for Pamela. With the help of two of the many African porters we loaded the luggage on the pickup. Knowing that our nearest shopping centre was Pietermaritzburg (which I always refer to as Maritzburg) Linda obtained provisions from a store in Pinetown whilst I got to know Pamela again and kept an eye on our luggage having already experienced the 'thieving hands' of the non-whites.

We now set off to Cato Ridge and Sunnyside Poultry farm. A railway line ran parallel with the main road and about five hundred yards from the station. We turned off the road immediately in front of a crossover on the dirt track round a bend, past a little Church and down a short way turning into a large area in front of the house. Sunnyside like the majority of houses had a corrugated roof. The three bedroomed house did not have many amenities but was adequate and most important of all – it was ours.

I lifted Pamela as Mary immerged from the native compound to help with the off-loading. Linda seemed quite happy with the prospects I had not painted too rosy a picture of the house.

"Darling, welcome to our home, there'll be a lot of work to do but at least it's ours."

"Don't worry, I'll soon make a home of it, I like the position, no neighbours to glare over the fence," she replied.

Our nearest neighbours were separated from our property by a six foot high fence and a lot of trees then a meadow so the three houses, built only a few yards apart, were not even within shouting distance.

Our staff lived in a 'compound' as did all native staff in Africa consisting of sleeping and eating quarters. All Africans like to cook over an open fire, the smoke they were used to, and covered in by a corrugated roof. It was all very rough but they had lived like this for generations. The householder supplies the mealie meal buying it in five pound bags. 'Mealie Pop' was the usual name and is the staple diet for all Africans. The householder also provides sugar, milk and meat.

Two of our labour force, Jackson and Samson lived away from the farm, the other two Joseph and Issack (most Africans have biblical names) lived with their wives and children in the compound at the end of the farm. Induna lived with his wife and family in African quarters at the station.

Linda left Pamela in the care of Mary but as she was sleeping in her new cot fitted with sides no harm could come to her.

We went for a look around our new home and farm. Linda had not been brought up on a farm and found many things unfamiliar yet interesting. Home Farm House had been free of any farming activity so Linda found this a lot different but I knew she would quickly adapt, being a worker. She was anxious to learn everything about our new venture seeing a great future ahead. The house was not as we would have wished but we had a roof above our heads and Linda was enthusiastic, "We'll soon put it altogether," she said.

We learned that our staff were all from different tribes. Jackson, who was Zulu and could speak a little English, told me that different tribes had different languages, coloured and Indian could speak English, Afrikaans and the African twang. Our gang had been at Sunnyside for several years with the exception of Isaak who had been with us for six months. Africans are fond of stealing fowls so the fowl houses had to be securely locked up.

We made our way through the peach orchard. It was small yet there was a lot of fruit waiting to ripen both the mangoes and paw paw, still green.

Linda had made a list of things needed urgently from Maritzburg the following day including rations and mealies for the fowls and scoff (African word for food) for the staff. We were short of furniture but Linda said, "We'll make do with the Stowe's leftovers for now."

"I bought this place at the wrong time of the year," I told her, "from now until February there'll be no income from day old chicks, all eggs being sold commercially. But it's only for a few months and I'm so happy, planning things ourselves. There's still so much yet to do, I think an extra incubator will be needed to cope with a surplus of eggs."

I told Linda more about Mrs Galtry and Mr Leroyd, she knew of them from my letters, mentioning my worries about the old 'Glevenum' incubator and thermostat, a 'Heath Robinson' affair, a poker at one end and a few washers threaded down a piece of wire on the other. 'Works Well' Mr Stowe had told me. I explained to Linda that if we could get another 'Secura' incubator on terms we could double up on the eighteen hundred eggs presently obtained from the existing incubator. Together with the six hundred eggs from 'Horace' the Glevenum incubator this would give us a total capacity of four thousand two hundred eggs per week producing approximately two thousand five hundred chickens.

Leghorns are in demand from May until October and the heavy breeds from March.

A lot of advertising would be needed to deal with the sale of the chickens, the main theme being disease free. I already had a good idea what I wanted to put in the advertisement.

"Where are we going to put another incubator?" Linda enquired.

I thought carefully about this, "I think at the end of the existing egg room," I replied. "We could build an extension."

The Indian manager of the farm next door had two sons one being a builder. He had already approached me about building and repairs.

"What about building materials?" asked Linda.

"The store at Camperdown will have cement and Sammy (the builder) will know about sand."

"That's good," exclaimed Linda.

We finished our tour to find Pamela still sleeping.

I invited Mr Glaum, the agent for Secura, to come up and see me and he offered me very good terms. I told Mr Kettle, the bank manager, and after giving him all the facts and figures, he approved, "laddy go ahead, you've worked hard and learnt such a lot in a short space of time."

I asked Mr Glaum to make all the necessary arrangements for the incubator to be at Sunnyside by the first week of March. He told me he would erect the incubator for me.

This was the beginning of a lot of work. Blood testing, mating, the culling of the fowls and an advertising campaign. Both Linda and Pamela were enjoying the warm weather but Linda was under a lot of strain, a new country, very few home comforts, if any, and a husband working all hours from six in the morning until ten at night. Still we were happy with our lot.

In one week Linda had changed the look of Sunnyside, it was now clean and the furniture had been moved around. Pamela was well and whenever possible Linda took her in the pickup to fetch groceries, taking Mary to help. She soon found Maritzburg was the only shopping centre to meet all our needs.

16

It was now December and becoming quite warm. Thunderstorms appeared, the rain freshening up the grass and weeds. Sammy was employed to build the extension for the incubator room and we chose asbestos for the roof as it would be cool. I was now busy blood testing and found that Issaak and Samson were a good team, it was a long and arduous job testing about five hundred birds each day. So far we had found one reactor.

Christmas came with a heat wave. The boys drank plenty of homemade beer, called 'Kaffir,' made chiefly from white mealies meal and allowed to 'ferment' giving it a 'kick.' We also gave them an extra meat ration. They are such happy people and certainly knew how to make the best out of the worst. We had a quiet Christmas having to check that the birds had enough food and water. After lunch we went to Mr & Mrs de Lange for mince pies. They only lived a few hundred yards down a dirt road. He was a stock inspector having to be present when the cattle were dipped once a week. The dip killed the blue ticks. Dave de Lange was a jolly chap, he and I became fond of shooting guinea fowl and rabbits, the rabbits being a cross between an English hare and a rabbit – at least that's what it looked like.

We saw the New Year in with the Buchanan's, a charming family, they kept the small dairy herd next door. On New Year' day Linda and I found the shops closed so I took her and Pamela to the 'Royal' for lunch. Pamela was so good. Linda and I enjoyed our lunch she had roast beef and I had guinea fowl. We then made our way back home as we knew the Kaffirs, as they were known, would still be 'under the influence'. After settling Pamela down we set about feeding and watering.

Early in the New Year the Tamworth boar arrived to join the six large white sows. Tommy had whitewashed the sties and repaired the gates so it all looked very smart. We were now waiting for the new incubator.

'Tough Times Never Last,
But Tough People Do

The weather was now hot about eighty degrees. The next day an envelope arrived in the post containing six one-pound notes. It was from a Mr Kraus in the Transvaal paying for one hundred Australorp day old chicks for delivery next July. I said to Linda, "This money will buy us a second-hand suite of furniture for the lounge, we'll go to Durban!" Linda chose a nice suite for five pounds, fifty, 'in cash' as the shopkeeper put it. So, with the change, we had a good meal by the sea and enough left over to purchase two gallons of petrol for the trip home.

The incubator room was finished in the New Year and we decided to build an office on the side of the house. I had begun advertising top quality disease free chickens ready in early March finding that the adverts were bringing in a response. I also had printed some propaganda on poultry keeping, it appeared that the poultry industry was still in its infancy, I had a lot of plans. The farmer's wives, who were our customers, were not used to being given advice on productivity, now they were told that when the disease free chicks arrived they should be kept warm, at ninety-eight degrees fahrenheit, away from draughts and fed with a balanced chick ration.

Slowly cash orders for fifty or a hundred Rhodes or Australorps began to come in. I found that in addition to the farm work and blood testing etc. I had numerous letters to write and bookings for chickens. Wednesday was hatching day, in the evening we sent them out by rail. Farmer's wives would be waiting at the station for the trains to come in.

Sammy set about building the office with breeze blocks cheap, yet strong and sturdy. He made the doors and I bought the windows. I advertised in the Farmers Weekly and wrote a few letters to the editor on the benefits of keeping a few chickens, in addition to the production of eggs, which helped with the groceries, the farmers wife always had a chicken for dinner on Sundays. Sunnyside was gradually building up into a household name. I knew the day was soon coming when I would need a typist to help me with the correspondence as numerous letters were coming in.

My working day began on the farming side of the business from six in the morning until six in the evening with a further five hours of paper work including the keeping of chicken records. My family was being neglected.

We were now spending a great deal of time blood testing fowls for BWD. I noticed an article about Mr H D Barley, in the Farmers Weekly, a well-known Rhode Island Red breeder in England. His birds continually headed the list of prize winners for egg laying tests and also in the showing classes. I wrote to Mr Barley enquiring if he could supply me with eggs knowing there was now a cargo air service by Sabena Airways from Croydon, London to Johannesburg a matter of five days. This would give me the nucleus of a new blood strain. Having paid and arranged all veterinary requirements we were set to receive such a valuable consignment of eggs. Five days later a Sterling bomber, converted to a cargo plane, touched down at Palmeitfontein Airport. I was there to meet it. I collected the eggs and conveyed them to Sunnyside where the incubator was ready and waiting at the controlled temperature. I gave the eggs four hours to settle before I set them, none were broken and all were two ounces in size. Twenty-one days later the one hundred and two eggs produced fifty-five chickens and were taken from the incubator and put in a readily prepared brooder with water and feed at a temperature of one hundred and one degrees fahrenheit.

It was now March and the weather was a little cooler as autumn was approaching. I had completed the culling and mating of all Rhodes and Australorps flocks. Early March was too early for my white Leghorns and those of Mr Leroyd's, the favourite month being August as Leghorns are early producers. Through advertising I found a steady demand for day old chicks, Australorps and Rhodes. All were strong healthy chicks, mortality being very low, and so far all had sold on hatching.

During March an advertisement appeared in the poultry section of the Farmers Weekly headed: *'The Only Way'– Aluminium Laying Cages from America For Sale Owing to bereavement. 50 sets of Cages, a set holding 50 birds. Great Opportunity for Egg Producers. All To Be Sold on the Kloof Poultry Farm, Kloof, Natal, Tuesday 23rd March 1948, at 12 noon together with numerous other cages and poultry equipment.*

Not that I wanted the cages for my own use but I knew I could sell them through Sunnyside. I discussed it with Linda we knew it was a gamble but 'nothing ventured, nothing gained'. Linda thought it was an excellent opportunity as long as we got the price right.

Linda could not come with me on the day of the sale as Pamela was unwell. I found the cages, all as new, displayed in a large paddock, in units of fifty, a total of two thousand five hundred. The feed and water troughs were also laid out neatly.

Much to my surprise the auctioneer decided to sell the nearly new cages first and a large crowd of farmers were standing in the first aisle. After a short description he stated jokingly, "One unit or the lot, what offers do I have in units of fifty. Fifty Pounds? Thirty Pounds?"

"Twenty pounds!" I shouted out.

191

Some members of the public were not happy about the auctioneer offering the cages for sale in units of fifty instead of ten and were openly critical of him. The auctioneer became annoyed and knocked the first unit down to me politely asking, "How many Sir?"

I replied, "The lot!"

He immediately knocked his hammer on the bench saying, "SOLD"

I made my way to the office and signed a cheque to the value of six hundred pounds arranging with a local haulier to transport the cages to Sunnyside. I then drove to the Standard Bank at Maritzburg to see Mr Kettle and told him what I had done, he agreed to meet the cheque. I promised that within two months I would sell the cages, doubling the money. It took a lot of hard work but that's just what I did!

In May Mr Glaum the Secura Agent telephoned to advise me that he had an incubator in store that was no longer required by his customer and offering to let me have it at a twenty-percent discount. The original incubator which I had ordered so long ago had been delayed on its journey over when the ship was in collision with another. I agreed and the incubator arrived. Mr Glaum erected it in the new incubator room and it was soon filled with eggs. A few days later Mr Glaum rang again to inform me that my original incubator had now arrived and asked if I would still be interested. I replied, "What would the price be?"

He paused and said, "Look I will make this a special deal and give you a thirty percent discount!"

"Can I phone you back after I've discussed it with Linda?"

I went and found Linda and told her about Mr Glaum's telephone conversation and the thirty per cent discount. "Where are we going to put it?" she asked.

I suggested the third bedroom and she readily agreed.

I telephoned Mr Glaum, completing the deal. The incubator arrived at Sunnyside within two days and Mr Glaum came and erected it. It was still early for hatching so I had to put some chicks in the brooder rooms and sold them as month olds. Now we would have three Secura incubators

Kilkington Manor. Birthplace of the author

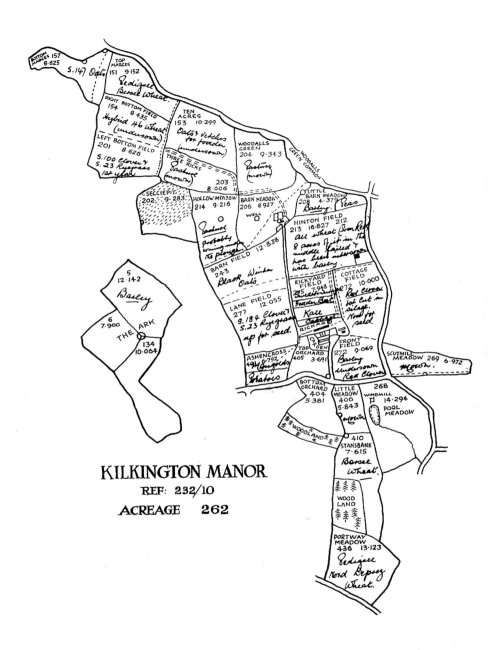

KILKINGTON MANOR

REF: 232/10

ACREAGE 262

Kilkington Manor Farm

KILKINGTON MANOR

Staunton–on–Wye

is believed that Kilkington Manor was one of the first
Manor Houses to be built in Herefordshire around the
sixteenth century.

Over the years, however, many alterations have been made
from which it would appear that oak beams at lower level
may have been used in a previous building. Timbers at the
upper level appear to show a 'wealthy' owner who was able to
afford to put in wide timbers with narrow brick works. It is
almost certain that these timbers came from the Kilkington
Estate.

According to hearsay, at the time of the Civil War, King
Charles II was supposed to have hidden in one of the
chimneys, which has a ledge on which he could have stood.

Jean Aged 14

Mum – Taken during her more happy days

Staunton-on-Wye Higher Elementary School

St Mary the Virgin's Church in which the author was christened and married.

International T3

Binder. A wonderful machine compared to the scythe

Left: *Thresher.*
Vastly different
to the modern
combine harvester

Right: *Side Rake.*
The author's father
fell off one of these
which led to his
death.

Left:
Various utensils used
for cider making.

THE PERSONAL TOUCH.

This business is the outcome of the winning by Mrs. Pantall of innumerable FIRST PRIZES for Foodstuffs at all the principal Agricultural Shows in England. Everything is made personally by Mrs. Pantall (or under her personal supervision), in the sincere endeavour to supply pure, nourishing, and appetising food in a manner and variety to tempt the most fastidious.

WHERE
"The LILAC"
Home-made Prize Products
are made.

The successful shop which belonged to the author's mother

*A Compendium of
nice things to eat
from the Pantry
of the*

LILAC Home-Made
Prize Products .

8b, Widemarsh Street
HEREFORD

: :

Mrs. J. WATT-PANTALL
Silver Medallist, B.D.F.A.

" Some hae meat and canna eat,
And some wad eat that want it,
But we hae meat and we can eat
And sae the Lord be thankit."

Burns.

The successful shop which belonged to the author's mother

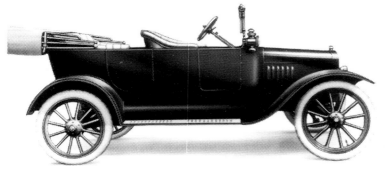

Left:
Model T Ford Ca...

Right: *Tax Disc*

Below: *Cup for puppy walking
Trueman 1936*

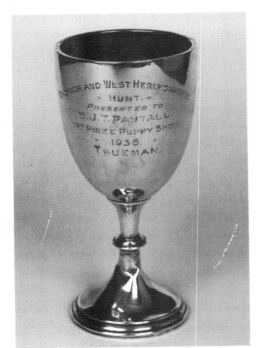

*Left: Jean, aged 25,
with dog and pet lamb.*

*Below Left:
The author, aged 20, in
Metropolitan Police Force.*

*Below Right:
The author aged 22.
Taken at Builth Wells Bridge
over River Wye.*

BERLIN GOES UP 7 PLACES

18.8.41.

Express Air Reporter

COLOGNE, fourth city in Germany, with a population of 768,000, ties with Berlin in earning more points this week than any other of the cities bombed by the R.A.F. in the Daily Express table.

Each receives eight points which puts Cologne more firmly in the lead and raises Berlin from fourteenth place to seventh.

Cologne earns three points for the heavy daylight attack by Blenheims and Flying Fortresses, and I have awarded two bonus points because the raid was in daylight, which is far more demoralising and effective than night bombing. Cologne also had a heavy night attack and a subsidiary raid during the week.

Berlin's 4½ millions receive eight points for one heavy night raid by the R.A.F. and two raids by the Red Air Force. This shuttle raiding earns them a bonus of two.

Stettin, 70 miles to the north-east of Berlin, appears in the table for the first time for attacks by the R.A.F. and the Red Air Force, for which I have awarded a bonus of one point. Brunswick is another newcomer to the table. It was raided once by the R.A.F.

I forecast that soon there will be big movements in the table when the R.A.F. and the Red Air Force get into their fully co-ordinated bomb stride, blasting the German towns by night and by day.

★ ★

Town	Total Raids	Very H'vy	H'vy	Others	Pts.
Cologne	21	3	16	2	47*
Bremen	13	3	9	1	30§
Kiel	11	2	8	1	27*
Dusseldorf	12	—	10	2	24§
Frankfort	8	2	6	—	21†
Hanover	9	—	8	1	17
Berlin	7	1	5	1	16§
Mannheim	6	2	4	—	16§
Munster	6	3	2	1	16§
Duisberg	7	1	5	1	14
Hamburg	6	3	2	1	14
Emden	8	1	1	6	13§
Aachen	5	1	3	1	12§
Essen	3	3	—	—	9
Wilhelmshaven	7	—	2	5	9
Osnabruck	4	1	2	1	8
Oldenburg	3	—	2	1	7§
Magdeburg	3	—	3	—	6
Bielefeld	3	—	2	1	5
Dortmund	2	1	1	—	5
Karlsruhe	2	1	1	—	5
Stettin	2	—	2	—	5‡
Bremerhaven	3	—	1	2	4
Hamm	2	—	2	—	4
Krefeld	2	—	2	—	4
Munchen-Gladbach	2	—	2	—	4
Rheydt	2	—	1	1	3
Vegesack	1	1	—	—	3
Brunswick	1	—	1	—	2
Leuna	1	—	1	—	2
Sylt	1	—	1	—	2
Rheine	1	—	1	—	2
Cuxhaven	1	—	—	1	1
Halle	1	—	—	1	1

Night raider blown to bits

Daily Express Raid Reporters

LATE last night one German raider ventured too low over London — and was blown to pieces by A.A. guns.

The German was flying fast when searchlights trapped him. At once the guns blasted shells at him.

At least one must have hit home. There was a terrific explosion and the guns ceased fire and the searchlights went out.

Last night was London's twenty-first blitz night. It began according to recent Nazi formula, with a single plane streaking fast across the London area and then other planes trying to start fires all round the capital.

Scores of incendiary bombs were dropped, with the object of lighting beacons to guide the raiders. Three or four fires were started, but they were soon put out.

Then the first high explosive bombs of the night were dropped. Six of them fell in a line in a dist— in north London. *(can see 97/3/6)*

one of those heavy(.)

Nov. 1940.

44,000 BRITISH PRISONERS-OF-WAR

About 44,000 British troops are held as prisoners of war by Germany and Italy, said Mr. Eden in Commons to-day.

Reports from American Embassy in Berlin and International Red Cross, most recent dated October 13 from Berlin, described arrivals of parcels of food, clothing and books to camps in Germany. Every parcel to British prisoners contained postcards for men to acknowledge receipt.

★

POINTS awarded are; 3 for a very heavy attack, 2 for a heavy attack, 1 for other raids.

BONUSES: 2 points for raids on three or more successive nights, 2 points for a daylight raid.

*IN THE TABLE. * means including four bonus points. † including three. § including two and ‡ including one.*

The table is compiled from R.A.F. communiques and official Russian statements, and is presented every Monday.

R.A.F. SHOW A PROFIT

AN enterprising Intelligence Officer has compiled a balance sheet for his R.A.F. fighter squadron, stationed in the South of England. Here it is:

DESTROYED

	£
10 M.E. 109's	50,000
27 M.E. 110's	270,000
1 Ju 87	10,000
6 Ju 88's	90,000
4 Do 17's	60,000
18 HE 111's	450,000
1 HE 113	10,000

Credit £940,000

LOST

26 Hurricanes ... 130,000

CREDIT BALANCE £810,000

SCORE-BOARD

Germany has now lost 2,957 'planes over and around Britain since the war began. Our losses are 829 'planes, from which 410 pilots were saved.

Losses officially announced during the past week, including seven Italian 'planes yesterday, are:—

	Enemy	Britisl
Sunday	14	5
(4 R.A.F. pilots safe)		
Monday	—	—
Tuesday	1	—
Wednesday	5	—
Thursday	1	1
Friday	2	—
Saturday	11	—
(Seven Italians)		
Total	34	6

Germany's total air losses since the invasion of the Low Countries on May 10 have now reached 5,586 'planes

KAAPPROVINSIE. CAPE PROVINCE.

Ordonnansie op Motor-	Motor Vehicle Ordinance,	Earl
voertuie, 1938.	1938.	
(Ordonnansie No. 15, 1938	(Ordinance No. 15 of 1938, as	Nº 98489
soos gewysig.)	amended.)	

BESTUURDERSLISENSIE. DRIVER'S LICENCE.

Klas motorvoertuig ten opsigte waarvan lisensie toegeken word	L I G H T	Class of motor vehicle in respect of which licence granted.
Drykrag	P E T R O L	How driven.
(Petrol, stoom of elektrisiteit.(Petrol, steam or electricity.)		

Uitgereik aan :   Issued to :

Familienaam   P A N T A L L   Surname.

Voornaam   C H R I S T O P H E R   Christian names.

ROBERT

Adres   39 St James Rd   Address.

East London

Bedrag betaal £1 10s. 0d. Fee paid.

Sertifikaat van Bekwaamheid :
Certificate of Competence :

No.   2 8 9 0 1   No.

Datum   1 8 - 7 - 4 7   Date.

C. R. Pantall.

Handtekening van bestuurder./Signature of Driver.

L.W.—Hierdie lisensie ... ... licence
oet onmiddellik op ... ... be signed by the
... deur die bestuur... driver immediately be
der geteken word. ... received it.

*   1 8 - 7 - 1947

Lisensie word hierby aan bovenoemde Licence is hereby granted to the above-
... ... wie se portret en handtekening named person whose photograph and sig-
... ... in 'n motor ... ... of class a ...
... ... is te bestuur. vehicle of the class described above.

G. E. Baker

Uitreiker van Lisensies. Issuer of Licences.

AANTEKENINGS. ENDORSEMENTS.

This is a life-time licence that the author uses when in South Africa

Above: *Sunnyside blotting pad. Pen and ink was used in the 1950s*

Right: *First ever Sunnyside
invoice.*

and: *First ever Sunnyside
receipt the money from
which was used to buy
furniture*

Above: *Cato Ridge where Sunnyside egg farm was situated.*

Below: *Advertising material*

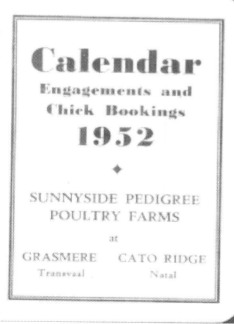

Above: *The author and Linda.*
V. C. flight to England on a
business trip.

SUCCESS STORY OF A HEREFORDSHIRE MAN

Farm bailiff to Sir R. C. G. Cotterell, Bt., at the home farm, Garnons, Herefordshire, in 1947—proprietor of a pedigree poultry business with a turnover of £70,000 gross in South Africa in 1952.

There are two milestones in a success story that is really only just beginning for 33-year-old Christopher Robert Pantall, a son of the late Mr. W. J. T. Pantall, of Kilkington Manor, Staunton-on-Wye, who flew into London Airport in the Comet a few weeks ago, and is flying back to South Africa via Rome next week.

His air trip to Johannesburg in the ultra-modern Comet will be vastly different from his original trip to the Union in June, 1947. Then he worked his passage in the good ship Umtata, as herdsman in charge of a bunch of 38 pedigree Jersey cattle, exported to Durban for the millionaire, Mr. H. G. Conrad.

Four years after he set foot in the Union, the man who had worked his passage on the Umtata was buying the 214-acre poultry farm that had belonged to the man who bought the Jersey cattle.

Mr. Pantall acts on a motto that has already brought him rich reward. It is, "Nothing venture, nothing gained." His story should be an inspiration to the young people of this generation.

SPIRIT OF ADVENTURE

Way back in 1947 this young man had what people called a good, safe job. But he also had a spirit of adventure which many of his friends could not understand. When he told them he wanted to emigrate and make a start on his own in a new country they told him not to be foolish, to be satisfied with what he had got.

But the spirit of adventure won. And when the opportunity of getting out to South Africa presented itself, he grasped it with both hands.

The cattle disposed of in Durban, this enterprising young man, who had had some experience of poultry farming in Herefordshire, began to look around the land of opportunity for a reasonable business proposition into which he could invest his available capital of £700.

About 40 miles from Durban he came across a small poultry farm in which he foresaw immense possibilities. With the assistance of a somewhat heavy mortgage, he bought the property and settled in as a poultry farmer.

"By November of that year my wife—she was a sister at the General Hospital, Hereford, before we were married in 1945—joined me," said Mr. Pantall in an interview with our agricultural correspondent this week.

"We worked almost 24 hours a day building up that poultry farm. It was terribly hard going, and every penny we made we put back into the business. In the following year we bought a five-acre plot adjoining the National Johannesburg-Durban main road.

"On this plot I built a large modern hatchery with an egg capacity of 180,000. This business began to expand very rapidly, and in a very short time I had the largest hatchery in South Africa.

"At this hatchery, Cato Ridge, I am producing somewhere between 20,000 and 30,000 chicks per week from February to October."

A tremendous stride forward in the Pantall fortunes was taken last year, when Mr. Conrad's 214-acre poultry farm, Grasmere, situated just outside Johannesburg, came on to the market.

A PIPE DREAM THAT CAME TRUE

Mr. Pantall saw a notice of the proposed sale in a newspaper, and was naturally interested because of his association with Mr. Conrad through the Jersey cattle shipment. But if any thoughts of buying the property passed through his head he dismissed them as a "pipe dream," far beyond his means. This farm comprised 300 poultry houses, built of face bricks, with the interior walls beautifully plastered, and the reservoir, constructed for irrigation purposes, looked more like a millionaire's swimming pool. The whole plant, of the very latest type, had a 65,000-bird capacity.

The farm did not sell, and was eventually offered to Mr. Pantall on most favourable terms.

Nothing venture, nothing gained. He bought the property. "And I have developed it into the largest and most modern poultry farm in the Southern Hemisphere," said Mr. Pantall. "There is absolutely nothing like it anywhere in that part of the world."

His enterprise is known as the Sunnyside Pedigree Poultry Farm, and early this year he developed it further by establishing at Bramley, Johannesburg, a 230,000-egg capacity hatchery, with the latest type Secura incubators, hatcheries, and offices.

All this has been done in five years. Exactly five years from the day he took over Cato Ridge, Mr. and Mrs. Pantall boarded the Comet for their flight to England. While the present is being used for consolidation, further expansion may follow.

The Sunnyside chicks are mainly Rhode Island Reds, Black Australorps, White Leghorns and crosses. They are being flown to-day from Palmietfontein aerodrome to customers in places as far apart as Cape Province, Southern and Northern Rhodesia, the Belgian Congo, Nyasaland, Kenya, Bechuanaland, and Portugese East Africa.

The original pedigree strains were imported from this country.

From Grasmere in the Transvaal to Cato Ridge in Natal is about 500 miles. But distance is no obstacle to Mr. Pantall. He, too, travels by air.

COLOURED WORKERS

In his business he employs 18 Europeans—three of his managers are English—between 80 and 90 natives, and 12 Indians. Asked why he has Indians on his staff, he replied that they were more intelligent than the natives, and were used to such jobs as egg setting, chick packing, and blood testing.

Mention of the coloured workers brought the policy of the Malan Government into the conversation, and Mr. Pantall made it clear that there was no discrimination against natives on his farms. "I always treat them fairly," he said, "and I find they are good workers. Incidentally, the wages paid to European workers in South Africa bear comparison with rates here. I pay my managers over £1,000 per year, and typists get from £40 to £50 per month."

"And what," asked our agricultural correspondent, "will be the next milestone in the Pantall story?"

The answer he received from this young man whose family have been Herefordshire yeomen for many generations, was: "A farm, say about 250 acres, in this grand old county, and as near the Wye as I can get it."

But Mr. Pantall is not talking about retiring. His idea is to spend eight months of the year mixed farming here, and four months overseeing his farms in South Africa.

How does he propose to do it? By Comet, of course!

and 'Horace' could be scrapped.

Our egg capacity was now seventeen thousand we were going to be stretched for eggs and orders for chicks. Fortunately I had written an article in the Farmers Weekly on BWD and how important it was to blood test and was already advertising 'Disease Free Stock – all blood tested'.

With extra advertising we sold all we produced over five thousand chicks a week. I decided to increase the two thousand New Hampshire hens by a thousand and to build more hen houses. The Barley chicks continued to thrive. What a healthy lot of chicks they were!

One summer evening when it was nearly dusk, Dave De Lange, my neighbour and friend rang me suggesting that we went guinea fowl shooting. Dusk was the best time so off we went towards the Thousand Hills about a mile away where there was a small forest, thick with trees and shrubs, well known for game. Almost immediately we lost our way in the thick bush struggling for an hour to find our bearings until, two hours later, we glimpsed a light in the distance and followed it eventually coming out close to a farm far from where we had entered. When we gathered ourselves together we were quick to realised how dangerous the wood was. It contained numerous snakes including the deadly Black Mamba. We just took jolly good care we did not go again!

We were now into the following March, Early April. Blood testing was completed with all birds being negative. I was beginning to fill all the incubators with the chicks all being sold. The new incubator was ticking over nicely with temperatures spot on. My problem was to try to keep on top of the correspondence Linda was a great help and Pamela was progressing well but Linda found herself more than busy. We decided to advertise for a typist who would live with us as family and, from the list of applicants, we chose an Australian girl called Patricia Yourell. She soon settled down, helping in many ways and, in no time at all, she had the correspondence up to date.

As Patricia was very capable Linda and I decided to motor up to Victoria Falls in Rhodesia in our new Chevrolet station wagon for a few days. We stayed at the Carlton Hotel, Eloff Street, Johannesburg the first night, it was the main shopping centre. We set off the next day for Rhodesia, over the Limpopo River that was full of crocodiles, then Beit Bridge and into Southern Rhodesia through Bulawaye and on to Livingstone. It was a vast country full of wild animals, Impala, Zebra, Lions, Kudu, deer etc. We stayed at a lovely hotel in Livingstone called the Victoria Falls Hotel for a couple of days. The 'Falls' were 'out of this world' and we got wet through from the spray. We returned over Beit Bridge going through Kruger National Park. What a wonderful sight we had of the wild animals. We stayed there overnight then returned home.

With an extra incubator I was able to cope with the additional orders. There was a demand for sexed pullets at day old but, unfortunately, sexing had not yet come to South Africa. We knew that a small compact machine was in the process of being made by Secura so Linda and I discussed ways and means, for her to fly over to Carlisle in the U.K to complete a two-week training course with Mr Fairbairn, the owner of Secura Incubator company.

The arrangements were made and Linda went off to Carlisle, where she was very well looked after, returning two weeks later fully trained. Mr Fairbairn grew Iceland poppies in his garden that, according to Linda, were beautiful.

Each week Linda sexed chicks and each week we sold about one thousand day-old pullets. The accuracy was about ninety-percent, later it was proven that hand sexing was more successful with ninety-seven percent accuracy. Each night at eight we had to turn the egg trays, this simply meant moving the trays by using a handle then moving them back into the same position at eight in the morning.

Linda was now very busy both in the household and two mornings per week sexing chicks and seemed to have got the knack of handling the chick-sexing instrument. In early October we had two girls helping in the house as the pressure on Linda was increasing, she was expecting our second baby and had to rest. I was now selling less of the sexed chickens but fortunately it was the end of the day old chicken season.

We left the farm in the hands of Induna and Patricia our secretary and went down to Umhlanga Rocks staying at the Oyster Box Hotel. Pamela and I spent some time together playing in the rocks. We soon returned home as Linda wanted to give birth to our baby in Durban. On the 10th November, in the afternoon, Linda began to have pains so I took her to the maternity hospital in Peitermaritzburg. I returned home to look after Pamela, giving her supper and a bath before settling her down to sleep. Patricia was happy to keep an eye on her whilst I went back to the hospital to be with Linda. We didn't have long to wait before a bouncing eight-pound baby girl was born whom we called Margaret. The birth was very successful and Mum was in good health.

It was about this time that I realised there was a good market for quality day old chicks having received many letters from customers thanking me for the quality of the chickens. One customer, Mrs van Heerden, had received two hundred and four and had lost none. I had greatly increased our stock and built six more poultry houses. Mrs Galtry had increased her stock by fifteen hundred, so it was all working out well.

Three days later I brought Linda and Maggie home from the hospital and after settling them in I had to go to Maritzburg to collect feed and mealies. On my return home I began off loading the mealies carrying a sack on my back up the steps into the feed shed. Suddenly in the corner a large rinkhals snake reared its head poised to strike. I dropped the sack rushing into the house to collect a gun. When I came back it reared its head again before I shot it. I have only ever seen about three of these poisonous snakes. The worst by far are the green and black Mamba. I shot a green Mamba lurking in one of our peach trees.

We were now a small family and needed all the rooms in the house so we decided to build another, much larger incubator-room, as we had no space to store chicken boxes.

During the Christmas period the owner of a big poultry

farm from the Cape came to see me. He knew I had expanded and, during our discussion, he remarked, "Your hatchery is a long way off the road and you are missing out on any advertising for Sunnyside. Why don't you build a modern hatchery alongside the main Johannesburg to Durban road?"

"Thank you for your suggestion. I'll certainly think seriously about it." I replied.

And I did! I knew there were about five plots of building land for sale on the side of the National road. Not wasting any time the following day Linda and I went to inspect the land and see the agent. After discussions we then went on to see Mr Kettle the Bank Manager in Martizburg. We wanted to buy a three-acre plot and build a modern hatchery installing three new Secura incubators. Each incubator would have a capacity of twenty-two thousand five hundred eggs. In total including Sunnyside's production, plus/minus this would give us twenty thousand chicks per week. After detailing our plans to him Mr Kettle approved giving us overdraft facilities and wishing us good luck!

When I told Mrs Galtry of our plans she said, "My son Harold is a builder. He will give you a quote for the work."

"Would you ask him to meet me next Monday morning at nine o'clock on the main road." I asked.

The meeting went well and I accepted Harold Galtry's quote. We carried on into Maritzburg to see the planning officer of the Perri Urban board to apply for building permission.

We were now in 1950 and it was hot with lots of thunderstorms. Linda was very busy and our young family was healthy and doing well. Pat had already taken a holiday and so she agreed to hold the fort whilst we went to Amanzimtoti for a few days break It was a popular seaside resort on the South Coast. Maggie was progressing and Pamela loved paddling and playing in the sand. Like all good things it was soon over.

The Perri Urban board passed the hatchery plans and Harold Galtry was soon on the project. The building was to have two front offices, a display window for poultry

196

equipment and a double door leading into the hatchery department. The hatchery department had racks included for the chicken boxes made by an Indian named Chintern who was to be in charge of the hatchery. Displayed on top of the building was to be a four-foot high neon sign shaped as a cockerell, and along the front of the building in neon:

SUNNYSIDE'S FAMOUS DAY OLD CHICKS
CATO RIDGE, TELE 13.

We did not plan to use the hatchery until May. Although it was only January the three incubators were on their way as we wanted to have them ready and running for April. Mr Glaum who was to erect the incubators had the plan well under control.

I spent most of January blood testing the breeding stock and by the end of the month I had completed Mrs Gantry's and our own. I left Mr Leroyd's Leghorns until last. I also began on the mating and culling with a strict cull of the hens and only kept the very best cockerels mating one with ten hens. Each pen had a 'foot bath' of disinfectant for everyone to dip their feet in and out. We improved the egg storage department making it cooler. Sammy was in charge of the farm hatchery and the brooders. During the whole of this time Patricia was coping with correspondence and telephone calls. Bookings were excellent for the coming year. We decided that as chick sexing was more accurate by hand we would employ a chick sexer as supplied by the British Chick Sexing Association. We engaged Mr Wally Wilkinson for two days a week and bought a new Commer van for transporting chicks and eggs etc. We were now into March and decided that we would start up one of the new incubators and followed on by running the three. On the family front both Pamela and Maggie were growing very fast!

By May the new incubators were going flat out and the farm incubators switched off until June when we hoped to sell our output. Advertising sexed day old pullets was proving to be a great advantage and orders were coming in fast. We were now using the Barley strain cockerels and multiplying our stock. I also had over two thousand New Hampshire hens the breed being very popular.

It was now July and we were working long hours but the business was well under control. We were selling more than four thousand, day old pullets a week, twelve thousand unsexed and four thousand cockerel chicks. I must admit that I did neglect my family for the business. Linda was a wonderful wife and worked so hard not only did she look after our family but she helped me in the office. I seldom took her out for dinner. When the chick season was in full swing it meant working twenty hours out of twenty-four for me.

17

After a very busy September, we turned off two of the incubators. On October 3rd I received a cable from my brother Richard in Staunton-on-Wye:

'Deeply regret Father died suddenly October 2nd.'

This meant that as Richard was the eldest he would take over Kilkington. The Will stipulated an equal share for each of us. Although I'd had to battle to borrow and raise enough money to start up myself with no help whatsoever from any member of the Pantall family, now my brother, sister and I were asked to leave our share in Kilkington for Richard to get established. He promised that he would pay us back 'SOME-TIME.' I have no record of him ever paying a penny of it back and as the years went by he became firmly convinced that, as the eldest, he was entitled to the lot! I could have done with the money to reduce my overdraft. I received only a battered cigarette case and a broken drinking horn. Father's gold and silver watch plus numerous other personal precious items I never ever heard of again. This confirmed that I worked for my father for sixteen years for 'nowt.' Father had been side-raking on a horse-raking machine, accompanied by Shook's three year old daughter who was sitting between his legs. They were enjoying themselves when the horse put its foot in a wasp's nest. All hell let loose, the horse bolted and Father, still holding Shook's daughter, was thrown breaking his collar bone. He received hospital treatment, having a pin inserted. About two weeks later he was ready for the pin to be removed but it caused a blood clot to go to his heart.

Kilkington was Jean's home. As Richard and his family had moved in she was under pressure to move out. Richard made her life 'very difficult' and much to his delight she packed up and made her way to me at Cato Ridge. We were very pleased to have her. I had already built two additional outside rooms for the chick sexers so we had sufficient accommodation.

One morning in early November Mr Kettle telephoned to offer me the sale of Mr H G Conrad's sixty-five thousand-bird poultry farm at Grasmere near Johannesburg. Mr Conrad owned a pedigree Jersey dairy farm and large pig farm. I had brought out his thirty-eight Jersey cattle from England. The Stock Market had received a sudden drop – one of the biggest falls the Johannesburg Stock market had ever experienced. The Standard Bank in Johannesburg held Mr Conrad's Securities and they had no option but to sell any assets belonging to him. I was taken by surprise and rather hesitant but I did promise to go up to the Transvaal and visit the poultry farm as it was now the off season.

The road to the Transvaal had not been tarred since my last visit some years earlier. I found my way from Heidelburg across to the Vereeniging road and then to Grasmere. The farm was one of the largest of its kind in the world and the building work had just been completed. There were three hundred poultry-houses (ten rows of thirty houses) all built of face brick with enclosed wire pens about thirty feet by thirty feet all with a gate. A large windmill kept a reservoir full of water piped down the ten rows with a tap in every pen. On the fifty acres of land stood a nice four-bedroomed house and a large brick shed for storing feed. Mr Conrad had been made insolvent before the farm could be stocked up with poultry. I estimated that the building costs would be around three hundred thousand pounds and knew, at this stage, it wasn't right for me.

I motored the five hundred miles back and telephoned Mr Kettle to check the price. He told me the bank was asking two hundred thousand pounds. I said, "Thanks for asking me but it's not for me at the moment."

Back in 1948 the United Party had lost control of Government to the Nationalist Party. They became stronger and stronger the longer they stayed in power, with apartheid soon becoming the Nationalist ruling theme until on May 10th 1994, Nelson Mandela became President of South Africa.

In 1961 the rand became S.A. currency replacing sterling at two Rand to the pound, never increasing above this even when Nelson Mandela first came into power.

A few years later I became alarmed at the dominance of the Nationalist Party and how they displayed anti British feeling at every opportunity. The Courts of Law were run by the Afrikaner, there were no English Magistrates or Judges. During two court hearings, although I was not a defendant, I noticed that anyone British did not get a hearing. Linda, like myself, was not in favour of the Nationalist Government. I decided that as there were no restrictions on currency as yet I would transfer some money to a London Bank.

On June 29th 1951 we became a family of three daughters. Maureen was born at the maternity hospital, Durban, a bumper baby she weighed over eight pounds. Both mum and daughter progressed very well, as we all did, the climate suiting us.

The new hatchery was a great success and two years after my visit to Grasmere Mr Kettle phoned me again to inform me that he had still not sold Mr Conrad's farm. It appeared that I was the dominant force in the South African poultry industry and would I like to make him an offer. So I motored the five hundred miles to Grasmere but this time I had a key to get through the gates. Once again I was impressed, the place had been built well although the entire area was overgrown and covered in weeds. I realised that I already had enough on my plate but also knew that Grasmere could be an outstandingly good supplier of eggs even though my main customers were in the Transvaal. In my plans for future expansion this farm could be ideal. I also appreciated the fact that although a large undertaking this farm would enable me to have sufficient eggs without having any other outside supplier. But what a journey! Another stumbling block was the fact that there was no electricity on the farm.

During the five hundred mile return journey I don't think I thought of much else and decided that it must be bought but at my price! I met with Mr Kettle and after a chat he said, "Are you going to make me an offer?"

"What's your asking figure?" I asked.

"Two hundred thousand!" He replied.

"No-one will offer you that. It's going to cost a lot to get it operational. I'll offer twenty thousand pounds and not a penny more and I'll require an overdraft for this amount – you can hold the title deeds as security."

Mr Kettle did not look too happy about this offer saying, "Well, as I've not had any other offers I'll have to accept yours."

I knew that this was my biggest deal yet.

Nothing ventured, nothing gained.

I did not sleep for several nights my mind was full of plans. I would hatch extra Rhodes, New Hampshires and Australorps, not Leghorns. I would set up brooders at Grasmere that I would take up there. Sammy would be put in charge with six Africans working under him and another four cleaning up the weeds. To start with we would send the chickens by rail. I would buy a second-hand Bedford truck for Sammy to use, Grasmere had a general store in the village but it was over a mile away. Paraffin heaters would also be needed for the chicks as there was no electricity at Grasmere and I decided to use the same make as I had at Sunnyside.

At Cato Ridge we now began hatching Rhodes, Australorps and Hampshire chickens for stocking up Grasmere with its capacity to hold sixty-five thousand birds.

All these chickens had to be transported by rail from Cato Ridge and although it was a good service it was far from ideal. Grasmere had no electricity and was too far off the beaten track. A hatchery was needed in the Johannesburg area.

I noticed that the demand for New Hampshire chickens was four times greater than a few years ago due to their golden coloured skin which made them look attractive as a table bird so we stepped up our breeding programme. I employed a secretary, bookkeeper, telephonist, non-Europeans to set eggs and chicken packers etc. One afternoon at about five o'clock when the staff had left I drove to Grasmere in the Wagon arriving well after midnight. Exhausted I used some empty mealies sacks in the storeroom and, laying them out, slept until six in the morning. After inspecting the farm and helping with the culling and mating etc. in the afternoon I decided to look for a site for a new hatchery. Not knowing Johannesburg I made for the direction of Orange Grove as the road led eventually to Pretoria and Rhodesia. Orange Grove was not a grove of oranges but consisted of a number of shops and a fairly straight road to Bramley, Wynberg and half way house. I travelled very slowly through Bramley which seemed a fairly progressive area and then on to Wynberg looking for sale boards. I wanted the hatchery on the main road. Spotting a sale board on the Wynberg road I pulled in on the verge to make an inspection. It was a one-acre plot with a four bedroomed corrugated roofed bungalow a windmill and a few nondescript fruit trees in the garden. I thought that for starters it would suit well. The sale board gave no agent particulars just stating 'apply Orange Grove tea room.' As it was now early evening and I was feeling hungry, not having eaten all day, I decided to go to Bramley where I found a cafe and had a good meal.

The Orange Grove tea room was well sign-posted and I went in to enquire about the sale. An assistant went to find the owner a Mr Isaac. We sat down at a table and during our discussion I discovered he wanted six thousand pounds for the plot, mains water, sewerage and electricity had just been installed. As I was interested I asked Mr Isaac for an inspection of the property and found the house was crying out for redecoration. The garden was a bed of weeds and the windmill was a relic! He had bought the property with a view to retire but had now decided to stay in his present home. Before we had concluded our business Mr Isaac said, "I'm sorry, I have to return to the tea room as I have a friend calling to see me about business at any minute."

Whilst he went into the back of the premises I had a pot of tea and a teacake and did a few sums. When his friend had gone we resumed. "The price is a bit steep," I told him. "I'll offer five thousand pounds."

"Six thousand, no less!" he replied.

We spent from half past nine until midnight bartering. Finally Mr Isaac said, "Mr Pantall, I paid six thousand for it two years ago and have put in all amenities. I won't sell at a lower figure!"

I decided to buy, producing my cheque book. "How much deposit?"

"Two thousand pounds." He replied.

I handed him the cheque, thanked him and made my way out back on to the Natal road.

I eventually got home at six in the morning and gave Linda the good news. I telephoned my solicitor in Maritzburg around nine to put him in the picture and told him I had given Mr Isaac a deposit for two thousand pounds.

"You did what!" he said.

"I gave Mr Isaac a two thousand pound deposit." I repeated.

"How do you know he's the registered owner, did you see the Title Deeds?"

"No."

"For all you know, it belongs to someone else. I'll telephone another Solicitor in Johannesburg and see what I can do."

Later that day he telephoned and confirmed that the deal was bonafide.

"Never do a deal like that again." He advised.

With the deeds now transferred to me and handed over to Mr Kettle for security I made my way to Wynberg again to seek permission from the Perri-Urban Board to build a hatchery. My application came back stating 'No Livestock'. All had been in vain. I now owned a four bedroomed house for which I had no use! I put my thinking cap on and made my way to the Perri-Urban Board's headquarters in Pretoria. Luckily I met one of their more helpful officials and informed him that there had been a mistake. My application should have read 'Warehouse for Storing Eggs.' The official not only assisted in filling out the application, he put it before the board and two days later it was passed.

I now had to find a builder and was lucky enough to meet George Olfin who took the contract on. Although a small firm he promised to have it completed by May only two months away. Four Secura incubators with a twenty three thousand capacity had been ordered by Mr Glaum and were, in fact, now packed ready for shipment. The incubators at Grasmere were not reliable but we made the best use of them we could. The Cato Ridge hatchery was going well and plenty of orders were coming in. The stock both at Cato Ridge and Grasmere had been blood-tested negative. I had trained staff to blood test both at Sunnyside and Grasmere and put an Indian called Grundy, who had a van in which to put the coups, in charge of a staff of four. At Grasmere, where we were building up the stock, I did the culling.

In early April I attended a meeting at Onderstepoort Laboratory, Pretoria, run under the direction of Professor Coles a very clever and popular veterinarian. The meeting was to emphasis the seriousness of Chronic Respiratory Disease, or CRD as we called it. This disease was also known as Pluro Pneumonia-Like Organism or PPLO. The birds that inherit the disease never produce eggs or weight as broilers but can, by blood testing in a similar method to BWD, be eliminated from the stock. During his address Professor Coles emphasised that every reactor must be eliminated, there was no other way. "You can make it a comparison to a young lady," he explained, "she can either be pregnant or not. She can't be a little bit pregnant!" After that meeting I was determined to have completely disease free flocks and so the testing for CRD began.

The building of the hatchery at Wynberg was progressing well but Mr Olfin was having difficulty in obtaining the asbestos for the roof. The incubators arrived and although May, June and July were usually dry winter months it could not be guaranteed by the 'weather-men'. I decided to take the gamble and Mr Glaum came to erect the incubators and set them working, imagine turning the eggs at night and looking up at the stars! I went with Mr Olfin to see the asbestos manufacturer and gave him a cheque: we got the asbestos three days later! Like the hatchery at Cato Ridge this one too had a big neon cockerel and the wording in large neon letters:

SUNNYSIDE PEDIGREE POULTRY FARMS
DAY OLD CHICKS.

I now realised that I needed an incubationist for the hatchery and I trained an Afrikaner named Andreas Venter, he moved into the house and all went well. I found that most of the business was in the Transvaal.

Around this time I met an accountant, Mark Walker, and his wife from Johannesburg. He was very keen on fishing and flew his Comanche aeroplane, ZS CLW (Charlie Limo Whisky) over Drakensburg Mountains down to Richards Bay on the North Coast. I went with him on a couple of occasions, not only was Richards Bay good fishing for salmon and grunter, three to five pounds in weight, the hotel was also excellent. I realised that if I had a plane I could deliver large consignments of day old pullets to customers near an airport. Although this would apply more to Cato Ridge the poultry business here could not be compared to that of the Transvaal and so I thought of selling the branch at Cato Ridge. Rand Airport was close to Wynberg and flying to Grasmere would save a lot of time. I put the thought of laying down a landing strip firmly in my mind.

206

After eight years Linda was unhappy in South Africa. I had to spend most of my time either at Grasmere or Wynberg and I did not have time to take her or the family out. Business always came first: I was a rotten father. I bought her a house in Bournemouth and willingly supported them. This was her choice, but my fault.

Looking back on it now not only was Linda a wonderful wife and mother but she was the one who worked hard helping me to get started. She deserved a better settlement, may my executors look after my wishes if not for Linda then for our children.

18

THE RISE AND FALL OF CHRISTOPER PANTALL
AND RISE AGAIN

I sold Cato Ridge after the family left for England and I was lonely and unhappy. I went to visit them several times. During a trip back to England I saw the Down Farm, in Tetbury, Gloucestershire and bought it. I knew I would not have time to live there permanently but saw it as an investment for the future. This lovely mixed farm joined the famous Arboretum and was situated at the end of a long drive lined with trees. It was a beautiful house with lovely lawns and gardens and at the rear stood twelve stables. I obtained the services of an old friend, Frank Jones, who was very capable. We stocked the farm with an Ayrshire milking herd and bought all the necessary machinery. I stayed at the Down Farm for a while very much enjoying farming again. I had a good manager in charge at Sunnyside during my absence and thought everything was under control. I should have known, and did know, that no one runs a business like the man who builds it up and owns it. One Day I received a telephone call from the manager at Sunnyside. The poultry at Grasmere had been stolen! I went straight to the Estate Agents, put the Down Farm on the market and, the same day, caught a plane to Johannesburg leaving Frank to sell the place and run it in the meantime. I would not be back as I had work to do!

During my absence the manager at Sunnyside had replaced the European farm manager at Grasmere with a coloured who had been selling the birds off each week. When the manager at Sunnyside visited Grasmere, instead of walking around the pens to check that the birds had food and water, he went only to the office! The farm manager had been taking advantage and had sold nearly all the birds, several thousand, and disappeared with the money from the sale. I gave the Sunnyside manager a month's notice and would have dismissed him immediately, had I not needed him to help me. I now had the task of beginning a re-stocking programme but first I needed fertile eggs from disease free stock. I managed to get these from a few local breeders and blood tested the stock throwing out any reactors. Fortunately one of these breeders had had the cream of my stock. We had to cancel and postpone orders for day old chicks. I worked twenty-five hours a day blood testing and inspecting breeding stock knowing that my competititors would be taking full advantage of the situation. It was a hard lesson but it served me right! At the end of the month we had achieved progress to recovery, and I had George Olfin to build me a small house by the hatchery. The manager came to see me and said, "We have made great progress, I can see now where I made the mistake, can I stay on?"

"You are due to leave tomorrow, you won't be missed!" I replied. He was not and within twelve months I had re-stocked Grasmere with our breeding stock and had the business back on course. The Down Farm sold and that was the end of my trying to farm and run another business. Sadly, the beautiful Down Farm, house and buildings, were burnt to the ground in 1995.

I concentrated on the Transvaal and worked hard expanding. I now had a large flock of laying hens at Grasmere and I trained a new group of blood testing staff. I bought a one-acre plot next door to the hatchery at Bramley and planned a processing plant but before doing this I bought thirty acres of bare veld land, with no surrounding houses, out on the Pretoria road at Harrowdene, about two miles from Bramley. I called this farm Mandalay. It had no water so I engaged a water-boring contractor and, on the fourth attempt, he succeeded in finding two thousand gallons per hour! Now I was ready for my next plan. Broilers in controlled environment houses, disease-free. A processing plant would follow later.

§

On September 24th, 1957, I went to Yorkshire to visit the Buxted Chicken Company. Their chief nutritionist, Mr David Faulkner, was very helpful giving me lots of advice on nutrition. I was already mixing all my own poultry rations and, on my return, would extend my purchase of vitamins. He showed me around their numerous broiler houses (broiler was the name the Americans gave to an oven ready chicken eight to ten weeks old).

The buildings were of timber, having an asbestos roof with no windows and thermostatically controlled electric fans placed in the roof and sides of the broiler houses. At eight weeks a four-pound table bird was being put through a processing plant. No wonder chicken became a popular meat, and cheap. I realised that genetic breeding of poultry in South Africa would have to improve. Western 'walk in' incubators, where the operator took off his shirt and worked at one hundred degrees fahrenheit, were popular. Another interesting item was the automatic processing plant, made by Gordon Johnson Stephens. It moved at a speed whereby the operators could pass on from one bird to another without taking the bird off the line. Wrapping oven ready birds for the housewife was also carefully thought out. In South Africa chickens were still being sold by the butcher 'on the hoof' and expensive by comparison.

Whilst at Yorkshire I decided that I must also improve my breeding stock and this meant a trip to the U.S.A. Mr Faulkner laid it on for me. I landed at New York airport, changed planes and flew up to Boston. I had left London at noon and here I was arriving at Boston, also at noon. I was met by a manager of 'Arbour Acres' Poultry Organisation, a pioneer in the genetic industry. They had produced a broiler in the advanced stage it was today. Others were in the race to sell the hybrid on licence throughout the world. At four o'clock I was taken by car to Connecticut, about one hundred miles into North America, to see their breeding techniques which were fascinating and very productive. Everyone was extremely hospitable giving me all the information they could. I told them I would have to give our poultry industry a 'good think over' and arrange with the 'powers that be' to put before our Government the benefits of importing breeding stock from the U.S.A. I decided to visit Professor Coles upon my return and get his opinion.

I had received an invitation from another pioneer – one of the Johnson brothers of Hyline Poultry Farms in South Georgia. He had telephoned Bramley and my secretary had informed him that I was already in the States. He had replied, "Tell him to come on down." Upon receiving the message I rang him and arranged a visit. I thanked everyone at Arbour Acres and bid them farewell.

I arrived at Atlanta airport at about seven o'clock in the evening, on October 7th 1957, and was met by Mr R Johnson of Hyline Poultry Farms. We drove for about an hour and a half and, on the way, called in to a steak house. I soon discovered that 'T' bone steaks in the U.S.A, washed down with a bottle of their beer, were *out of this world*. We arrived at midnight whereupon I excused myself. I was tired and needed sleep.

I learned so much during the next three days. If importation was not allowed then I was advised that Cornish Game and White Rock were heavy broilers and if not as good as a hybrid they would be better than Rhodes. I spent a good deal of time looking at their management systems and was greatly impressed. They were charming people and enjoyed being helpful. I bid them farewell and caught a plane to New York, London, then on to Johannesburg.

Upon my return, after a general look at things, I went to see Professor Coles. He told me that the veterinary department would not recommend importation because of several poultry diseases found in both the UK and USA. He advised me to keep my poultry disease free by not using imported stock. I knew of a farm north of Pretoria that stocked Cornish and White Rock poultry and, after blood testing, introduced fifty Cornish Game cockerels to cross with Hampshires. I knew it would take a couple of years to get a flock of these established.

The following year there was a big demand for day old New Hampshire pullets. The Sunnyside entry in the laying test had done well along with the rest of the entries. Mandalay was to be the new broiler plant and I had thought of starting by producing Hampshire cockerels for their attractive yellow colour. For the customers who preferred white flesh they would be catered for in due course by Cornish Game and White Rock. In England and the States their hybrid was processed at three and a half pounds, taking seven weeks, whereas our Hampshire's were processed at three pounds, taking nine weeks. Rocks and Cornish were yet to be tested but they would be disease free!

I decided the first thing to build at Mandalay would be a large shed, we could use part of this building for mixing our poultry feed. A new mill was to be installed and the mixed ration would be taken, by lorry, to Grasmere. The ingredients to be used would be the same as always, ground yellow mealies for a yellow flesh and vitamins which were so important in poultry feed rations. Vitamins were the only ingredients imported. In spite of the press report I had recently read, stating that according to feed manufacturers offal was a necessity to egg production and weight gain in all livestock, I was not in favour of its use. I discussed this with Professor Coles who agreed that a good deal more research was needed on the subject, advising me that as I could mix my own poultry feed, I should exclude offal from it its mixture. As a producer I was prepared to forfeit extra production because offal was thought to be one of the main causes of salmonella and I was adamant that our birds and eggs would be disease-free – it was top priority.

As soon as our broiler production began the mill would be flat out in production. Our aim was one hundred thousand disease-free Sunnybrand oven ready chickens per week with our own broiler producing farms.

The first broiler house at Mandalay was built and completed with all the electrical equipment. The first chicks went in during April 1959. It was the first controlled environment poultry house in Africa. We were also the first to use controlled feeding systems and a regular flow of water by means of a dripping nozzle although some houses had fox valves. The first crop was experimental but looked so successful that George Olfin carried on building a second house until a total of twelve were built. I estimated that it would take ten weeks for our present breeding stock to attain the required weight and two weeks to rest the houses (in order to kill all bacteria) so, in all, we needed twelve poultry houses per crop of birds. We were ahead of schedule for the broilers and as the processing plant was not yet ready I sold the birds live to Bolnick Brothers – later they bought processed birds.

The building for the processing plant was completed and the Gordon Johnson processing plant was on its way from the States. I had arranged for an engineer from England to come over and erect the plant. I decided that as Government permission to import breeding stock was a 'no go' I would start building up my pure bred Cornish Game and White Rocks. There was a good deal of experimental work involved in building up our pure bred lines, crossing dominant White Rock males with New Hampshires and crossing Cornish Game males with White Rock females both sexes to be used for processing.

In early 1960 a South African Railway lorry was pulling a trailer and travelling down the Pretoria road. When it was opposite Sunnyside the trailer became detached and crashed through the wire fence demolishing an office adjoining the hatchery. Fortunately no one was in the building at the time!

Much damage was done with equipment and records being destroyed. The South African Railways sent a letter asking me to fill in an enclosed claim form. I handed this to my manager who then attended to the claim. I did not need to go through it for it was only a minor claim. The office was rebuilt and the damaged equipment either replaced or repaired.

I had kept in touch with the Galtrys and Leyroyds, they were supplying the new owner of Sunnyside, Cato Ridge, with eggs. Grasmere was now a very productive breeding farm with our largest numbers being New Hampshires.

About this time, with the proposed opening up of the 'oven ready' chicken in South Africa which would be a big step forward, I realised that I needed more incubation space in order to keep the day old chick business flowing. I got on the telephone to England and ordered two Western 'walk-in' incubators, fortunately they had two in the process of manufacture agreeing to sell and fly out an engineer to erect them. As it was January when they would arrive, being off-season we would be able to shut down and dismantle two Secura's which I would then sell. The capacity of the Western was three times greater than the Secura.

The hatchery had ample room as I built it larger than our requirements. Next came 'Harrowdene' a thirty acre farm close to Mandalay where we could have completely controlled environment breeding houses and would be the farm to supply Grasmere's breeding stock. Mandalay could not give us enough broilers and it had been recommended, overseas, not to build too many broiler houses in one area. I had decided that twenty-four broiler houses would be enough for one unit. I went further afield to look for more land. In the Halfway House direction, between Johannesburg and Pretoria, I found thirty acres of veld land about fifteen miles from Bramley being close to Halfway House. There was water and electricity on the farm.

I still banked with Standard Bank at Bramley but the branch manager, Mr Geldenuys, was not like Mr Kettle. Far from being encouraging he was over-cautious. The business

214

was running on overdraft facilities and he was not happy
with my rate of expansion, expressing concern. The bank
held the title deeds to all properties with the exception of
'moveable' assets, which were not covered. I went to see the
manager of Barclays Bank just over the road from the
Standard Bank where I spent a great deal of time with its
manager pointing out to him what a wonderful future the
poultry business had. I explained that I wanted to be the first
person to give South Africans the oven-ready chicken and
Sunnybrand mini turkey. I took him to Mandalay and
Harrowdene to convince him that my plans were profitable,
asking my accountant to supply him with a balance sheet.
He did his homework and came back with a 'YES'. I then
transferred my account from Standard Bank to Barclays and
PROGRESSED!

I found that although the management at Grasmere was
good I needed to be there more often than twice a week. The
traffic on the Bramley to Vereeniging side of Johannesburg
was always heavy and it took me more than two hours to
reach Grasmere and the same back. I had been flying to
Richards Bay with Mark Walker at weekends and decided to
learn to fly myself. I bought a Piper PA 22, four-seater
ZA CRP (Charlie Romeo Papa) arriving at five o'clock each
morning at Rand airport for an hour's lesson with a qualified
pilot, returning back home to have breakfast and be in the
office for eight. After a month I completed my first solo flight
and passed my flying test, receiving my pilot's licence. The
following day, on December 13th 1960, I was presented with
my Wings by my instructor, Mr John Moller. We had a little
party to celebrate attended by Mary and Mark Walker.

The following Thursday, on hatching day, I decided to
deliver eight hundred day old Black Australorp pullets by
plane to a Mrs du Plessis who had a farm five miles away
from Bloemfontein. I arranged to meet her at the airport and
then accompany her back to her farm to see the poultry.
With the assistance of my hatchery manager I loaded the
chick boxes onto the plane (I had asked him to accompany
me and he had replied, "No thank you.") I completed an

estimated time of arrival (ETA), checked the plane and was ready for take off. I started the plane and taxied onto the runway, noting the sock direction as take off must be into the wind. I then called the operation tower, controlling Johannesburg airport, "Charlie Romeo Papa, ready for take off to Bloemfontein airport, ETA 1200 hours."

"Charlie Romeo Papa, call after take off," they replied.

I took off, my direction finder set and climbed quickly to the required height. "Charlie Romeo Papa, airborne heading for Bloemfontein, over and out."

"O.K Charlie Romeo Papa, call Bloemfontein for permission to land, over and out."

I found this very exciting, just a little plane cruising at eighty miles per hour. The wind tried to take me off course but it was soon righted. When I got to within twenty miles of my destination I called Bloemfontein airport control for runway directions. It was a beautiful day and I made a positive approach to the runway and a perfect landing before taxing to a stop. Mrs du Plessis arrived with a van and we loaded the chickens, reporting my arrival to the control centre before we drove off to her farm.

Everything was prepared very well for the chicks' arrival and we placed them under an electric brooder. Mrs du Plessis only had a few hundred poultry as the farm grew mainly mealies. "Eggs pay for the household expenses", she explained. She took me back to the airport where I filled out my ETA for arrival back at Rand airport, doing everything by the book. I asked the control tower for permission to take off and was told to taxi to the stop point on runway three and await take off instructions. Within two minutes I was instructed to take off and report when airborne. I arrived back at Rand airport in good time and, being a small airport, there were no landing instructions. I called Johannesburg control. After filling the plane with petrol I made my departure!

The following day, at Grasmere, after the usual inspection of the poultry houses and egg records taking a couple of hours, I took four boys and the manager to where there was a large piece of flat land between row one and the railway line. A perfect landing spot! The only problem was that it was West to East! As there was no room for a runway elsewhere we set about making it stock proof and bump free. One of the boy's, Charlie, was put in charge of keeping it clean and animal free.

Harrowdene was now all set and pure Rocks, Cornish Game, New Hampshires and Black Australorps were hand selected for pedigree breeding. We had decided not to expand on the Leghorns. The chickens produced from Harrowdene were for Grasmere. Weather permitting, I continued to fly out to Grasmere three mornings a week leaving Rand airport about six and arriving at Grasmere ten minutes later. I had to watch for wind direction and always looked down at the windsock before making an approach. Sometimes I would return to Rand airport as a crosswind could be dangerous.

On March 22nd 1961 Sunnybrand, together with Sunnyside held a party at the Rosebank hotel to celebrate completion of the building and the opening of the Sunnybrand's processing plant. Due to apartheid this only applied to the European staff and builders such as George Olfin and his wife, other tradesmen and the press. The non-Europeans were not allowed in the hotel. As they were the backbone of the business we held a party in my office and the hatchery at nine o'clock in the evening. Gallons of beer along with their 'favourite drinks' were consumed.

During March the Police called in to see me. They were aggressive being very much 'Afrikaners'. They told me that they had a warrant for my arrest for fraud. It involved a claim for fifteen pounds for a typewriter. They alleged I had made a claim on the grounds that the typewriter had been destroyed in the accident when obviously one of the staff had made a mistake and not deleted this item when it came back from the repairer. But there was more to it than that. I employed as few Afrikaners as possible but there was one employed in the hatchery that I knew to be anti-British and jealous of my success. Instead of deleting it from the claim form he had purposely reported it to the police. I knew nothing about it and would certainly not have claimed fifteen pounds for a typewriter. The police took me to the station and a charge was made. They then took my passport which they retained. To sum up how ludicrous it was to hold on to my passport: I owned and ran a large business, would I try to escape the country for fifteen pounds? The Afrikaner police were arrogant I had never met one that was otherwise.

The court hearing was held on April 17th. Nicky Schneider, a well-known lawyer in Johannesburg, defended me. The magistrate was known to be very anti-British. Nicky pleaded with him that the case should never have been brought before the court using the logic that, even if I'd known about it, would I make a claim for fifteen pounds for a typewriter? But here was an Englishman and justice had 'to be seen to be done'. To find him guilty of fraud, possibly extradite him, making him a criminal. Here was an Englishman that had pioneered where an Afrikaner had neither the ability nor brains to venture such a project.

During the recess Nicky said, "I'm sorry we've had to have this Magistrate, we don't stand a chance." The Afrikaner I had employed began speaking in Afrikaans. Nicky objected. He then went on to say that I had known of the claim because I had signed the claim form. In actual fact, as I owned the building, I had to sign but I left the contents to the manager. After two days the magistrate announced that he would give his verdict on the following Saturday at ten o'clock.

At the appointed day and hour Nicky and I went before him again and without any summing up, treating me like a criminal, he declared, "Guilty!"

Immediately and without hesitation Nicky answered, "We wish to lodge an appeal."

Two weeks later Nicky went alone to Pretoria, reporting back to me afterwards, and sat before three Judges who heard the case from beginning to end. They expressed deep concern stating how appalled they were that the case had ever come to court. In addition they apologised that such anti-British feeling had been shown. Our appeal had been upheld. Nicky also informed me that they had recommended that the Magistrate be demoted from sitting in court and that he be transferred to the registry of Births, Marriage and Deaths.

19

I had been thinking of introducing mini turkeys and asked a turkey producer in Bryanston to supply me with two hundred per week. The breeder set up an expansion programme althoughshe already had a big setup. I would market them as the 'Sunnybrand Oven-Ready Mini Turkey'. Added to the chickens we now advertised 'Sunnyside Pedigree Poultry Farms – Disease Free – Delicious Oven Ready Turkeys and Chickens. Bolnick Brothers agreed to distribute them into stores such as OK Bazaars and many others. We also tried ducks but found the dressing of them to be difficult.

The processing plant was a huge success and we found ample staff being close to Alexander Township. I had three managers to help me, working closely under my direction. I had to watch the supply of eggs from Grasmere and now that I had a plane I could go out there and do a day's mating and culling. The new broiler plant at Halfway House was being built and nearly ready.

On Friday November 2nd 1962, I flew BOAC to London and then went on to the Westbury Hotel to collect my shooting gear, guns and warm clothes, having previously arranged that a friend would drop them off there for me. I then caught the night-sleeper from Euston Station arriving at Aviemore in Scotland on the Sunday morning. I was met at Aviemore by Richard Waddington's chauffeur, in the Rolls-Royce, who drove me to Blairfindly Lodge, at Glenlivet, Bauffshire. The weather was cold but dry and although there was snow on the mountains, everything was green and lovely. I knew in this kind of weather pheasants would fly well. The cost of travelling and staying at Blairfindy Lodge for the week including the shooting was only a few hundred pounds. The shooting, food and drink was all very good. Richard was an excellent host.

On Wednesday, whilst shooting at my peg, some very high pheasants came over and one that I shot fell with a bang onto the corrugated roof of a shed. After the drive was over I went to explore how I could retrieve the bird. Lo and behold inside the shed, standing out like a sore thumb, was a yellow Rolls-Royce! Richard came over to join me and, whilst the keeper retrieved the pheasant, he told me that the car had belonged to Dorothy Pagett and pointed to the sides of the car indicating her racing colours and, fixed to the rear chassis, the specially made luncheon box. Many a bottle of champagne had been supplied from there, particularly when Golden Miller, the famous racehorse, won the Gold Cup at Cheltenham as well as the Grand National. Like his owner, Golden Miller was very well thought of and held in high esteem by the racing world. "What are you doing with it?" I asked, shooing the hens off their roosting place on top of the Rolls.

"I had big ideas for that Rolls but I've never had the time to do anything about it!" he replied. "I'll sell it to you if you want it."

"Price?" I enquired.

"Three hundred and fifty pounds," he replied.

The following morning Richard's chauffeur, armed with petrol and a battery, took me down to the shed. He poured petrol into the tank and coupled up the battery as the car had not been started for a long time. He pressed the starter and the engine started immediately, ticking over as if it was used only yesterday. It registration number was GP4680, chassis number, 48GX. I had it sent to Rolls-Royce at Crewe to be serviced then shipped over to South Africa. It arrived in Johannesburg three months later. I had a lot of pleasure from the car taking part in many rallies. I believe that this Rolls thought we were on our way to Cheltenham and that every horse was 'Golden Miller'. In 1964 I won a silver cup at Johannesburg Festival Rally for 'best performance'.

One afternoon I went to visit Grasmere in order to inspect the production records. I had a young lad with me in the co-pilot's seat and we took off as usual. As I flew over the sock at Grasmere I knew it was blowing slightly North to South and I would have to allow for a slight cross and tail wind. I flew the usual square approach to land over the road, reduced speed to forty miles per hour but, because the cross wind was greater than I anticipated, and although I was making a perfect landing, I was approaching faster than usual. I reduced speed to twenty miles per hour and was about to touch down, being careful not to stall the engine, when suddenly the plane caught a gust of wind. I hit the deck and bounced back up but I did not have time to open the throttle and make a new approach for yet another gust wind turned the plane upside down. We extracted ourselves from the broken glass and debris with only the odd scratch!

I made my way to the farm office and telephoned the aircraft accident branch and they came out to inspect the plane and take a report from me. It did not deter my enthusiasm for flying and, within a week of the insurance company agreeing to carry the loss of the accident, I bought a new Cessna 172 Skylark ZS CPU, and soon got used to flying it. Mark Walker had on many occasions made me fly blind using only instruments, as I had no pilot ratings, but this plane had extra instruments including an ADF (auxiliary directional finder) and was much easier to fly.

A few days later I went to the Magistrate Court and asked for my passport. A different Magistrate was sitting but, apparently, he had possession of my passport. I explained to a court official that I needed it to travel to England. I heard the court official ask the Magistrate for Mr Pantall's passport as he wished to travel to England and I heard the Magistrate reply, "Who in their right mind would want to go to England!" The official spoke Afrikaans badly so English was used.

About a week later I used one of the vans and went out to Grasmere to collect a quantity of eggs and, after my usual tour, I loaded the ten boxes into the van and set off for home avoiding the heavy traffic by taking the Grasmere Roodepoort road. I was travelling at my usual speed of about fifty miles an hour on the left-hand side on a good straight road. About ten miles from Roodepoort I saw a car rapidly approaching at speed on my side of the road. He was about ten yards away when I took the urgent decision to avoid him, turning into the opposite lane. He struck the rear, near side of my van turning it upside down in the veld. Covered in blood and eggs I managed to climb out through the window, the other car was upright in a ditch but the driver was missing. A passer-by kindly gave me a lift to Roodepoort police station where, after a wash and clean up, an officer drove me back to the scene of the accident. Several people at the spot kindly helped me to put the van back on the road whilst the police-man went looking for the driver of the offending car, finding him asleep in the veld. He said that he had been in a fight with his wife, got drunk and decided to kill himself by driving into a vehicle travelling towards him regardless of any thought for the other driver, in this case, me!

The policeman told him that he would be charged with dangerous driving and took him off to the station, instructing me to attend Roodepoort Magistrate Court at ten the follow-ing morning.

Fortunately my van started up and I was lucky not to be injured, just shaken up and minus a good few eggs and next day I drove to attend the hearing. At my request the Afrikaner policeman gave evidence in English in front of a glaring Magistrate, still fighting us in the Boer War. He asked me if I was sober at the time of the accident to which I replied, "Yes Sir!" Turning to the guilty party, another Afrikaner, he advised him not to fight with his wife and gave him a 'caution' on this occasion. Disgusted I left the Magistrate Court. I remarked, "Is this is what the Afrikaners call JUSTICE?"

Bolnick Brothers were successful suppliers to the retail market and Sunnybrand oven ready chickens were a great success, and although as yet our breeding programme was not completed, the New Hampshire made a very presentable bird.

Each Monday the manager of each department would attend a meeting in the boardroom. Mrs Rubin, my secretary, would sit beside me making notes. In total there were nine managers of Sunnyside and Sunnybrand farms and production plants. We would discuss problems (too many to put in this book) but between us, we always found a solution. Jean, my sister, and her husband Jack was in charge of Mandalay, the best-run farm in the organisation. I believe Jean lived in the houses when the chicks were put in, she was so conscientious.

I had been flying the Cessna for some months when I flew Mark Walker down to Paradise Island on a fishing trip. As it was Portugese East African territory we had to land at Lorenco Marques and report our existence, then on up the coast to Paradise Island where a yacht *Melody* was waiting to take us across to the Island about ten minutes from shore. The following morning we boarded *Melody* and sailed out into the deep black Indian Ocean, full of Marlin, catching grunter, swordfish, barracuda and many other species on the way. When we reached our destination we used two rods trailing behind the *Melody*, baited with Spanish mackerel sometimes attracting a huge shark. When a Marlin struck it was great sport. The Marlin would go down deep then when wound up would 'tail-walk' on the surface before taking off with the reel screaming and rod half bent. We would take it in turns to sit in a revolving seat as the skipper kept the yacht alongside the Marlin occasionally leaping up out of the water and tail-walking the surface, a fantastic sight to see.

After four hours we finally got the four hundred and

POULTRY FEEDS

Last July the Farmer's Weekly published an article I wrote on Hybrid Poultry and Poultry Feeds. I am limited for space in this Annual but would like to give my customers the benefit of using the same ingredients for Poultry Rations as I use on my Grasmere Farm.

If you wish to mix your own rations, this will not only save you a lot of money, but **you know what is in it.**

CHICK MASH

46 lbs.	Yellow Mealie Meal.
10 lbs.	Pollard.
13 lbs.	Bran.
8 lbs.	Lucerne Meal.
10 lbs.	Fish Meal (60% Protein).
6 lbs.	Sunflower Oilcake Meal (42% Protein).
3 lbs.	Fermavite Yeast.
2 lbs.	Oyster Shell Powder.
3 ozs.	Fine Salt.
4 ozs.	Vitamins.

98 lbs. 7 ozs.

CHICK-CHICK No. 1 also fed.

LAYING MASH

158 lbs.	Yellow Mealie Meal.
12 lbs.	Lucerne Meal.
25 lbs.	Bran.
20 lbs.	Pollard.
16 lbs.	Fish Meal (60% Protein).
5 lbs.	Sunflower Oilcake Meal (42% Protein).
2½ lbs.	Bone Meal.
3 lbs.	Oyster Shell Grit.
2 lbs.	Fermavite Yeast.
½ lb.	Fine Salt.
10 ozs.	Vitamins.

244 lbs. 10 ozs.

NO MEALIES FED.

This is a High Energy BROILER MASH
(used from 8 weeks to slaughter).

48 lbs.	Yellow Mealie Meal.
5 lbs.	Pollard.
5 lbs.	Wheaten Bran.
5 lbs.	Maize Germ Meal.
5 lbs.	Lucerne Meal.
13 lbs.	Fish Meal.
7 lbs.	Sunflower Oilcake Meal.
1½ lbs.	Lime of Oyster Shell Powder.
½ lb.	Common Salt.
2 lbs.	Fermavite Yeast.
1½ lbs.	Bone Meal.
2 lbs.	Sugarcane Molasses.
4 ozs.	Vitamins.

96 lbs.

CRUSHED MEALIES also fed.

The Laying Mash is an all mash ration and no mealies should be fed. Vitamins are very important and because of difficulty in obtaining these I stock the same brand as I use at Grasmere. Each tin of 5 lbs. is sufficient to mix approximately 2,000 lbs. of feed. This is a V.M.P. product.

FOR CHICKS
5 lb. tin £1.

FOR LAYERS
5 lb. tin 16/8.

FULL DETAILS ON TINS.
Cash with order.
Railage Paid.

FOR BROILERS
5 lb. tin £3/3/4.
Contains Coccidiostat and antibiotics
Nitrofurazone
Penicillin
Aureomycin

If you are not getting good results from your merchants' balanced Poultry Feeds then you can add vitamins to each bag of feed. These Vitamins are obtainable from Sunnyside Pedigree Poultry Farm. If you are not satisfied with the weights of your Broilers I suggest you ask your merchant to sell you feed minus vitamins and antibiotics. Obtain these from me you certainly then know what quantity of Vitamins your birds are getting.

BETTER RESULTS FROM BETTER FEEDING

As recommended to poultry farmers by the author

Despatching day old chicks to the Belgian Congo

*Some of the processing plant empoyees with the author's plane –
'Charlie Papa Uniform'*

Packing the plane with day old chicks for air delivery

Taken in the boardroom with Mrs Rubin, the author's secretary

In the process of being built

Little Sunnyside. The author's private residence

Sunday morning out with fox hounds using a drag

Salmon caught on *River Wye – Rock Cottage*

READ THIS!

The Next Five Minutes Can Change Your Life!!

The company needed something new to attract the public's attention. It worked!

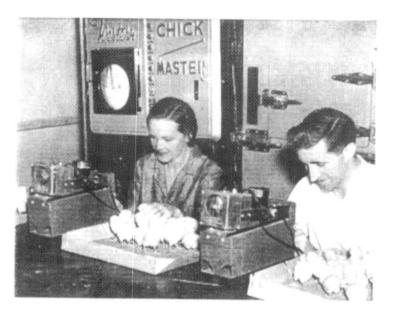

DE-BEAKING SERVICE

TO PREVENT TOE PICKING, FEATHER PICKING and CANNIBALISM, we will de-beak all your Day Old Chicks BEFORE DESPATCHING, with our new American de-beaking machines, at only 10/– per 100. A perfectly harmless operation, and will make your chicks grow faster.

De- beaking

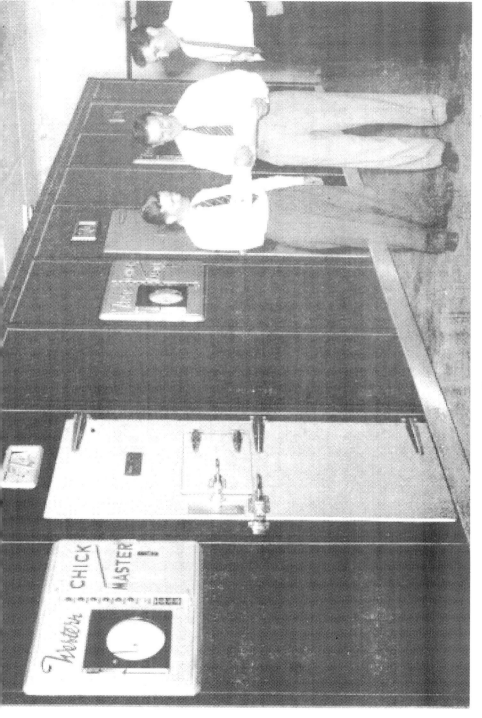

Progress

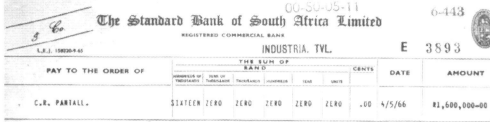

Top: *Processing plant*

Above: *Payment to the author for an 80% stake in Sunnyside.*

Right: *The author receiving cheque from directors of UTC on behalf of BAT*

MR. G. T. G. Moorhead, chairman of the United Tobacco Companies (South) Ltd. (left), signs a R1,600,000 take-over agreement of Sunnyside poultry enterprises with Mr. C. R. Pantall (right). Looking on is Mr. M. H. McRae, a director of United Tobacco. In terms of the transaction, United Tobacco acquired an 80 per cent interest in Chican (Pty.) Ltd., the holding company for Sunnyside Pedigree Poultry Farms, from Mr. Pantall, who built up his poultry empire over the past 19 years. Mr. Pantall, who retains the remaining 20 per cent interest, will stay on as managing director of the new company.

FLIGHT CREW MEMBER LICENCE
VLIEGPERSONEELLISENSIE

Signature of Holder
Handtekening van houer

The Holder of this licence
Die houer van hierdie lisensie   C.R. PANTALL.

is hereby authorised to exercise the privileges of the licence, ratings
word hierby gemagtig om die voorregte van die lisensie, grade en
and certificate attached hereto
sertifikate hierby aangeheg, uit te oefen

Given at   Pretoria   this   15th   day of
Gegee te   op hede die   dag van

December   60.

Commissioner for Civil Aviation
Kommissaris van Burgerlugvaart

With this licence the author was
able to fly his plane unaided all
over Africa

Johannesburg Festival Rally
1964
Best Performance
Rolls Royce

Down Farm. A beautiful residence adjoining Arboretum in Gloucestershire

Tapster Mill. Home of the author upon returning from South Africa.

A good morning's sport

Grouse shooting at Invercauld Castle. The first view of grouse approaching

Above: *Ballingham fishing lodge adjoining Rock Cottage.*

Below: *Fishing on the mighty Vosso River, Norway, 1976*

The author caught twenty-two Salmon in two days on the River Tweed in 1971

Thailand – receiving trophies

Not the author's scene

Top and below : *Umhlanga*
The author spent many hours in this enjoyable part of the world.

Top left and right:*The author's beloved daughter Demelza*

Left: *Demelza. taken as student a St Andrew's University in Scotland*

Lugwardine House. The author's favourite home.

Above: *Pheasant shooting in Hungary – where the people wer hungry*

Above and Right: *Jean, still in Krugersdorp South Africa today.*

The author's lovable companion Lolly

The author and a 450lb Marlin
which was caught off Paradise Island in the Indian Ocean

twenty-pound monster to the side, a crew of four hauling it up with gaffs. The Indian Ocean was usually very calm and today we were lucky. On the way back into port the crew, who were given the catch, flew a black flag signifying a Marlin catch.

Next day we flew home interrupted stopping only at Lorenco Marques to check out. When we were flying over the Drakensburg Mountains Mark covered my eyes with a scarf and instructed me to fly blind with only the use of my instruments a precaution in case I was ever caught in a storm and needed to fly by instruments.

At the time I gave poultry tips on the radio – there was , as yet, no television. Day old chicks were exported as far as the Congo and Kenya and sold well. Chick 'sexers' from overseas were sexing twenty thousand per week. Wally Wilkinson and Beryl Coles were now resident here and Lizzie Mitchell from Maidstone came for five months.

Bolnick Brothers were doing well with sales from the processing plant. O.K. Bazaars stocked Sunnybrand oven ready chickens and turkeys and we sold our output. The products were all fresh as we did not as yet have frozen facilities. Being disease and salmonella free the public were eating a lot of chicken and at a cheaper price than beef, mutton or pork. All our vans, lorries and buildings were painted in red checker-board which was extremely eye catching. We now employed sixty-two people and I had a photograph taken of some of the staff beside the plane at Rand airport.

It was now 1965 and, in addition to Mandalay, we had three further broiler plants at Halfway House, Harrowdene was also going very well. I found I had an excellent general manager – he had two managers working under him.

On Thursday morning I took a telephone call from a customer at Ladysmith who wanted one thousand New Hampshire day old pullets. Bernard, my incubation manager, was standing by my side. He was short of space for brooders so a sale was needed. "Shall we fly them down there?" he asked.

"Do you have an airport near you Mr Van Rooyan?" I asked the customer.

"No, but there's a landing strip on my land that was used years ago, I could see that it was in order", he replied.

I told him that I would telephone back regarding the landing strip but that if we decided not to use the plane then the chickens would arrive by train. Bernard and I then planned to go down early Saturday morning, drop off Mr Van Rooyan's chicks before flying on to Richards Bay for some fishing; returning home on Sunday. I confirmed the details with the customer explaining that the runway must be long enough and free from potholes. He assured me that it was a long strip so I told him not to bother to measure as I could pin point a spot for landing.

The chicks were sexed, packed and ready for despatch on the Saturday morning. We took off from Rand airport and about two hours later were flying over the Drakensberg Mountains. At 08.30 hrs we flew over Van Rooyan's farm where he was waving a flag to mark the point of touchdown. I flew over it twice thinking it was a bit short for a landing strip so I came in very slowly just above stalling speed, hit the deck where he had indicated, applied the brakes coming to a standstill about ten yards from an open ditch!

"This is the last time I'm flying chicks out to a farm," I told him as I got out of the plane, "you left me a few yards from disaster!"

We off-loaded the chicks, Mr Van Rooyan handed me his cheque and we climbed aboard again. Although heading in the right direction we would now be taking off into a small breeze. Mr Van Rooyan hadn't got a clue, everything he had told me was completely wrong. Taking off at full throttle with a lighter plane I eased the stick back at forty miles per hour and we climbed rapidly into the sky thanking God for his deliverance.

My ETA to Richards Bay was 09.30 hrs. It was a beautiful morning and at 09.15 hours we could see the sea, flying up the coast until Richards Bay came into sight. Flying out to sea I turned and came in to make a perfect landing. We were met by our ghillie who then took us to our hotel for a good breakfast of bacon and eggs before fishing. We caught a few grunter and salmon, fishing all day. In the afternoon we put the three-pound grunters which we had caught overboard in a landing net tying them to the boat to keep the fish fresh. Suddenly there was a loud splash a big shark had bitten through the net devouring our fish together with most of the net! We caught sight of the shark's fin above the water making its way towards a small inlet. If I'd had my gun I could have shot him!

We both enjoyed the break and the flight down. I found Bernard good company as we relaxed with plenty of Lion ale. We went out early on the Sunday about six am and caught a couple of four pound salmon and grunter. Our ghillie had got us shrimps for bait. As we went in for breakfast I asked the office to give us a weather forecast for our trip back and was told 'forecast was good'. We had breakfast and at about ten o'clock packed our fish and gear made out an ETA and took off heading for home.

When airborne I tried to locate Johannesburg airport and although having an excellent radio, I couldn't make contact. The plane did not have an automatic pilot known as 'George'. We flew on for about another couple of hours and where Drakensburg Mountains should have been located I saw only a blanket of cloud! If I flew above I still had no idea what the weather would be like and to drop below the cloud could court disaster. My ADF (auxilary directional finder) would take me to Johannesburg but having managed to contact control the forecast was cloud and rain. I decided to turn around and head back to Richards Bay where I expected clearer weather but a huge cloud had closed in behind us. I told Bernard to keep calm and I set my ADF on Eshowe controls (no voice contact) and the plane flew this course. We then ran into a thunderstorm with hail beating against the windscreen. Bernard was crouched with his head down into the back of his seat and being tossed about. He was very unhappy and certainly not enjoying the flight. I did my best to keep him cool, calm and collected. It was now that all the 'flying blind' instruction by Mark Walker came in. I had to believe my instruments although at times I was convinced that we were flying upside down. When my speed increased I pulled back the stick to normal speed and watched the ADF, it was difficult! I knew that once we exceeded the normal speed we would be out of control in a 'graveyard spiral' resulting in certain disaster. After enduring this for at least an hour the ADF went 'beep beep', the loveliest music I have ever heard. Fortunately I had made a compass setting for the coast in my ADF book. I set it quickly flying to the same height, by my watch nine minutes, before dropping down through the cloud as slowly as possible. Suddenly the sea appeared and we headed out towards it. We were only about fifty feet below the cloud, to our left about a quarter of a mile away was the shore.

I turned the plane towards the shore and flying up to Richards Bay the cloud was very low. Had I come down through the cloud any sooner we would certainly have crashed! I had to look carefully for Richards Bay or I could fly past it but there it was in all its splendour and glory. I circled, came in and made a perfect landing. Bernard was as white as a sheet as he got out of the plane and holding his pants he made for the hotel taking his overnight bag with him. I called after him jokingly "Don't keep em!"

I went into the hotel and ordered two treble whiskies neat! I then went looking for the female member of staff who had given me the weather conditions only to find she had gone 'off duty' so I decided to write to the hotel and advise them in future to give pilots truer information when it was required.

Although I'd been in contact with Johannesburg control during our return flight to Richards Bay I telephoned them again to confirm that we had arrived safe and sound. After a good lunch we said a prayer to God for our deliverance and fell soundly asleep.

Next morning I telephoned Johannesburg control, the weather was now clear and cloudless. I informed Richards Bay hotel reception that they were unreliable, before flying back over Drakensburg Mountains in a bright cloudless sky then touching down at Rand airport.

A few days later I flew out to Grasmere in the afternoon and being very busy had left my return a bit late. Unlike England there is no twilight and it falls dark in twenty minutes. I took off, soon reaching Rand airport where the light was fading. Coming in to land I realised that there were big heavy electric cables directly in my path. I opened up the throttle, pulled the stick back and went over them, did another turn for landing but this time on a different runway. After landing I decided there and then that this was the end of my flying career. I knew of a pilot looking for a Cessna, he was not only interested but bought it!

In 1965 Linda and the girls decided to emigrate to New Zealand North Island. Alan, my younger brother, had emigrated to South Island at the same time that I had emigrated to South Africa.

§

Sunnybrand chickens were not only popular but known for their keeping quality. I attributed a lot of this to the feed. No offal was added to the feed which, in turn, meant that no part of the chicken, even when the intestines were removed, had any bacteria left to cause an immediate 'going off' i.e. deterioration.

One afternoon Al Challoner a poultry keeper and a great friend of mine came into the boardroom with a bundle of papers underneath his arm. He supplied Sunnyside with commercial breeding eggs and kept an immaculate farm. Al used my saying "Do you keep poultry or do poultry keep you?" Sitting down he said, "Chris, would you like to buy my farm. It's in excellent order and showing a good profit."

"Al, I have enough on my plate but thanks for the offer. I'll bear it in mind."

After a cup of tea made for us by Mrs Rubin he made his way to collect his egg boxes. When Mrs Rubin came into my office I said, "Mrs Rubin, what shall I do, keep expanding and be the richest man in the cemetery or sell up go back to England and be miserable in comfort?"

"I know your answer!" said Mrs Rubin smiling, so we discussed it. Other processors and feed merchants would be interested but they would offer a cheap price. "United Tobacco Company are diversifying into food," I said. "They have recently bought Willards Chips. They could be interested."

We discovered that a Mr Moorhead was Chairman and Managing Director of United Tobacco Company, an offshoot of British American Tobacco – B.A.T. – who were world famous. I gave him a ring and finding him at his desk congratulated him on entering the food world before outlining the reason for my call. At the end of our conversation I offered to send him photographs and a brief synopsis on Sunnyside for which he thanked me.

§

In due course Mr Moorhead, along with the deputy Chairman Mr McCrae, accepted my invitation to visit Sunnyside and Sunnybrand and were suitably impressed. I invited them to be our guests during our weekly board meeting on a Monday when all the senior members of the staff would be present for a general discussion.

Mr McCrae attended the meeting surprised how one farm manager from the hatchery could help another from the processing plant in an exchange of ideas especially when it came to transport. United Tobacco's accountants came in to scrutinise the accounts, they were very interested. We were now in early 1966.

I told them that I ran Sunnyside on Buxted Chicken lines, getting David Faulkner to lay on an invitation. So we flew to London and then went by train to Yorkshire. After a two-day visit, which they found very informative, we went back to London and stayed the night at the Westbury Hotel where I held a dinner for all my guests. Next day it was home by BOAC. During this time, frequent visits were being made by both senior staff and accountants from United Tobacco.

I was invited to lunch with the Director of UTC at one of their restaurants within their grounds. During luncheon Mr Moorhead told me that they were interested in buying Sunnyside but would I write to him stating the asking price and confirmation that if asked I would be prepared to spend one month per year working at Sunnyside. I went back to my office and penned a letter back to Mr Moorhead stating that my price to include all farms, processing plant, hatchery and equipment, lock, stock and barrel was a very reasonable R1,600,000. My services for one month a year for a period of three years would be £20,000 per year. The sale to be eighty percent of the negotiated price with the remaining twenty percent being retained by me. I then posted the letter.

United Tobacco Company was in agreement and the deal was made! In deciding to sell Sunnyside and Sunnybrand I took into consideration that although owned solely by me it was big business and so vulnerable with many competitors 'knocking at my door.' The bank held all my assets even with a sale of this amount the overdraft at the bank was huge and had to be met from the proceeds of the sale. It only required one of my competitors to undercut my production costs and the bank would foreclose and I would end up with 'nowt'.

On May 4th 1966 Mr G T G Moorhead, accompanied by Mr M H McRae on behalf of the United Tobacco Company (representing British American Tobacco) came out to Sunnyside and we signed an agreement before I was handed a cheque to the value of R1,600,000

Thus, after nineteen years of hard work with my slogan 'Nothing Ventured, Nothing Gained, I could say:

MY VENTURE HAD GAINED.

PART V

HUNTING, SHOOTING AND FISHING

20

Two months later, when I was satisfied that the Sunnyside organisation was on course and could manage without me, I travelled to Ireland. The previous year I had visited Dublin with the South African Show Jumping team and found it a very 'easy going' country. I stayed at a Hotel near Bray overlooking the sea and spent the evenings mackerel fishing. It was a great sport, so much so that I bought a rowing boat with an outboard motor and rented a stretch of salmon fishing, spending the days fishing the River Slaney. I hired a Vauxhall motor car serving my purpose very well considering the fact that the roads and lanes were narrow and barely accessible.

On my first visit to my rented stretch of water on the Slaney I came across three Irish fishermen each with a bucketful of worms. They were poachers paying nothing for their fishing yet the tenants, like me, paid all expenses including rates. I did not want a fight or a quarrel so I let them stay as all Irishmen consider the rivers in Ireland belong to them. The Slaney was a fast flowing river, excellent for fly-fishing, and I waded out about ten yards into the stream. My second cast reached the normal length and the fly rod bent and the real screamed, I was 'playing' a fresh fighting salmon. What a thrill! This is what I had been looking forward to all my life. For about twenty-five minutes I kept a tight line in the fast running water before gently bringing the exhausted salmon to the net in about a foot of water. I did not use a gaff being against the use of such a weapon. Glancing towards the bank I suddenly noticed that my 'uninvited guests' were sitting with their worm buckets watching. They always use worms, so it was the fly versus the worm. They did not know that not only was I a novice, this being my first salmon, but I had no idea how to fish using worms. On this particular day the salmon were not taking their worms preferring the fly and I caught two more, one was a smaller fish but gave me quite a fight.

> *God grant that I may catch a fish so big that even I,*
> *when talking of it afterwards, shall have no need to lie.*

Content in the knowledge that this had been 'my day' and as it was seven o'clock in the evening I decided on a finish. I was standing on the bank when a lovely big fish jumped in mid-stream. I needed to be above the salmon and I walked about fifteen yards upstream then waded about ten yards in the water. I cast my line and the salmon took the Stoats Tail fly, it was a large fish, about eighteen pounds. I fought for about twenty minutes but was too hasty bringing it in and the hook came out. I went back to the hotel with my three salmon weighing nine pounds, twelve pounds and fourteen pounds. I fished for most of the following day and did not have an offer, yet my 'guests' with their worms caught four. After dinner I went mackerel fishing catching nine.

A fisherman at the hotel, Patrick Murphy, was going down to the Blackwater Lodge and invited me to join him for a couple of days fly-fishing in the Blackwater River, County Cork. I followed him down in my car the next day but as we drew a blank after the two days I returned to Bray. With my 'guests' still for company I continued to fish the Slaney finding the larger fish in the main stream. Although I did lose some, with the hook coming out, I put this down to inexperience and the majority, which I caught, down to sheer luck.

Whilst at Bray I had to go to the local police station but needed directions. I drove passed a woman walking along with several children and pulled up alongside her, asking her for directions. "Yer see that toining left up there?" she pointed.

"I see a turning on the right." I replied.

"Oim sorry Zir," she said, "It's the roight I mean!"

"Why is it that the Irish don't know their right from left?" I said, smiling.

"Mister," she replied, "If you had six kids running around yer, yer wouldn't know yer roight from yer left."

Things were not going too well at Sunnyside so I decided to fly back for a short visit attending the Monday afternoon meeting in the boardroom. It appeared that the 'Rainbow Poultry Farm' in Natal were bringing oven ready chickens to Johannesburg. Rainbow had just started in the business copying my methods yet I held to my belief that quality would always hold the market. The meeting went very well. Bernard was pleased with the Western walk-in incubators. During the visit I helped with blood testing, mating and culling being a very big task. I was pleased to see that the White Rocks and Cornish Game had flourished so well being PPLO negative with no reactors to CRD and BWD.

It was imperative to keep the stock disease free.

I still owned Little Sunnyside, my residence in Summit Road. Letty and Hudson were looking after it and were very pleased to see me as were Jean and Jack still at Mandalay. I had some poultry houses built at Little Sunnyside in which to keep the White Rocks, Cornish Game and other special pedigree stock. The plant was well protected with burglar-proofed pens and looked after for me by Joseph under the supervision of Sunnyside's manager, as the breeding stock belonged to Sunnyside Poultry Farm.

Little Sunnyside was close to Bryanston Country Club where I had been a member for several years and I managed to play a round or two of golf. I was proud of the fact that I was a South African citizen holding both a South African passport and identity card.

I returned to England as Sunnyside was now well under control. I would be revisiting again in a few months. Arriving in England I travelled straight to Scotland by overnight sleeper for a weeks grouse shooting on the moors of Invercauld Castle. This was an annual event costing very little and worth every penny. Captain Farquarson, was the owner and Laird of Invercauld Castle and I was invited to join a party of ten. After an enjoyable day's shooting ending at four in the afternoons I would take my fourteen-foot fishing rod and fly fish for salmon in the river Dee that flowed through the grounds of Invercauld. The average weight of my catch was thirteen pounds and I caught one that weighed in at seventeen, they gave me a lot of sport. I caught several salmon that Mrs Farquarson was delighted to cook as we often had salmon on the menu. I had a wonderful week's grouse shooting!

At the end of my stay at Invercauld Castle I went on to stay with Sir Robin McEwan at Marchmont. Marchmont was an elegant house and large estate with beautiful lawns and grounds overlooking the Tweed Valley. Princess Margaret often stayed there. Dinner was a scene to behold! Waiters in full livery attended to the guests and the food was delicious. These sorts of shoots were available in the nineteen-fifties at very low prices. A week's shoot including accommodation and food could be obtained for a few pounds to a very high standard. Many famous faces would be present as guests one of which was Robin Maxwell, a well-known BBC commentator and author of 'The Black Raven'. Like me he was there for the week's shoot. I was fortunate enough to have many such weeks at most good shoots including that of Earl Haig on whose water I caught a sixteen pound sea trout, the average weight being four to six pounds. I also stayed at the Earl of Dundee's, a wonderful pheasant shoot. Sir Alec Douglas Hume and the Earl had to interrupt the shoot for two or three days to attend to important business at the House of Commons. I found Sir Alec to be a very charming man. Other shoots included Major Richard Waddington, Blairfindy Lodge and Glenlivet a wonderful grouse moor.

Whilst shooting with Sir Robin McEwan, double guns, my loader, Bill Braithwaite remarked, "Do you see the River Tweed below?"

"Yes, it looks lovely!" I replied.

"That fishery is part of the Tweedswood Estate, one and a quarter miles of fishing, both banks. It's a lovely estate, made up of two farms, Kittyfield and Leaderfoot. The owner is looking for a private sale wishing to move to the Isle of Skye."

When the shoot was over I telephoned the owner making an appointment to meet him. The Tweedswood Estate had recently passed to its present owner through the death of the father in a fatal accident abroad. We negotiated a sale and I informed my accountants in London to make the necessary arrangements for its purchase. I fished the water regularly but it was at its best in the autumn.

It was now the season for shooting and, as I had caught many salmon at Tweedswood, I decided to sell the fishery as fishing clashed with shooting. I had bought Tweedswood fishery for forty-eight thousand pounds and sold it a couple of years later at a record price of two hundred and six thousand pounds under auction.

In November I went to Lord Elliott's Estate at Saltash in Cornwall for a week's shooting and houseguest. This was a lovely estate with thousands of pheasant and numerous foxes. I so enjoyed the week!

Yet my favourite stay was at Lord Dundee's shoot at his lovely mansion. He was a wonderful host always insisting that his guests called him 'Jimmy'. I took my ghillie from Ballingham to load for me finding him accommodation nearby. The pheasants were driven out of the covers flying over the guns at about sixty feet in height making it difficult to shoot. During one such drive I was lucky to draw a good number seeing many pheasants over my two guns. At the end of the drive Gerry, my loader said, "This is the best shoot I've ever seen!" The head keeper came over saying, "Zir, you had four birds dead in the air before the first one touched the ground. I've never seen that before!"

I longed to get back into farming and bought The Manor Farm at Claverdon, near Henley-in-Arden. I stocked the small farm but found help very difficult to obtain as, being so close to Birmingham, workers preferred to work in the city.

As per my contract with United Tobacco Company, I had returned to Sunnyside on several occasions in an advisory capacity. However, I found the running of the farms was not going to my satisfaction with no notice being taken of any advice I was giving. I was treated like a stranger. I made an appointment to meet Mr Moorhead and asked him to release me from the remainder of the contract. Shortly afterwards, not to my surprise, United Tobacco Company disposed of the Sunnyside organisation.

At this particular time I saw quite a lot of David Faulkner whom I had met a few years before. David was interested in pig production and ran a company called Nutrikem, suppliers of vitamins to feed manufacturers. I had bought vitamins from him whilst at Sunnyside. We decided on a joint venture and formed our own company called 'Pig Pac' keeping pigs in controlled environment houses, many sows per house, breeding piglets. At ten weeks old they were sent to the bacon factory, a steady weekly supply of pigs to the factory. I erected a controlled environment house at Claverdon Manor, although this type of business paid very well I eventually found that, yet again, I had no time for fishing, shooting or golf. It was all work and no play! I decided to quit farming and sold the piggery to a well-known pig farmer. I had worked hard all my life and wanted to spend the rest enjoying it.

Yorkshire was one of the largest producers of oven ready chickens in the country and pig production was becoming a large industry. David Faulkner had been asked by farmers to supply them with pig and poultry rations so he approached me with a view to us setting up our own mill supplying feed to the farmers at a lower price. I spent a lot of time investigating the project and we went ahead and erected the mill. We called the new feed, FEEDEX still well known today.

It became a tremendous success. At this time I held twenty-percent of the share holding.

I sold Claverdon Manor and heard that Tapster Mill, a lovely Georgian house at Solihull, was for sale. The Rover Motor Company had merged with British Leyland and Mr Smith the Managing Director who resided at Tapster Mill would be vacating the house. On September 16th, 1971, I bought it for a bargain price and moved in the following March. Tapster Mill stood in seventeen acres of land. It had a gardener's cottage, a lovely vegetable garden, flowerbeds, lawns and a long sweeping drive leading up to the double garage and stables. I added a billiard room and indoor swimming pool. It was beautiful, I wish I were still there now!

I had bought Middle Ballingham Fishery (a one and a half-mile stretch of fishing on both banks, at Holme Lacy, Hereford, three miles from Kilkington) in August 1969 and I now had time to fish it. It had a low to average catch of salmon.

Lord Bradford owned a large estate close to Shifnall and Telford in Shropshire, only an hour away from Tapster Mill. I spent a pleasant evening at his lovely mansion discussing, amongst other things, the letting of the Tong Shoot. It was agreed that for the next three years I would take over the shoot. It was good agricultural land with many pheasants and wild partridges. Partridges were always found in packs, usually about ten per pack, were wild and flew extremely well. I invited guests to join me, my neighbour Tom Bates a farmer, Nick Irens, my accountant, Clarence Powell and many others. We were usually eight guns and employed beaters to drive the partridges over hedges where our guns would be waiting. Although partridges fly anywhere there were so many of them that we always had good sport. We had a full-time keeper but only shot once per week.

I was now settled in Tapster Mill, enjoying it. I had a housekeeper who was a good cook and looked after things. In 1973 Elizabeth Mitchell who had sexed chickens for me at Sunnyside called in to Tapster Mill to see me. She was working in Russell and Bromley shoe shop in Bond Street,

London. We had much in common and enjoyed each other's company. Although I always had plenty to keep me busy I must admit that I was, at times, very lonely. It was autumn and in the November I took part in a great deal of shooting.

On December 12th 1973 Lizzie joined me and we went to Zermatt in Switzerland staying at the Matterhoff Hotel. Lizzie could ski but I was a beginner. My instructor gave me my first lesson and I started off down a slope but he did not show me how to stop and I went crashing into a hut. I wasn't injured but I gave the skis back to the instructor and bid him farewell. Lizzie was not around so I went down the lift to the hotel and had a stiff coffee. This was the end of my skiing career. In the evenings Lizzie and I went to the theatre or to whatever else was going on. We spent a short time in Zurich before returning to London, taking the train to Solihull then home to Tapster Mill.

Christmas arrived and with it the shooting parties. I was never one for parties and drank very little. I did like a glass of wine, Chablis being my favourite. Christmas day was quiet and next day I held a shoot at Tong. Beaters were scarce so we only drove the small covers. January was quiet. On the business front my shares in Feedex 3452 were up to forty-six pence but I did have some which were down.

In February Lizzie and I flew to Johannesburg to get married. On February 7th we went to the Registry Office joined by a few friends including Mark and Mary Walker and John Moller. After the reception at the Carlton Hotel we flew down to Durban and honeymooned at the Beverley Hills Hotel, Umhlanga.

A few days later we flew back to London before going home to Tapster Mill. I had a gardener and his wife living in the cottage in the grounds who were not up to scratch. The wife, who worked in the house, had a soft spot for a 'wee' dram unfortunately it did not stop at the wee. All liquor had to be locked up!

Shortly afterwards we changed our gardener at Tapster employing Cedrick and his wife Ivy. Lizzie and I went down to Ballingham and stayed at the lodge. Gerry, our ghillie, looked after everything. Lizzie learnt to cook. I caught a salmon weighing over fourteen pounds. Then the rains came and we left the lodge in the care of Gerry.

In April I went to Banbury market and bought eleven Hereford Cross bullocks to graze the grass at Tapster Mill, now well grown. A few days later we flew to Barbados staying at the Sandy Lane Hotel where, once again, I could play tennis and golf whilst Lizzie enjoyed sunbathing, a relaxed occupation which I could not apply myself to. A week of this extravagant living was enough so we came home.

I became a member of the Ladbrook Golf Club enjoying playing a little. I gave Lizzie tennis lessons and after a while she played a reasonable game. As it was summertime and the evenings were long we often invited friends, especially Margaret and Ted, along to join us in a game.

In June we drove to Scotland to fish the Tay at Murthly and Ballathie, just beyond Perth but this time of year was not good for fishing salmon on Scottish rivers, so we went down to the lodge at Ballingham. We stayed for three days and I caught five salmon weighing between twelve and sixteen pounds each. I caught the salmon on Devon Spinners and put them in the deep freeze at the lodge for smoking later. Then – back home in the Mercedes 450 SLC, what a motor car! We never ever went to London by train always using the Merc. We had driven to Scotland and back, twenty-five miles per gallon. I used the indoor swimming pool – which I'd had built onto Tapster Mill – early each morning and found the exercise not only enjoyable but a good way of keeping fit. In August we found the fishing on the Wye was not good for the river was too low. We went instead to the River Tay staying at Ballathie House. The food was extremely good, all managed by Colonel Brassey and his wife Pat. I caught two salmon before lunch fly fishing below the bridge using a 'Munroe Killer' fly and nine salmon after lunch, all between eleven and fourteen pounds. I was to beat this record later. One afternoon I caught fifteen salmon, using a 'Munroe Killer'fly, landing them with a net myself. Lizzie was not keen on fishing but loved riding so she used a 'borrowed' horse. We went for drives but, because the fishing was so good I was glued to the river, making up for those days when I fished with a heavy greenheart rod for chub weighing half a pound – three pounds if I was lucky. It was a beautiful spot, just a few miles below Loch Tay. The River Tay flowed to Dundee then out to sea. Both banks of the Tay were always full of fishermen. We caught fifteen fish in that week one weighing twenty-eight pounds!

We made our way home travelling down to Builth via Rhyder and the Rhyder Reservoirs which supplied water to Birmingham, Wolverhampton, Hereford, Worcester and other towns. We motored down the Wye valley joining up with the Leominster to Solihull, a long way round but Lizzie enjoyed driving. We had dinner at the 'Feathers', Ludlow.

On January 7th 1977 I flew, along with eleven other golfers, to Bangkok in Thailand, staying at the Asia Hotel, Pataya Beach. We played golf at the Siam Country Club and I won three cups. It was a wonderful week's holiday, the sea was calm and so clear that when I went swimming I could see fish gliding through the water below. Each evening we would sit on wooden benches at the edge of the beach and select, from the live aquarium, the fish we would like for dinner. It would then be lifted out in a net, despatched, and fried – delicious with a glass of Bankok beer. All the caddies were girls and so efficient. Mine would hand me the club to use, enquiring, "Yes? No?"

In February 1977 we flew to Barbados staying at the Sandy Lane Hotel. The airfare, return, was one hundred and sixty-eight pounds. Our holiday was to celebrate Lizzie being pregnant. We had hoped it was not too late for a baby as Lizzie was in her thirties. It was a grand holiday with plenty of good food, swimming in a lovely pool and tennis in floodlit tennis courts which we now both enjoyed. We returned home a fortnight later looking forward to July.

I thought is was about time I put a couple of horses in the stables and asked a friend of ours, Graham Cleaton, who hunted with the North Warwicks to help. We found two hunters, both three-quarter thoroughbreds, pure thoroughbreds being more difficult to handle. The horse I chose had a habit of rearing up then dashing forward so I returned him for a good hunter quiet and a joy to ride. Lizzie's hunter was also quiet but, being pregnant, she was restricted to riding only an hour each day. Accompanied by Graham I often went for a day's hunting although it was now the end of the hunting season and I still rode around the locality nearly every day.

The lawns, gardens and flowerbeds at Tapster were quite extensive so I helped the gardener quite a lot. One warm sunny afternoon I was emptying the wheelbarrow in a tip at the end of the garden when I saw a large black snake. I collected a gun from the house but the snake had disappeared in a big heap of rubbish. Next morning it was again warm and sunny and I crept to the dump. There were two snakes, one coiled with only its head showing, as black as the ace of spades. I shot it, the other snake making a get away towards the rubbish, but I gave it the second barrel, killing it. They were about four feet long and the species unknown to me. How they got there was a mystery. They must have come from abroad perhaps in a box of fruit and the box then dumped on the heap of rubbish. I set fire to any burnable rubbish standing waiting with my gun but did not see another snake. I inspected this dump every day and Cedrick, the gardener, also kept his eye on the site.

Ballingham Rates for 1977 – River £364.23
Fownhope side of River – £201.04
The Lodge – £140.33 half year – A full year £290
Tapster Mill – £361.59 half year
Cottage – £58.67
Lodge Cottage – £69.77 – A full year £980

On good Friday April 8th, I played golf with Richard Andrews. I played off a handicap of eighteen and he off fourteen and beat me.

On Wednesday July 13th Lizzie started to have labour pains, her specialist in Solihull advised me to 'bring her in'. On the way Lizzie's pains increased as did my speed in the Range Rover. About two miles from Tapster, travelling along the Solihull road, a Round-Robin three-wheeled Reliant came out from a side road and we collided. The Reliant turned over and landed in a ditch. The occupants, a man and his wife, climbed out through a window with no injury.

Lizzie was taken to a house opposite whilst we awaited the arrival of the police who came very quickly. After taking details we left for the hospital where her specialist took over. Next day, at half past two, Lizzie gave birth to our baby girl, five pounds twelve ounces, both mother and daughter doing well! I was not at the birth as there were complications and baby was taken to intensive care. A nurse and I walked the corridor lined with glass rooms each containing a tiny cot trying to find her. Without looking at the label I suddenly said, "There she is!" She had the Pantall nose and other features. I told Lizzie this as she had not yet seen her. We had already discussed names and at the time Poldark was a very popular series on the television. We had decided that, if it was a boy he would be christened Ross and, if a girl, Demelza – so Demelza it was! I spent most of my time with them at the hospital and, after five days, brought them home.

From then on I loved Demelza so much that I took over looking after her, changing nappies and feeding her at night with Cow and Gate milk. On August 1st she weighed six pounds six ounces and was referred to as 'Melz'. On August 24th she weighed eight pounds four ounces. On Sunday 2nd October 1977 baby was christened at Lapworth Church, Demelza Jane Pantall, we had quite a party at Tapster Mill after the christening. Margaret Mitchell, Lizzie's sister-in-law and Ann Bendall, a family friend were Godmothers and Steve Bendall was Demelza's Godfather. There were over fifty guests including Mr & Mrs Mitchell, Lizzie's parents, Margaret Mitchell and her husband Godfrey, Lizzie's brother (also known as Tizzie) Clarence and Gwen Powell, who gave

Melz a sovereign in a satin box. On October 28th Melz had climbed in weight to twelve pounds ten ounces. Her Dad was now fully into the routine of feeding twice in the night, changing nappies and taking her for a walk during the morning up the drive in a beautiful cream pram that I had bought from Harrods. On November 27th Melz cut her first tooth

I was playing golf on various courses and shooting once a week. I was now a member with the North Warwicks and hunted once per week.

Lizzie's parents arrived at Tapster on January 23rd 1978 and Lizzie and I, together with our friends Steve and Ann Bendall, flew to Johannesburg staying at the President Hotel. Whilst staying here I bought Lizzie a gold watch from Chas, Greig.

Three days later we went on to Cape Town staying at the President Hotel, Sea Point. On the 30th we hired a car and left for Plattenburg Bay where we rented a house on the sea front. We had a lovely holiday with staff to cook and look after us and the bathing was wonderful. Like all good things it had to end and on February 15th we motored to Durban from where Steve and Ann left returning to England as their daughter was ill. Lizzie and I stayed on at the Beverley Hills, Umhlanga Rocks, near Durban until the 23rd when we flew home to find Melz very well and adored by her Granny and Grandad.

During March I was busy with cattle dealing. I bought and sold forty-five making a good profit. At the beginning of April we went to the lodge where I caught three salmon, eleven pounds, twelve pounds and twenty-two pounds. They were sold for seventy pounds.

On June 17th Lizzie and I went to Norway to fish the mighty Vosso. We flew to Bergen and then by train up to Voss where we stayed at the fishing lodge. The River Vosso was fast flowing, originating from the mountains and fishing here was exhilarating. From a wide bank I would cast my line using big shrimp as bait and the line travelled quickly downstream. When the fish took the weighted bait I would have to run about fifty yards – holding my rod up to keep the hook in place – to a boat that was waiting, my ghillie already aboard. Once I scrambled aboard we followed the salmon. The boat was swept about half a mile to the fiord below where the water was still; then after playing the salmon for about twenty-five minutes the boat was eventually rowed ashore and we jumped out before beaching the fish. I caught one fish weighing thirty-eight pounds, two weighing thirty-five pounds and three at thirty pounds, six for the week. I sold them to the fishery. It was a glorious holiday. Lizzie caught a thirty and a thirty-eight pounder! We made our way back at the end of the week. Grandma and Grandad were looking after Melz.

We had five days of freezing weather, hard frosts and snow in early January 1979 and, although the central heating was on, the pipes in the roof froze. When it thawed, at two o'clock in the morning, the pipes over the third and fourth bedroom burst and the ceilings caved in onto the beds. Melz was asleep in her cot in a bedroom close to ours, undamaged by the catastrophe. I turned the water off to prevent it flowing everywhere. Next day a firm of plumbers and insurance assessors arrived – it was a big job. Lizzie took Melz to her parents in Kent who were delighted to have them whilst I held the fort. It was not until February that the cold wintry weather disappeared and it became warmer. All repairs were completed with new carpets and beds and the central heating renewed with more modern equipment. Lizzie returned with Melz after being away over a month and seemed indifferent to Tapster Mill. She wanted me to sell the place and for us to live in Kent. I was extremely upset as I loved the place as I loved my wife and precious daughter. After this she began making visits to Kent every month. Lizzie's mother and father were fantastic parents, lovely God Fearing people. They had seven children all of whom I liked. After one such visit Lizzie told me that she disliked Tapster Mill – as it was too close to Birmingham – and she also disliked its people. It became clear that if I did not do as she asked I would lose both her and my adorable Melz. Lizzie made it clear that she would move anyway. One evening we were playing tennis when the telephone rang in the house. Lizzie ran to answer it and I followed. I found Lizzie crying, her mother had suffered a heart attack and died. I comforted her as much as I could then went to bring Melz in from the tennis court where she was sitting in the pram.

The funeral was Friday June 8th 1979. Lizzie now became determined to live in Kent. I gave way putting Tapster Mill on the market and began looking for property in Maidstone. I was broken-hearted. Lizzie found a property called The Elms, occupied and owned by relations of hers. A lodge at the entrance, a big shed half way up the drive, then a lovely Georgian house, it sounded nice. We went to view. We found that the Lodge had in fact been sold off – the new occupant had left his car parked on the drive for us to some-how manoeuvre around – and the shed had been sold to a fruit and vegetable dealer. This dealer kept fowls in a pen at the back of the shed that stank all the way up to the house. The first thing I noticed was the guttering and spouting, it was falling down – some already had. There was also no garage. The whole place was neglected by the occupiers, Lizzie's relations, only in their forties yet too lazy to do any maintenance work. Lizzie insisted that I buy it and kept saying, "Don't barter with them!"

We had arrived in the Mercedes and her attitude was one of, 'look how well I married'. Melz had been left with Lizzie's sister at Maidstone. The Elms was at Yalding, a few miles away. I desperately wanted to keep the marriage together. I had acquired a great love for Melz whilst looking after her at Tapster Mill.

I bought The Elms at their price. I won't say what the price was because it hurts! I worked hard to make it a home putting up with the stench from the fowls. Ironically just before we moved in, Lizzie's relations had left a note saying, 'HEREWITH THE ELMS, TAKE CARE OF IT!'

The painters, decorators, carpenters and other workmen were there for days! On August 8th Melz developed German measles.

In October, we asked Lizzie's sister to take care of Melz and we flew to Venice. We stayed at the Danieli Hotel then on to Rome enjoying it so much we went from there to Vienna – the city of my dreams. We went every night to the theatre, staying at Hotel Sacher where the food was 'out of this world'. After a few days we flew back and for the next couple of months Lizzie seemed to be her old self again.

On December 19th Lizzie's brother 'Tizzie' joined me in a days shoot at Lamberhurst, our bag for nine guns was two hundred and forty seven pheasants, one hundred and forty-two ducks, seventeen partridges and four woodcock. On December 27th we took Melz to a Pantomime in Tunbridge Wells. Although only two and a half years old she so enjoyed this treat.

In the autumn of 1980 I was preparing fishing lettings for the 1981 season – January until the middle of October, there was always a big demand. I let four rods on the lower Ballingham stretch, Hawthorn, Gravel, Brooks Mouth and the Wood Stream and two rods on the top beat, Rock Cottage Graveyard and Rock Cottage Stream. I did a lot of shooting in the autumn and winter.

On January 20th 1981 I flew again, via Bangkok, with Tony Fisher's golf party to wonderful Pataya, taking part in pro-am golf on Navatance golf course just outside Bangkok. We stayed the evening at the Oriental Hotel and it was interesting watching the Thai girls parting company with their night's companion. The evenings here were very much 'a man's world'. I did not take part at any time in such 'manly' activities. Next day we went to Pataya and stayed at the Asia Hotel. I played in the golf competitions at the Siam Country Club whose clubhouse was luxurious, a swimming pool adjoining. Because of the heat every fourth golf hole had a rondovel (a thatched hut) in which to quench one's thirst. The Thai people are extremely nice in fact I would say the loveliest people I have ever met. After a successful and enjoyable week's golf in which I won three cups we flew back to Heathrow arriving early in the morning on the last day of January 1981. In the middle of February I caught a nineteen-pound salmon at Rock Cottage to be followed by a twenty-eight and a half pounder.

On March 10th Lizzie persuaded me to take advantage of an off-season offer at the Cabana Beach Hotel, Durban – thirty rand, or fifteen pounds per day for the three of us. Meals cost extra and we ate at the Beverley Hills Hotel. Melz loved the big breakers and shrieked with delight as they pounded over her. Lizzie loved her sunbathing and Melz her swimming in the sea. We had a lovely family holiday and flew home on April 7th.

21

On April 23rd Colin Manning, of Sunderlands Estate Agents at Hereford, telephoned to say that they had just the property I was looking for, Lugwardine House, two miles from Hereford. I made arrangements to visit. As I drove up the beautiful long drive I said to myself, 'This is to be mine'. The house was set in a beautiful spot looking right across towards the Malvern Hills and no neighbours! Mr Manning, the Estate Agent, introduced me to the owner, Mrs Wood Power. Mr Wood Power had operated on me on May 7th 1930, removing my appendicitis. I was shown around the house, it was marvellous, a lovely dining room, drawing room with a superb open fire and a snug also with an open fire. Upstairs five bedrooms, three en-suite, four bathrooms etc., as we looked around a list of improvements went through my head, the large playroom would make a brilliant billiard room. Outside lawns and shubbery, stables, tennis court, swimming pool, kitchen garden (sadly neglected) and a large greenhouse with cold frames. Fourteen acres of meadowland including about four acres of land adjoining the River Lugg with one hundred and thirty-yards of fishing rights. There was also a back drive leading on to a bye-road. We went to the pool area which also housed a bar, for a gin and tonic and then our discussion. I mentioned that a great deal of work was needed on the house and that I would have to wait for the survey but we came to an agreement in principle on price. I travelled back looking forward to telling Lizzie about Lugwardine House. I then put The Elms on the market but did not find a buyer. Luckily Nick Irens, my accountant, was looking for a larger house himself so I sold it to him enabling me to complete on the sale for Lugwardine House. The survey took place, everything was fine and I engaged a firm of builders to do the necessary alterations and repairs.

Melz could now attend the much thought of 'Margaret Allen' Preparatory School, only two miles away from Lugwardine House, there were stables for a pony and a swimming pool for the summer. When the repairs and alterations were complete, the billiard table erected and the chandeliers put up it was a lovely home and it all looked absolutely wonderful.

That autumn Clarence Powell and myself became joint tenants of Lymore Park, a very good shoot in Montgomeryshire, Wales. An hour and twenty minutes drive away from Hereford, we shot there twice a week. It had two thousand acres and employed two keepers.

On January 3rd 1982 Lizzie, Melz and I flew to Durban staying at Cabana Beach, Umhlanga Rocks where the three of us had a lovely holiday and Melz learned to swim without armbands. Whilst staying at Cabana Beach we motored up through Zululand and visited Rorkes Drift and other sites of the Zulu War. On the return journey we went through Umfolozi Game Reserve seeing lots of Impala, White Rhinos and Zebra etc.

I played golf regularly during most of 1982, once at Royal Wimbledon and St Georges, Surrey, both lovely courses, fishing and shooting as usual.

On February 9th 1983, Melz had to lose fifteen days at school as Lizzie wanted 'a change of scene', so we flew to Durban then to Umhlanga Rocks and the Cabana Beach Hotel. Seventy-two to seventy-eight rand per day, including breakfast – off season only, the fifteen days costing one

251

thousand, one hundred and sixty-four rand, paid by First National Bank Umhlanga, from annuity payments received twice yearly from Southern Life Assurance. We thoroughly enjoyed our holiday making the most of the sea's big breakers, excellent for water skiing, being very popular.

On our return home I went to Banbury market and bought eighteen bullocks. Each year I bought bullocks making a good profit when I sold them in October. Melz broke up from school in July and the following week we took a trip to London booking in to see 'Cats'. It was excellent and we thoroughly enjoyed it.

On December 8th I went on a pheasant-shooting trip to Hungary, organised by Malcolm Hammond. We were due to fly to Budapest but could not land due to the snowy conditions landing instead at Vienna airport, where we spent the night. Next day we flew on to Budapest passing easily through customs where our guns were examined before we boarded an old ramshackle bus that was to transport us miles out into the countryside. We were 'much needed foreign currency' the government having spent so much money rearing pheasants for foreign visitors. All farming was government controlled with no private ownership – an example of government versus private farming. The further we travelled the thicker the blanket of snow covering the land and, being a farmer myself I was interested to witness the ricks of corn and hay, not thatched or covered but left fully exposed to the weather. Cultivation was the worst I had ever seen. At last we reached our lodge and after a drink of sour wine we were asked to board a trailer complete with our double guns and cartridges. Pulled along by an old tractor we drove to some big woods where, after a drink of hot coffee from flasks provided by Malcolm, we spread out to our allotted peg number. I had a Hungarian loader who did not speak English, when the Captain blew his horn he handed me gun number one loaded with two Hungarian cartridges. The pheasants came over the wood in hundreds, I fired both barrels at the pheasants but I think the birds went on, I could not see for smoke from the cartridges. Fortunately I had my cartridge bag, I had brought about a thousand Eley's and we quickly reloaded. I shot so many pheasants that the barrels of both guns were hot, some comfort, as it was so cold.

I noticed my loader and one of the 'pickers-up' covering pheasants with snow. Apparently that night the loaders would come back and collect the birds to be dressed and eaten by all the villagers later. My loader marked twenty-two pheasants on his report card, I knew that I had shot far more than that. Each day we had lunch sitting on a wooden bench, sour wine, black bread and cheese which my dog would not eat – we ate it because there was no alternative. Dinner was the same but fortunately Malcolm and others who had been before had brought along tinned food, butter and sugar. However the shooting was really fantastic with high birds. A hunting horn would sound to start the drive and again when it was over. As soon as the loaders were ready we boarded the chariot and on to the next drive straight to our pegs the horn sounded and the birds came over. There were about a hundred beaters on a drive with a new set on each drive. It was pathetic how the people lived, or survived. At the end of the day the pheasants were laid out, two brace each, and counted. Every day it was over one thousand – add to this the number covered with snow and the amount must have been fifteen hundred.

In spite of the third class accommodation and food we all enjoyed it. It did not snow during the day only at night. At the end of the week we had to make our way back to the airport travelling through villages and towns. The people were starving and it was so cold. Shops were practically non existent as money was the same. After a good many delays we finally boarded the plane to London.

On Friday May 11th 1984 we had the pleasure of Hugh Falkus to stay for the weekend. He fished Rock Cottage but the river was not in good order after rising due to recent rains. He was possibly the best fly-fisherman in England having written many books on fishing and produced films for television such as 'The World about Us' and 'Salmo the

Leaper'. He also developed the 'Spey' cast. Salmon are becoming scarce due to the use of drift nets on the high seas. The whole world is using this netting, in 1983 Norway caught approximately eight hundred and twenty-six tons, imagine the volume other countries are catching. I foresee a day in the near future when the Atlantic salmon becomes extinct and although the housewife will still be able to buy farm salmon reared in Scottish lakes, they will not have the taste of the wild Atlantic salmon.

I still played a lot of golf and was the secretary for the seniors at Belmont Golf Club where we played competitions every Tuesday with a monthly medal on the first Tuesday in the month. We also played other seniors from clubs all over the county. I won several competitions other than playing with the seniors.

On February 11th 1985, Tizzie, Lizzie's brother, had a terrible accident. He was driving his lorry in London moving forward as the traffic lights changed. A left-hand drive car tried to cross the lights on red striking Tizzie's lorry in the passenger side so hard it forced his door open and he fell onto the pavement badly fracturing his skull. There were no witnesses. He was taken to hospital where part of his brain was removed. He was one of the kindest men I'd ever met, a great shooting and fishing companion. I visited him at the Royal Free hospital in London; now partially blind and not able to converse or do anything, he always remained cheerful.

At the bottom of our front meadow adjoining our land was a bog belonging to our neighbour, Mr Phillips. Sheep and cattle used to get stuck some dying. I offered to buy the one acre bog and my offer was accepted. I employed the services of Reid Brothers of Hereford who used heavy-duty machinery to bulldoze out a huge amount of sludge, to a depth of five feet, forming two islands that made a lovely trout lake the overflow being piped via a mains drain down to the River Lugg. I fenced around the one-acre lake and put in fifty rainbow trout, stocking up every year. Using a light nine foot rod, with light tackle, we caught rainbows up to nine

– Tim Jessop did catch one that topped nine and a half pounds. The lake gave myself and invited friends a great deal of sport.

Melz had a lovely pony called 'Wesley'. I bought her a Rice trailer and she took part in many pony competitions being successful enough to decorate her room with many a red and blue rossette. However, anxious to impress upon my daughter the importance of animal welfare from an early age, all tack cleaning and mucking out was executed by the jockey herself.

On April 6th 1986, accompanied by my friend Ken Clegg, I hooked and netted in the 'Graveyard', Rock Cottage a thirty-three pound salmon, what a fight and what a thrill! Three days later on the lower beat – 'The Gravel' – I hooked and landed in the net, which bent, a thirty-eight pound salmon. It took me forty-five minutes.

On April 27th I heard the cuckoo. One Friday at the end of May I caught fifteen salmon in Rock Cottage stream mostly on a 'Munroe Killer' fly, they weighed between eleven and seventeen pounds each, what a wonderful day's sport! The river was full of salmon and one could see them travelling up stream in shoals, never to be seen again. 1986 was a record year I caught over a hundred salmon.

In 1987 I went to Banbury several times buying and selling cattle. There was a big demand this year and I sold the lot, some at one pound twenty per kilo and some at one pound thirty per kilo.

22

On April 7th 1988, Edwina Curry M.P. brought to the notice of the public, in an article in *The Times*, 'Salmonella in eggs'. Because of the seriousness of the bacteria in eggs it had to be rectified. Poultry farmers were up in arms at this accusation worried about a serious effect on their industry. The House of Commons was in uproar, many MPs demanding Edwina Curry's resignation. The Farmers Union stated that, as far as they were aware, there were no reported deaths from salmonella. However, for the first time, the public was advised to buy eggs from free-range hens. But hens could not be put out to free-range so quickly, in most cases, poultry farmers did not have land in which to free-range their hens. In any case the number of hens would be limited as production of eggs from free-range hens could not be compared to the production of eggs from hens in cages. In my opinion the cause of the trouble was in the feed fed to the hens. How much offal was put in the ration and of what quality? These were questions put before the Government. The feed manufacturers maintained that the offal used was of top quality and a limited amount used. Offal is flesh from animals, how long those animals had been dead before the offal was processed could have had an effect, causing salmonella. For twenty years, whilst at Sunnyside in South Africa, I had owned the largest poultry organisation in Africa (see Part IV – Pioneering the Poultry Industry). My organisation made all the rations for the thousands of bird's both broilers and layers. Not one ounce of offal was ever used (flesh is for dogs and not chickens). I would not risk bacteria going into the egg from the birds' intestines and we had no disease of any kind. The uproar from the public increased – they wanted an answer to their question, 'Is it safe to eat eggs'? I was retired and did not particularly want to become involved but on April 11th I called in at the offices of the National Farmers Union in Hereford and asked an official if I could speak to its Secretary. Unfortunately he was not available so I spoke to another official and passed on my experience and knowledge of salmonella acknowledging that Edwina Curry was doing the public a great service. Although having no experience she nevertheless had all the expertise at her fingertips and knowing the facts and serious consequences of salmonella she felt it her duty to 'go public'. I left, having given my opinion and I presume that the feed manufacturers reduced the offal in the feed as the salmonella issue died down. Edwina Curry resigned the following December. She had done her duty at the cost of her job.

Mad Cow's disease commonly known as BSE (Bovine Spongiform Encephalopathy) I believe is linked to animal offal. How much care and attention was given to the animal feed at the time of the first outbreak? What quality was the flesh and how long had the animals been dead before processing? These items I believe, from my vast experience, are linked to DISEASE.

On July 14th 1988, it was Melz eleventh birthday and we held a party for her in the swimming pool room. It was a large room plenty big enough for the fourteen children to play in. They swam, used the diving boards, played tennis on the courts and held ball games on the lawns.

On September 1st Melz started school at Malvern Girls College. She was a 'day girl' which meant travelling a total of fifty-six miles there and back each day. The train service was unreliable and so Richard, my general handyman who was a very good driver, had the task of driving Melz to school. The road to Malvern was steep and, in the winter, could be 'skiddy'. With the safety of Melz in mind I bought a new Mercedes 300E, F501 JVJ, complete with the new anti-skid mechanism. I was, at the time, without a Mercedes for the first time in years. That autumn I joined Glen Usk Shoot at Abergavenny, one of the best shoots in the country, the mallard on the River Usk giving good sport.

On March 17th 1989, at eight in the evening, whilst playing snooker with Ken Klegg, 'Sooty', my black Labrador, came unnoticed into the snooker room, although he had been trained not to do so and lay on the carpet in the right hand corner. I was standing the other side of the table and walked around to play the shot tripping over 'Sooty' as I did so and stumbling against the fixed shelving beyond the table, injuring my left shoulder. I was in pain for days, an X-ray finding nothing. Nearly three months later, on June 8th, Mr Ian Reynolds examined my shoulder at his residence, Mouse Castle, Old Eign Road, Hereford and found that I had torn a muscle. Six days later he had me in the Nuffield Nursing Home and operated, repairing the three-inch tear and keeping me in bed for three days. It was very painful. Two weeks later the stitches came out and for two or three months afterwards it was extremely painful.

July 16th was a sad day. Sooty was run over by a car on the Ledbury road. He was looking for a bitch in season. Richard and I collected his body and buried him beneath the lawn.

From August onwards I had to have physiotherapy twice a week on my shoulder it was still so painful. About this time I was walking down Capler meadow passing Capler cottage on my left adjoining the Fownhope Road. I saw a man in his garden and said, "Good Afternoon" to him. We had a chat during which he mentioned that he was thinking of selling the cottage. He took me through his orchard leading down to the riverbank. Immediately my brain started working and I saw a wonderful opportunity. I had thought of selling the

Capler side of the fishery for some time and here was now the opportunity. I could buy the cottage and make a roadway down through the orchard to the riverbank. My investment company, Wye Investments, already owned the fishing rights at Ballingham Fishery so we bought Capler cottage. It was in a dilapidated condition having been split, making a double dwelling for two families, who were all farm workers. Capler was a good fishery and Hugo Mason, one of the most clever and successful fishermen on the River Wye, was catching a lot of salmon up to thirty pounds each; yet to me Rock Cottage, where I fished, was more accessible. I decided to sell three quarters of a mile of the Ballingham/Fownhope fishing together with the cottage, doing no improvements to the cottage as I had reasoned that any puchasers would prefer to make improvements to their own liking. I put in on the market – 'offers over six hundred thousand pounds' and over six hundred and thirty thousand pounds it did make! It is now a beautiful weekend cottage but the drift netting at sea has deprived us all of our salmon fishing. I still kept Rock Cottage, one of the foremost salmon holding pools on the River Wye and which I fished regularly.

God grant that I may love to fish until my dying day
And when it comes to my last cast I will most humbly pray
When in the Lord's safe landing net and peacefully asleep
That in his mercy I'll be judged as good enough to keep

After two years at Malvern Girls College Melz was unhappy. The boarders at the school resented the 'day girls' and Melz could not settle. In 1991 she became a pupil at Hereford Cathedral School.

On November 13th 1991 I went to see Dr Patrick Ramage, a great fishing friend, as I had been having cramp in my feet, something new to me. After a blood test and a thorough examination of my feet he said, "Chris you have diabetes...."

I was thunderstruck, "But Patrick, no one in my family has diabetes, how could I have developed it?"

"Lots of things can trigger diabetes Chris, particularly

stress. Take two Tolbutamide tablets a day, one in the morning and another at night, massage your feet in warm water twice daily, have a strict diet and no sugar. You can forget strawberries with cream and sugar. There's a booklet in the surgery about diet but you will have diabetes until death do you part."

I came out of Dr. Ramage's surgery feeling very depressed and for the rest of the year I enjoyed as much shooting as I could fit in, sometimes twice a week. Glen Usk was a wonderful shoot as was our own at Lymore.

Melz went to a pony club at Cabalva where she either won or was in the running with 'Samuel Whiskers' in most events. She also won a glass trophy at a pre-novice event at Midland Horse Trials on 'Stanley'.

On September 5th 1993 Melz started school at Millfield in Somerset. Education here is to a very high standard and Melz was allowed to take along her horses. She continued to compete, enjoying the excellent sporting facilities the school was able to provide.

I changed the Range Rover – for a Peugeot Estate 405 – in 1994 as it had been giving me a lot of trouble. I sold the Range Rover to a Mr Frost, delivering it to Tintern and whilst there I visited historical Tintern Abbey in Monmouthshire. It was fascinating. I could imagine the fifty or so monks living in the cold Abbey in the eleventh century with no central heating but at least food would have been plentiful. The Abbey was surrounded by land, about five hundred acres and in the woodland game and deer would be roaming. The River Wye flowed along the boundaries so fish and salmon could be caught for the pot.

On February 7th 1995 I flew to Melbourne in Australia, arriving in Adelaide two days later, before flying on again to Mount Gambier. The purpose of my journey was to visit Pamela, my daughter. She had been ill and was now out of hospital. I asked Lizzie to accompany me but the plane journey was too long. Pamela met me at Mount Gambier and took me to her home at Millicent where she and her husband, Ron Oliver, ran dog kennels and a cattery keeping up to twenty-five dogs and ten cats. It was very hot, ninety-eight degrees fahrenheit and no rain but the kennels were fairly cool. I visited lots of places including some farms, one of which, near Millicent, belonged to John Bullman. It had a magnificent herd of pedigree Hereford cattle. One morning he took me in his boat out to sea to inspect his lobster pots. We had great success and brought ashore eight lobsters, the fishing grounds in Victoria State off the coast of the Tasman Sea, are extremely productive.

What an enormous country Australia is, we spent some time touring, visiting Mount Gambier and Adelaide, where Pam, Ron and I stayed over one night. Adelaide is a lovely seaside town. I found it all very interesting. On February 28th I flew out from Adelaide to London, via Singapore. I found Singapore airlines excellent.

Melz was enjoying Millfield, her exam results always good. She is a clever girl inheriting her brains from her grandmother. My mother, Janet, came from the Watt-White family famous for inventing the steam engine and free-wheel bicycle. Melz completed her schooling at Millfield with her 'A' levels including English, History, Business Studies and General Studies. Until September 1997 she was at a Business College in Oxford from where she was accepted at St. Andrews University, Fife, Scotland, on a four-year course studying English, Economics and Psychology.

I had not seen my sister Jean for some time, and as I had some business to attend to in Durban and Johannesburg I decided I would fly to Durban. I had an injury to my left shoulder caused by a heavy gate swinging back and, in spite of physiotherapy, the shoulder did not improve. I decided to pay John Taylor a visit in Santon, near Johannesburg. I had known John for years, he was an excellent physiotherapist and I knew he would be pleased to see me again. Before leaving I had an X-ray taken at the Mount Stuart Hospital and took this with me.

I flew to Durban and concluded some unfinished business with a bank, flying out the following day to Johannesburg. This five hundred-mile flight was such an improvement, that the service was operating every hour with the planes always full.

I went to see John who confirmed that, although nothing could be seen on the X-ray, there was bound to be severe bruising. He recommended that upon my return to England I should visit my specialist, Mr Ian Reynolds, and have cortisone injections. It was a question of time and plenty of rest.

My sister Jean had a small broiler raising plant out at Krugersdorp about fifteen miles north of Johannesburg. As I drove through the suburbs I saw that most homes and factories were not only fitted with burglar alarms but some resembled Fort Knox and were surrounded by barbed wire. Africans were now carrying handguns, the police could not keep pace with the number of Europeans being killed. The armed Africans were not particular whom they shot so long as they were white!

I arrived at Jean's farm, her husband Jack having died last year. Although her farm was completely surrounded by barbed wire it had not kept the Africans from breaking in. She told me that two weeks ago, at eleven o'clock at night, four of them had broken in, rough handled her and locked her in a small shed. She had not been able to make anyone hear until, at seven the following morning, her workers had arrived. The intruders had stolen everything they could lay their hands on. There was not a television or a video machine as these had been stolen on two previous robberies! They had stolen her pick-up truck but it had been recognised four miles away parked outside a shed and the police returned it to my sister but they did not catch the thieves. This was not the South Africa that welcomed me in 1947, and it was not the South Africa I had left twenty years later.

I tried desperately to persuade my sister to come back to England but she had six dogs and umpteen cats and lived for their affection and love. As it would be difficult for them to go into quarantine in England together with the problems of shipping them back, it was her wish to stay in South Africa. Such was the love between the dogs and their master.

United Tobacco Company had sold Sunnyside Poultry Farms to a large feed firm at Vereeniging who had moved all the equipment to their new premises. Now, along with the other processors, they were able to flood the market with oven ready chickens. I left South Africa with a sad heart, and drove to the airport with poignant memories of my great adventure. The love I had for my African and coloured workers whether living or dead would always be in my heart. I hoped their memory of me would be that I treated them fairly and with kindness, had it not been for the Afrikaans it would have been as equals.

I returned to England where I had planned to live for a few years and then return to Umhlanga Rocks, Durban and live the rest of my life in South Africa.

Oh! to be in England now September's here
The salmon and the trout passing through the weir
The falling of the leaves, the crispness in the air
This and every other thing that I hold dear
Is the image of love with nothing to compare.

EPILOGUE

I am sitting in my study surrounded by a towering pile of hand-written manuscripts, pencils, pens, photographs and documents – each one a fragment of my life, reminding me of another story, another face, another adventure. However, it appears I have exhausted my library of diaries (sixty so far and half way through 1998!) and must trust that you have enjoyed reflecting upon my history.

Lying at the side of my desk is my faithful companion, Lolly, who must surely be the most patient Black Labrador to date. Throughout the gestation of this book, he has never once left my side and is always punctual in his demands for a tea break and a breath of fresh air.

Those typing the manuscript have worked tirelessly and diligently to decipher my 'artistic' handwriting, compiling it into a neatly typed copy which everyone could understand, hence the completion of this book.

INDEX

INDEX

INDEX

INDEX

INDEX

INDEX

INDEX